Debating Women's Equality

Debating Women's Equality

Toward a Feminist Theory of Law from a European Perspective

UTE GERHARD

TRANSLATED FROM THE GERMAN BY
ALLISON BROWN
BELINDA COOPER

RUTGERS UNIVERSITY PRESS
New Brunswick, New Jersey, and London

Library of Congress Cataloging-in-Publication Data

Gerhard, Ute.
    [Gleichheit onhe Angleichung. English]
    Debating women's equality : toward a feminist theory of law from a
European perspective / Ute Gerhard ; translated from the German by Allison
Brown and Belinda Cooper ; foreword by Linda M.G. Zerilli.
      p. cm. — (Rutgers series on women and politics)
    Includes bibliographical references and index.
    ISBN 0-8135-2905-0 (cloth: alk. paper)
    1. Women's rights—History. 2. Women—Legal status, laws, etc.—History.
3. Liberty—History. 4. Equality—History. I. Title. II. Series.

HQ1236 .G4713 2001
305.42'09—dc21   00-067363

British Cataloging-in-Publication data for this book is available from the British
Library

First published in German in 1990 by C.H. Beck'sche Verlagsbuchhandlung,
Munich, Germany. Copyright © 1990 C.H. Beck'sche Verlagsbuchhandlung.

English translation copyright © 2001 by Rutgers, The State University

This translation was supported in part by Inter Nationes, Bonn, Germany

Manufactured in the United States of America

To Nele, Ulrike, Gesine, and other daughters

Contents

Foreword

LINDA M. G. ZERILLI

U TE GERHARD'S *Debating Women's Equality—Toward a Feminist Theory of Law: A European Perspective* is an important contribution to feminist scholarship. Originally published in Germany, the book was written in a national context in which feminists have tended to view a rights-based strategy of social change as extremely limited and dangerously state centered. Although American feminists, in contrast, have by and large accepted this legal strategy as an important dimension of political struggle, they too have raised concerns about the restrictions it places on feminist theory and practice. These concerns turn primarily on the question of difference: the difference between women and men, on one hand, and the differences among women, on the other hand. Indeed feminists in both countries are skeptical of the principle of equality because—apart from the obvious gap that exists between the ideal of equality and the tenacious reality of inequality—that principle appears to establish sameness as the condition for women's legal recognition and social justice and, consequently, to erase multiple articulations of social and sexual difference.

Ute Gerhard is sympathetic to the concerns that motivate feminist criticisms of equal rights, but, she argues, we should examine the extent to which they may be grounded both in a series of misconceptions about the principle of equality itself and in an inadequate historical understanding of the struggle for gender justice. Reminding us that "equality is neither an absolute principle nor a firm standard, but a relational concept," Gerhard insists that equality is not reducible to identity and thus sameness. Although one can express this difference mathematically—"the formula for identity would be a=a, while equality would be a=b"—the purpose of Gerhard's book is to weaken the hold that abstract logic has on our thinking and to enhance our capacity to make political judgments.

To appreciate the complexity of every (historical) claim to equality, Gerhard suggests, we need to shift the debate from a philosophical idiom to a political one, in which the abstract character of equality claims is tempered by an awareness of "who or what decides which characteristics or particularities suggest comparison and equal treatment." This simple but decisive move entails a change in perspective, for now we are asked to focus not on the (social) objects being compared (e.g., a and b; men and women), as if they alone determined the standard of comparison, but on the subjects making the comparison and the sociohistorical context of their judgments. To emphasize the importance of standpoint and context to feminist accounts of equality, in other words, is to consider the specific circumstances in which a claim is made as well as the social location both of those who make it and those who decide what shall count as the standard of comparison. If that standard does not inhere in the object itself, as Gerhard argues, it cannot be obtained by means of a logical operation. Rather, every claim to equality calls for a political judgment that is, historically speaking, based on precedent but by no means given or knowable in advance of the act of judgment itself.

Emphasizing the necessity of a third party, a *tertium comparationis*, Gerhard shows that the demand for equal rights between the sexes does not reduce to making women like men: "This third party can never simply be 'man' or the status of men; it must be a standard that is fair to both genders." She does not deny that this reduction has in fact taken place—the rich historical account offered here gives numerous examples of it on the part of lawyers, politicians, and, at times, feminists themselves—but insists that an alternative story of rights can be gleaned from history, one which points beyond the deadlock of the sameness-versus-difference debate that is familiar to American feminists. This story—told through the lens of the first- and second-wave German women's movement—entails a political notion of equality that, unlike the philosophical principle of identity, is premised on and constituted through an appreciation of social and sexual differences.

The difference-versus-sameness debate tends to assume that equality claims confront and are at odds with claims about difference. We are thus faced with an either/or proposition: to claim equality is to eliminate difference, and vice versa. Joan Scott has recently argued against this way of thinking about feminist political claims, which, she maintains, are characterized not by contradiction but paradox: "Feminism was a protest against women's political exclusion; its goal was to eliminate 'sexual difference' in politics, but it had to make its claims on behalf of 'women' (who were discursively produced through 'sexual difference'). To the extent that it acted for 'women,' feminism produced the 'sexual difference' it sought to eliminate. This paradox—the need both to accept *and* to refuse 'sexual difference'—was the constitutive condition of feminism as a political movement throughout its long history."[1] Like Scott, Gerhard argues that equality claims do not (simply) eliminate difference but (also) articulate it, that is, they shape what will count as socially and politically significant difference. Equality claims, in other words, do not confront and oppose a static field of already existing differences; they transform socially recognized differences of sex and gender into politically meaningful ones that are contestable and thus subject to change, and, further, they bring into existence new social differences which, in turn, may be transformed into political ones.

Attending to the play of difference in the polyvalent historical articulations of equality as a political and legal principle, Gerhard distinguishes equality from identity (or sameness) and argues for equality as a potentially progressive principle that is vital to feminism. She is appropriately critical of the highly philosophical character of the sameness-versus-difference debate in American circles, which has tended to neglect context and to elide crucial national differences of history, culture, and law. Gerhard takes feminist legal theorists like Catherine MacKinnon to task for, first, interpreting the question of equal rights strictly according to American legal institutions and then generalizing this interpretation as if it were a global problem of Aristotelian legal reasoning (according to which equality amounts to treating likes alike). MacKinnon's conclusion that the legal concept of equality presupposes "sameness" or identity, cautions Gerhard, cannot be indiscriminately applied to European countries, whose constitutions never embraced this sort of reasoning.

Gerhard's critique of the sameness-versus-difference debate in American feminism is meant to highlight once again the importance of contextualizing equality in contrast to determining its meaning "at the level of doctrinal formulas and 'argumentative logic.'" If "equality is neither an absolute principle nor a firm standard [but] a dynamic, discursive concept," as Gerhard argues, it may indeed be premature to proclaim the death of rights-based feminist projects. The approach to equality that Gerhard finds and celebrates in the closing declaration of the Fourth World Conference on Women, held in 1995, in Beijing, takes as its empirical and theoretical starting point the experiences of women and their political expression in various women's movements. Employing Winfried Brugger's phrase "exemplary experiences of injustice," Gerhard attempts to clear an intellectual space in which it would be possible to reconstruct an argument for equality that avoids the twin pitfalls of abstract universalism and cultural relativism. She does not produce a formula for equality or a model of legal reasoning that could be applied in rule-like fashion to every particular case. Rather she directs us to attend to the social and political context in which equality arguments are made and to the importance of a third party for making claims with universal validity. More importantly, she reminds us that equality claims are political judgments that "cannot be imported or prescribed; they apply only if the people involved are in a position to claim and defend them as rights." In short, *Debating Women's Equality* directs us back to the quotidian practice of feminist activism.

Acknowledgments

THE AMERICAN EDITION is, in large part, a revised and updated version of my German book *Gleichheit ohne Angleichung* (Equality without Assimilation), which was published in 1990. The book owes a great deal to all those I worked with in women's and gender studies and in the social sciences during that time. First of all, I want to thank my students and young scholars at Frankfurt University for their intellectual curiosity and criticism, especially with regard to feminist theory, the feminist movement, and the great debate on equality, difference, and woman as a subject of law. I am grateful for all the support I received in organizing conferences, such as the international conference "Human Rights Have no/a Gender" in 1989, which opened up international contacts and facilitated networking. All these debates and initiatives are embedded in feminist networks that helped me to be surer about the need to intervene intellectually and politically, and to rethink what seems to be a matter of fact.

Among those I wish to mention particularly are the members of the editorial board of the interdisciplinary feminist journal *Feministische Studien*. I am especially pleased to thank Claudia Honegger, Christel Eckart, Mechthild Rumpf, Heide Schlüpmann, and, again and again, Eva Senghaas-Knobloch as well as Ulla Wischermann for their reliability and many inspiring cooperative efforts. The board of the feminist historical journal *L'Homme. Zeitschrift für feministische Geschichtswissenschaft*, including Karin Hausen, Edith Saurer, and Regina Schulte among others, is also a congenial team. I wish also to acknowledge my long-standing friendship and intellectual relationship with the members of the German Women's History Group in New York, especially Marion Kaplan and Renate Bridenthal. I want to thank Angiolina Arru for her long-lasting friendship in all situations of life and work. In recent years, the international cooperation within a European network on citizenship and social policy has been very stimulating and encouraging about crossing borders of the mind, of disciplines, and of countries. In this context I enjoyed the intellectual solidarity of many brilliant scholars, especially Jane Lewis, Arnlaug Leira, Trudie Knijn, and Birte Siim. I would also like to thank Heiner Bielefeld, who offered competent suggestions on the English translation of Kant quotations. Jürgen Seifert, Joachim Perels, and Oskar Negt, my advisors during completion of the first version of this book as a postdoctoral thesis, provided early encouragement of my studies of legal theories and history, and I would like to thank them again here. Last, but not least, I want to mention my colleagues at the Frankfurt Center for Women's and Gender Studies, who in the last three years have been the most important circle for my academic activities as well as for feminist theorizing.

In all these activities I could rely on the professional skills and personal warmth of my secretarial staff. It is a pleasure for me to thank again Lotte Rahbauer, Anja Weckwert, and particularly Marion Keller, who helped me update the bibliography and took care of all the details that were necessary to enable a translation as well as for preparing the index. And I thank both translators, Allison Brown and Belinda Cooper, for their committed and careful work, whose quality the reader may discern.

As always, Klaus Gerhard has been an endless source of patience and support. Finally, I owe a debt of gratitude to Linda Zerilli, for the American edition would not have been possible without her generous recommendation to Rutgers University Press, and to the Press's director, Marlie Wasserman. I combine my words of thanks to the publisher with the hope that the book may help facilitate greater understanding of gender and women's studies from a European perspective.

Debating Women's Equality

Introduction

THIS BOOK DEALS WITH equality as a principle and practice of law in history, and legal theory from a feminist perspective. Consequently, its focus is on the legal status of women, on gender, and on the history of the women's movement. I would like to explain why equality still matters, despite differences—even among women and others than those related to gender. My analysis makes a case for equal rights, although in the past and present this principle has continually been implemented without sufficient regard for women's interests. It has failed and still fails to impose equality in legal and social practice.

Although it may seem paradoxical to formulate this as an objective, I would like to discuss why equality remains indispensable as a standard of justice. Moreover, I assume that the paradoxes and contradictions in society correspond better to the social situation of women than clearly defined assumptions or strategies. Even law has two sides and an ambivalent function, since it can serve the liberation and emancipation of the individual as well as control and the preservation of power.

My thoughts are based on the worldwide feminist discussion on equality and/or difference. The German history of feminism and law serves as a concrete example by which to further this discourse. Feminist epistemological and philosophical debate has helped explain the relationship between equality and difference by showing their characterization as opposites to be a false alternative, thus radicalizing the concept of equality to include differences. Nevertheless, international and interdisciplinary feminist criticism of the androcentrism of law has all too often neglected different historical and legal contexts. As a result, this criticism has made generalizing statements, despite all the talk of differences, and failed to take adequately into account the role of social movements, especially of feminist movements and their struggle for rights, as a driving force in the history of law.

Against this background I will develop a contextualized and dynamic understanding of equality with respect to gender difference in the German context. Based on this example, I intend to delineate the institutional obstacles to, and legal achievements toward, the implementation of equality. Instead of focusing on a particular or national standpoint, I will attempt to show the meaning and influence of European legal developments and of international feminist discussion on this specific domain of law.

By placing the issue of women's rights at the center of legal philosophy and legal theory, this book attempts to combine two diverse discourses and histories: a so-called general, that is, male, history of law and legal philosophy, and a history of struggle for rights, which since the mid-nineteenth century has been supported by women's rights activists and several women's movements. Their story to date has appeared only in the context of gender studies or perhaps social history, but not that of legal studies or legal history. A new chapter in the history of law has thus to be written, incorporating the subversive history of women's movements of the nineteenth and twentieth centuries into the history of law and political theory. Since more is at stake than simply justice in a general sense, this investigation requires much attention to detail.

The book consists of two parts. Part 1 deals with the theoretical question of whether, and if so to what extent, the traditional conception of equality as the basis of a human rights utopia ensuring the liberty of *all* people at the beginning of the modern age is still appropriate as a standard of criticism of unequal, hierarchical gender relations, and even whether law and laws are a suitable tool to empower women and establish more just relations. In this context, the history of the concept of equality and its significance for women will be developed. In particular, the male bias in legal philosophy will be critically examined. My analysis identifies traces of an opposing concept of equality, including women's equality, since antiquity; it critically follows the footsteps of modern philosophers such as Jean Jacques Rousseau, Johann Gottlieb Fichte, and Immanuel Kant. My comments on a feminist theory of law are centered around Olympe de Gouges's "Declaration of the Rights of Woman and Citizen," written in 1791. The minimal—and yet significant—deviations from the so-called universal Declaration of the Rights of Man of 1789 allow this female counterproposal to be read as a program of modern feminism, offering orientation and a basis for evaluating the politics of both the first and the second-wave women's movements. The question of human rights as women's rights thus forms the common theme running through my analysis of legal history and the legal struggles of the women's movement in Germany, which first entered the public arena around the time of the 1848 revolution with demands for equal rights and indivisible liberty. The different currents of the movement grew into a mass movement, following and in cooperation with the other women's movements in the western world. But it was not only class contradictions—in Germany especially, the rift between middle-class and proletarian women's movements—that led to seemingly insurmountable differences of opinion. The question of to what extent the emphasis placed by the women's movement on gender difference was even compatible with demands for equality prevented a united feminist politics. Part 1 concludes that women need to be recognized as both equal *and different.*

Part 2 is made up of three in-depth studies on particular legal issues. Chapter 6 focuses on the legal struggles and legal critique of the radical wing of the German women's movement around the turn of the twentieth century. With their program of equal rights as human rights, their politics of sexual reform, and their peace work, these women seem to be the real precursors of modern feminism, yet they remained a minority. The chapter underscores the significance of women's public rights, especially suffrage as a paradigm of rights. Chapter 7 on gender tutelage analyzes women's legal capacity in private law. Identifying a blind spot in the history of law, it also explains why private law—with respect to women, especially family law—played such a decisive role in the constitution of civil society, which today still contains the paradox of gender hierarchy. Finally, chapter 8, on women's human rights, an issue in the current international campaign of women's movements, places my historical and theoretical findings within the context of the present feminist debate on law and reviews the dimensions of today's feminist thought toward a feminist theory of law.

All in all, my legal criticism is an appeal to use law to facilitate more just relations. It is founded upon a dynamic and discursive understanding of law. Equal rights that are fundamentally based on political agreements deriving from a democratic process have, despite all obstacles, continued to question unequal relationships and violent arrogance and provided the impetus for diverse changes. "Rights are relationships, not things; they are institutionally defined rules specifying what people can do in relation to one another. Rights refer to doing more than having, to social relationships that enable or constrain action."[1] In view of the diversity of interests and the extent of injustice in the world, I believe women cannot afford to give up the chance to make legal agreements instead of tolerating violence and injustice. Even though law in its present form is still largely a domain of male discourse, and even though women are correct in continuing to view the discursive power of the law skeptically, they must intervene, getting involved in the process of jurisprudence and legislation, to write their own, ultimately more universal, story of law, and thus create legal rules different from those prevailing today.

Part I

The Meaning of Equality with Regard to Difference

Chapter 1

THE QUESTION of the meaning of equal rights cannot be answered without considering the conditions under which the question is posed, or without taking their history into account. To avoid the most common misconceptions about equal rights, it is helpful at the outset to explain a term that, though thought to be well defined in legal scholarship, nevertheless bears constant reiteration.

Equality is neither an absolute principle nor a firm standard, but a "relational concept." It expresses a relationship between two objects, people, or conditions and determines the respect in which they are to be viewed as equal. That is, equality must first be sought, demanded, and established, and it presupposes that the objects being compared are different from each other. Otherwise, the principle of equality would be unnecessary and absurd. Logically, however, this can only involve partial equality, that is, equality in specific respects. Absolute equality would mean identity. If one were to illustrate the difference mathematically, the formula for identity would be $a = a$, while equality would be expressed as $a = b$.[1]

What seems plausible so far is complicated in Western equality discourse by a legality that derives from Aristotle's concept of equality of justice, which has caused conceptual confusion into modern times. According to this rule, only "things that are alike should be treated alike, while things that are unalike should be treated unalike in proportion

7

to their unalikeness."[2] Even in this apparently straightforward definition, it is not clear who or what decides which characteristics or particularities suggest comparison or equal treatment and in respect of which traits difference is determined. "In a comparison," wrote Wilhelm Windelband bluntly in his fundamental, clarifying work on equality and identity, "in each case it is the reflective standpoint that determines what shall be essential or nonessential for the comparison."[3] However, this means that comparison is by no means a logical operation, but is instead the result of an assessment, a value judgment, whose criteria may very well be controversial. If one sees law, in the words of Carl F. von Savigny, "as human life itself, viewed from a particular perspective," then equality as a basic legal concept is "nothing more than abstraction from a given inequality from one definite point of view."[4]

The "definite point of view" or concrete respect in which the comparison is made is thus decisive; it must become the standard of comparison. But this standard is not inherent in the comparison. It is dependent on the context and the perspective of those making the comparison and should by no means be oriented toward only one of the objects to be compared. It requires a third party. Lawyers therefore speak of *tertium comparationis*. Although this phrase is initially an empty formula, this distinction reveals the standard of evaluation and helps to expose some premature conclusions.

In terms of legal equality between men and women, this preliminary clarification means the following: The principle of equality assumes that men and women are different and that they will not become identical as a result of equal treatment, but will be able to preserve their difference. The 1949 Basic Law (constitution) of the Federal Republic of Germany explicitly guaranteed the legal equality of man and woman, including private law for the first time, and thus invalidated the Aristotelian rule in this regard. Because of this, Erna Scheffler could declare—to the applause of those present at the thirty-eighth lawyers' conference in 1950—that "it is precisely because men and women are psychologically and physically different that [the legislature] has adopted special laws ensuring their legal equality. The principle of equal rights despite sex difference cannot be restricted using the argument that the sexes are different. That contradicts the inherent logic of the principle of equal rights."[5] And yet, in the equal rights debate in West Germany, high court judges' subsequent consideration not only of "biological" but also of "functional"—that is, division-of-labor—differences between the sexes opened the door to supposedly "legal" unequal treatment.[6] Not until the 1970s were there new developments in case law; it was no accident that they coincided with the emergence of the new women's movement. The prevailing legal opinion now accepted an interpretation of the equal rights article that encouraged acknowledgment of gender differences in implementing equal rights.

But the talk of "making everyone the same," the constant assurance that only "equal worth" is meant, the denunciation of "mechanical equality," all miss the point.[7] And the necessity of a *tertium comparationis* tells us that the standard of comparison must be provided not by one of the two sides but by a third, impartial point of view. This means that equal rights for women cannot take men as the guideline; it cannot mean "attaining the status of men." Therefore, the following statement in a leading commentary on the German Basic Law by Maunz, Dürig, and Herzog is incorrect: "We must remember that equal rights for both sexes, beyond the equal worth of the sexes in human dignity and human rights (which are seen by the Basic Law as 'timeless'), has a *specific historic starting point*: women's demands to attain *the status of men*."[8]

Aside from the fact that "attaining the status of men" was never the "specific historical starting point" of women's efforts to gain equal rights (see chapter 4), this wording reveals an error that has become traditional and is not limited to lawyers: the conflation of "person" and "man."[9] Only a short time earlier, in a general discussion of the basic equal rights provision in Article 3 sec. 1 of the Basic Law (GG), the Maunz, Dürig, and Herzog commentary emphasizes that the *tertium comparationis* of the principle of equality is the individual human being, or the "dignity common to all men"; yet in the concrete application of such rules of interpretation, the situation of the individual is conceivable only as the "man's status."[10]

As I hope to show in the course of this book, this erroneous conclusion, which violates the inherent logic of rules created by lawyers themselves, continues to have serious consequences for the legal status of women. For now, however, it is sufficient to repeat that enjoying equal rights does not presuppose assimilation into men's status and lifestyle.

Instead, it must be based on a superordinate standard, a degree of free-dom possible for all people (men and women). The respect in which people are to be considered equal depends on the "reflective standpoint"; in more precise, contemporary terms, it is a political issue.[11]

The significance of the issue can be inferred from the philosophi-cal efforts and legal acumen expended over the centuries to resolve it, one-sidedly, excluding the majority of human beings, especially women. For the apologists of inequality, only the opportunities or the examples have changed. Thus a constitutional law scholar, Konrad Hesse, pon-tificated in 1951: "A multitude of rational arguments may be furnished, for example, in deciding what should be determinative in resolving the issue of equal voting rights for men and women: the equality of their humanity or citizenship or the inequality of their sex. Ultimately, how-ever, it is a personal decision that cannot be made using the tools of reason and can only be answered within the context of an *idea* that de-termines the essential criteria."[12]

This concept of an "idea" of law, always contested, was "turned right side up again" quite vividly by Karl Marx in his critique of bourgeois law as class law. His purpose was to expose legal illusions and "all the mystifications of the capitalistic mode of production," according to which the unjust exchange of "labor power" [*Ware Arbeitskraft*] between wage worker and capital hides the real conditions of exploitation and power behind the appearance of law, by disregarding, or abstracting from, unequal economic conditions and property relations.[13] In his *Cri-tique of the Gotha Program*, Marx attempted to protect the Social Demo-cratic Party from such legal illusions, writing: "Right by its very nature can consist only in the application of an equal standard; but unequal individuals (and they would not be different individuals if they were not unequal) are measurable only by an equal standard insofar as they are brought under an equal point of view, are taken from one *definite* side only, for instance, in the present case, are regarded *only as workers*, and nothing more is seen in them, everything else being ignored."[14] Marxist legal theory, which placed the "worker" at the center of its analysis of society, tellingly failed to consider the unequal legal status of women and their exploitation; at most, they were relegated to a sec-ondary contradiction. For Marx, "women's work" was an especially de-testable example of "capitalist exploitation," which the worker sells to the capitalist as a sort of "slave trader"; but more generally, it was viewed as a private exploitative relationship that outlives various social forms and is subordinate to the class contradiction.[15] Yet Marx's characterization of law highlights a crucial point: If and because equality as a form of law sees human beings "from one definite side only," it was and is capable of disregarding significant—for example, material—inequalities. Which concrete relationships between people are taken into account and considered important for legal purposes depends upon their significance for the respective relationships of dominance and dependence. The judgment of equality depends on perspective and social context, especially in relation to the rights of women. Thus, if equality is to be more than an empty word or a political slogan, logical deductions will get us no further; instead we must consider its historically determined message, which is constructed by a particular context and specific social relationships.

Chapter 2

In the Footsteps of the Philosophers

The Historical Significance of Equality

"EQUALITY" IS A leitmotif of modern times; not until the beginning of the modern age and the transition to a capitalist economy did equality come to be considered the epitome of social justice. Of course, there were some worthy and emotional precursors to the idea of human equality that are significant for the cultural heritage of women. I would like to name those I consider most important, not simply to reiterate all that has been thought and passed down on the subject, but rather to identify traces of the historical development within the jungle of definitions of, and obstacles to, equality. This requires placing the legal demands of women within the context of legal history, which to date has erroneously been referred to as "general" history. Up to now, two totally isolated histories have existed, each displaying virtually no knowledge of the other; however, it is the authors of the established history, the scholars of jurisprudence and legal philosophy, who are particularly unaware of the distinct, subversive history of women. Aside from concrete examples of criticism and indignation, feminist researchers have long been reluctant to embrace law as "their cause" or subject it to comprehensive analysis. This is not only because law and jurisprudence have traditionally been considered masculine domains, but also because the interests and values they embody are still primarily male. Who would dare to challenge what Ernst Bloch referred to as the "powerful reification of cunning invested in jurisprudence"? As Bloch continued in his social critique, filled as much with masculine pride as with socialist ideology:

> This cunning more than anything else has made the law into
> such a masculine discipline, into something full of definitions,
> formulas, something so elaborately formed, into a discipline
> that—looked at from its point of view—is too good for those
> students who study in order to earn a living, and just perfect for
> exceptional logicians. But none of this obstructed the positive
> law from doing the dirty work: protection of the private
> property of the means of production.[1]

The role of law as a tool to do the dirty work, including that of male interests, was not Bloch's concern. This issue, however, determines an essential principle of law—that is, its claim to universal validity—since the issue is not merely one of justice in general but of specific legal questions and decisions, "of greater justice in the gradual work with details."[2]

I would like to start with a brief outline of relevant legal criticism from a historical perspective. I have been very selective, with no claim to comprehensiveness.[3] My aim is to find systematic reference points for a theory of law that could also apply to women. I hope thereby to shed light on the question of whether, and to what extent, the traditional concept of equality can even be employed to communicate the demands on present-day society expressed by women and the modern women's movement.

Humanity versus Reasons of State: Antigone's Opposition

The historical foundation for our understanding of equality was laid during the Greek enlightenment period of the fifth century B.C.E, when the Sophists "turned [their focus] to human beings."[4] Protagoras's claim that "man is the measure of all things" became the self-confident and socially critical starting point of the opposition to tradition, to the arbitrariness of human conventions and the myth of the gods.

> Protagoras's words marked the birth of natural law. The
> opposition between "physis" and "nomos" means nature versus
> convention; it means true law that humanity is born with, that

hangs in the starry heavens and that man brings down to
earth . . . versus the law that a few rich and powerful scoundrels
have introduced. Natural law has emerged as a revolutionary
instrument.[5]

And yet it is no coincidence that the human being as a subject was
imagined exclusively as male from the very beginning. Thus there arose,
side by side with the creation of a political sphere separate from the
private, an explicitly "misogynist tradition," which would from then on
become a standard element of occidental philosophy in Greek democracy and the theories of state and democracy based upon it.[6] The gender conflict still found mention in mythology and literature, forming,
together with the triumph of the patriarchy, a prerequisite for the male
will to rule.[7] In the heyday of Greek democracy, Sophocles created a
symbolic female figure in his tragedy *Antigone*. Antigone's actions and
statements for women and their rights offer a rare female role model.
Antigone rebels against the law proclaimed by the male tyrant Creon,
according to which she was forbidden to bury her deceased brother. "I
did not think your edicts strong enough / To overrule the unwritten
unalterable laws / Of God and heaven, you being only a man." And
she refuses to heed her sister Ismene's warning to "think, Antigone; we
are women; it is not for us / To fight against men." Unwavering and
insubordinate, she refuses to conform to reasons of state, but obeys another set of laws, the laws of compassion and sisterly sympathy, of humanity. She calls these the "laws of God and heaven." "They are not
of yesterday or today, but everlasting, / Though where they came from,
none of us can tell."[8] This is a poetic way of expressing something "unwritten and binding," an eternal basis for inalienable human rights that
predates the existence of the state.[9]

Even the merely fictional Antigone evidently posed a challenge to
the codified law of the state, made by men, and has given rise on numerous occasions to legal and philosophical interpretation. Georg W. F.
Hegel saw in her the embodiment of "family piety[,] . . . the law of
woman, . . . the law of the inward life."[10] For Johann J. Bachofen, the
story illustrated the struggle between maternal and paternal rights.[11]
And for Ernst Bloch, natural law, "warm and human" and "soft and femi-
nine," remained recognizable in Antigone's rebellion, "despite its oth-

erwise masculine dignity."[12] It is obvious that in all these dichotomies "blood ties" and "bonds of blood" are assumed to play a role in Antigone's motives. These are biologistic—that is, fundamentally sexist—explanations, which eliminate reason or female consciousness from the outset in explaining the opposition she offers out of belief in a different law.

All of these are, in fact, male projections of a difference between man and woman—"the supreme opposition in ethics and therefore in tragedy"—that is justified, or at least considered immutable, in these interpretations.[13] Even Sophocles explained why Creon had to break the resistance of a woman in this tragic conflict—"We'll have no woman's law here, while I live"—and offered the basic justification for a two-thousand-year-old patriarchal philosophy of law and the state: "He who is a righteous master of his house / Will be a righteous statesman."[14] In her conversations with women on politics, Rossana Rossanda explains that in this "story of a key figure," Antigone "brings democracy to her people, but death to herself—she hangs herself in a cave—as if no communication were possible between the unwritten, 'natural' law personified by women and the law agreed upon among men. Is this true? One really must ask if this 'natural law' had not also been agreed upon, albeit in the distant past. . . . That is not what concerns us here, but rather the situation that this ancient dispute threatens to break out again in our day."[15]

Starting in the fourth century B.C.E., the natural law of the Stoics invoked the cosmopolitan idea and the unity of humankind more decisively than the elitist and exclusive democracy of the Athenian polis did in the fifth century B.C.E. Their humankind was no longer comprised only of Hellenists and barbarians, but of slaves as well, though only rarely did this explicitly include women.[16] The "law of nature," now united with universal reason, found its way into Roman law via Stoic philosophy, and thus into Western jurisprudence.

"Equality before God" in a Church of Lords

It is difficult to reconstruct how early Christianity, with its concept of "equality before God," paved the way for the idea of the equality of all people. Addressed to an ancient world characterized by social inequality and Greco-Roman patriarchy, the sermons of Jesus of Nazareth were incredibly revolutionary, as he gathered tax collectors, plebeians, lepers, and whores and other women around him: "There is neither Jew nor Greek, there is neither bond nor free, there is neither male nor female: for ye are all one in Christ Jesus."[17]

It would be dangerous and misleading to blame Judaism in particular for the androcentrism of the ancient world, thus inadvertently basing feminist insight on "anti-Judaism"—that is, on traditional Christian anti-Semitism.[18] "Viewing the Jesus movement as a movement of renewal *within* Judaism, that is, as an *intra-Jewish* alternative to prevailing patriarchal structures,"[19] supports the view of social and Church historians that Jesus was, from the very beginning, a "dangerous egalitarian."[20] His uncomfortable and inflammatory messages were reinterpreted and passed down incorrectly, starting with the first men who followed him. The command to "Let your women keep silence in the churches"[21] was widely circulated and initiated a "fateful course in history." [22] It can only be interpreted as a reaction to what was seen from a male perspective as women who spoke, preached, and prophesied too much in the original Christian community.

Having achieved state power and established itself in the hierarchical and patriarchal order as the "church of lords," the institution of the Church proceeded to totally quash, again and again, any hopes of equality in this life. In a process of exclusion that continued for centuries, the Church fathers, theologians, and popes grounded their power and doctrine in the ostracism of everything female as the personification of Eve, original sin, a nature driven by physical desire, and sexuality. "The female is . . . a subordinate creation, . . . not created in the image of God,"[23] preached the Church fathers. As Thomas Aquinas put it, with reference to Aristotle (De Gener. ii, 3), "the female is a misbegotten male, misbegotten or defective."[24] According to canon law—codified in the corpus juris canonici—on the basis of his conjugal rights a man could beat his wife and declare their marital vows null and void, and the woman was supposed to follow him anywhere, even to parts unknown, even to the grave. However—and here, in particular, lay the supposedly moralizing moment—both woman *and* man were obligated to satisfy their marital duties, including fidelity.[25] The witch trials at the close of the Middle Ages represented the height, but by no means the end, of the misogyny spread by the Church. The cult of the Virgin Mary, which emerged at about the same time, could not compensate for this mass murder; it was simply "the other side of the obsessive belief in witches."[26] Nevertheless, today's feminism—which has claimed the history of witch burning as an important reference point for its own historical identity—runs the risk of underestimating the role "of the Biblical heritage in [women's] culture and rebellion"—indeed, in the women's movement itself.[27]

New feminist theology is making up for the previous lack of religious criticism, uncovering a revolutionary women's tradition from under the many layers of partriarchal editing, reception, and interpretation.[28] A subversive, antipatriarchal history of women's emancipation is being discovered, including the "women around Jesus," disciples with equal status, apostles in positions of leadership, and the first bishops.[29] This feminist perspective reveals how much has yet to be researched on the cultural and social significance of convents and women's orders, the Beguines, and the conspicuously high level of participation by women in religious protest movements and heresies.[30] This grassroots history of the Church does not end with the Reformation or the Enlightenment. It was not the great theorists of civil society, not Hobbes, Locke, or even Rousseau, who led the women's movements of the modern era to demand rights for women. Quite the contrary; in times of change and insecurity, women repeatedly looked to the Christian faith as the "religion of freedom." The concept of "equality before God" gave them the courage to think for themselves and fight the "tyranny of dogma, convention, and the family."[31]

This context and motivation have been documented in many autobiographical works and other sources from the women's movements.[32] For example, Louise Otto, a devout Christian who was well versed in the Bible—by no means typical—called upon her sisters to be "true Christians" in order to serve the cause of freedom—that is, "love of humankind."[33] The debate over *Was die Pastoren denken* (What the Pastors are Thinking)[34] and "Anfrage an die Herren Theologen Deutschlands aus den Kreisen christlich gebildeter Frauen" (Questions to the Gentlemen Theologians in Germany from the Ranks of Christian-Educated Women)[35] played an undeniable role in raising women's awareness of their own rights and their struggle for equality.

Natural or Civic Equality: From Natural Law to a Law of Reason

Theories of equality according to classical, rationalist natural law in the seventeenth and eighteenth centuries nevertheless laid the groundwork for women's demands for rights, even if women's rights were not an issue for the major proponents of such law and found mention, at most, hidden in matrimonial law. The legal darkness brought about by the witch hunts, belief in the devil, and horrendous methods of torture began to lighten, even for women, in the early eighteenth century, when witch trials started to decrease in number. One person who contributed to this improvement was Christian Thomasius, law professor and natural law scholar at the University of Halle. He first encountered the witch hunts when an affidavit was requested from his university department. From then on, his writings and lectures attacked the fanatical spirit of the times, condemning heresy, torture, and the witch trials. Not "until the days of Thomasius"—according to popular tradition—"could women once again grow old in peace."[36] His venture was a thoroughly courageous one for the time, since he himself could have faced charges of heresy and blasphemy. Above all, it demanded a sense of reason. This no longer referred to a universal reason delivered "from above" or supported by dogma, but reason as a subjective critique, a "systematic doubt" of all tradition (René Descartes), as well as logical deduction or proof through empirical and historical certainty.

Thomasius's famous dissertation *De Crimine Magiae*, published in 1701, called for an end to all witch trials, since witchcraft was a fictitious crime. In 1631, the Jesuit priest Friedrich von Spee had already anonymously written a sensational treatise condemning the torture and inquisitorial procedures used in the witch trials, but he did not call the existence of witchcraft itself into question.[37] Thomasius, on the other hand, took up the battle against the belief in witches, in particular belief in the devil. In 1712 he published *Historische Untersuchung vom Ursprung und Fortgang des Inquisitionsprozesses wider die Hexen* (Historical Investigation of the Origin and Course of the Inquisitional Trials against Witches), "wherein it is clearly proven that the devil who seeks mistresses and leads them to the Block Mount is not more than a century and a half old."[38] In other words, Thomasius showed that witchcraft and the so-called pact with the devil were figments of the imagination that were no more than 200 years old. The date can be confirmed through the papal bull issued in 1484 by Innocent VIII and the *Malleus Maleficarum* (Witches' Hammer), written by Jacob Sprenger in 1487, which was based on it. In 1716 Thomasius's work led to a Prussian royal edict stating that the death penalty could not be carried out for crimes of magic without first being approved by the ruler. The last witch burning in Prussia took place in 1728; the last on German soil took place in Kempten in 1775.

Such support by a legal scholar for the cause of women was extraordinary, and by no means a matter of course. Not only did it cause Thomasius to lose favor with his contemporary colleagues; he remains in disrepute even today.[39] Although the new Age of Reason challenged superstition and prejudice, it celebrated the emergence of modern science above all as a "masculine birth," according to Francis Bacon in 1603.[40] A clear line had been drawn between intellect and nature, reason and emotion, and rationality or so-called scientific objectivity, in contrast to irrationality and subjectivity, which were plainly attributed to women. Discourse on the essence of witchcraft was an expression of the fear of women and female sexuality.[41] Thus it was no coincidence that this debate played a constitutive role in perceptions of science in the competing disciplines of the new sciences; for example, among alchemists and mechanists or among pietists, early Enlightenment thinkers, and materialists.

In the words of Francis Bacon, science was a "chaste and lawful marriage between Mind and Nature, . . . to bind her [Nature] to your [man's] service and make her your slave." That is, it was by no means a collaboration between mind and nature, which would imply a mixture of the male and the female—as the alchemists believed—but a virile force, the goal of which was control and domination of nature, especially the female nature.[42] It was precisely this segregation of women, not only ideologically but in practice—as "nature" as it were, as an object rather than a subject of study—that was to advance the natural sciences to science par excellence. Max Horkheimer and Theodor Adorno explained where such inconsistencies led in their *Dialectic of Enlightenment*, referring to Bacon: "The concordance between the mind of man and the nature of things that he had in mind is patriarchal: the human mind, which overcomes superstition, is to hold sway over a disenchanted nature. Knowledge, which is power, knows no obstacles: neither in the enslavement of men nor in compliance with the world's rulers."[43]

This significant chapter in the history of science between the sixteenth and eighteenth centuries is closely tied to the development of the Western doctrine of natural law into a law of reason. But developments in law, legal theory, and especially legal practice took neither a regular nor a linear course. Quite the contrary: the legal situation during this period was confusing and complicated due to a multitude of legal sources and conventions that were as varied as the social and political conditions.[44] Legal scholarship and practice in Germany were influenced by the Usus Modernus Pandectarum (contemporary application of Roman law), a mixture of Roman legal sources incorporated little by little and local German law, also called customary law.[45] Deliberations about a better, more reasonable system of law were triggered by the questionable nature of the traditional legal order; its unity and legitimacy had broken down in face of new ideas about the world, such as the discovery of the Americas, and centuries of religious wars.

Modern doctrine on natural law took up many aspects of the cultural tradition and social teachings of the Greek philosophers, the Stoics, and the Christian concept of natural law.[46] First and foremost, it offered emancipation from Church tutelage and moral theology. It broke with all prevailing authorities of the time, both human and divine, and viewed reason per se as the only standard of criticism. It promised liberation and appealed to a higher, just law that served as the foundation, contour, and guideline for the improvement of concrete historical and social conditions. The unique aspect of the new legal doctrine lay in the fact that it came on the scene as anthropology, the philosophy and science of human beings, and thus had very little to do with the practice of law. On the other hand, it claimed to be legal theory and thus to influence the legal conditions of human beings. Its methods corresponded to those of the newly developing natural sciences, and its goal was to establish a comprehensive system of rights and obligations on the basis of logical, systematic deductions and mathematically precise constructions of legal concepts. The model that formed the foundation for numerous variants of the "natural law" of society was the social contract. It marked the transition from natural to social, "civil" conditions, not necessarily as a historical fact, but as a "parable of consistent foundation of law."[47]

In his famous treatise *De iure belli ac pacis* (On the Law of War and Peace, 1625), Hugo Grotius (1583–1645), humanist and pioneer of the Enlightenment, defined justice as that which is "not contrary to the nature of a society of rational creatures."[48] According to natural law as expressed by Enlightenment thinkers, the gift of reason basic to all individuals was the foundation on which to base the equality of all humans. It was innate and unrestricted, though only imaginable in "status naturalis," the state of nature. The state of nature served the new political theory only as a backdrop against which to explain the necessity for a social contract. This necessity arose as a consequence of "human nature." Because of social drives, neediness, or ruthless egotism, human beings needed to enter into a contract to compensate for the insecurity of the "state of nature." In this contract, the members of society unite and surrender their freedom of action to an absolute authority. It is through this social contract that a collective will is theoretically created, along with a compact of rule and thus a state, which provides its citizens in "status civilis" with order and security. Otherwise, "they are in that condition which is called Warre; and such a warre, as is of every man, against every man," according to Thomas Hobbes;[49] or the "Preservation of their Lives, Liberties and Estates"—for John Locke (1632–1704) this meant above all "Preservation of their Property"[50]—could not be guaranteed.

From the very beginning, this natural law theory combined different concepts of equality. On the one hand, there was the idea of an "original" natural equality of all individuals, an equality that is not necessarily granted under civil, state conditions. On the contrary, a particular inequality—for example between propertied and property-less individuals—is presupposed and justified, according to Locke for example, by a social contract.[51] On the other hand, there was the legal demand for social equality, which opposed social distinctions with the belief in an original, natural equality of all human beings. In this latter sense, historically, equality became a social, political, and legal concept, used in particular to criticize a privilege- and estates-based society, but by no means implying that all individuals are equal in their natural aptitudes and abilities. Instead, it signified that all individuals have the same worth and the same rights in relationship to one another. This is why Christian Wolff, in an essay on the foundations of natural and international law, stressed that all human beings are equal, not only "on the basis of nature," but also with respect to "moral reason."[52]

In any case, we must ask why these models of society have remained exclusively male, even though the equality of all individuals has been rationally and theoretically grounded and has become a principle of modern political theory. That is, why have women, as human beings "endowed with reason," never been considered equals or partners in the social contract? Reference to women's "nature" has not served to justify their autonomy and liberty. In fact the opposite is true; it has led to their explicit exclusion and subordination, albeit under new and different conditions and with new justifications.[53]

Because the "natural" liberty and equality of women was presupposed in principle, however, their unequal treatment and subordination under civil conditions demanded at least a legal explanation. This justification was supplied not by the social contract but by the institution of marriage.[54] The significance of marriage as a special institution that stabilized social conditions, "as the nursery of humankind" (Samuel von Pufendorf), was emphasized by all authors. Matrimonial law received special attention from proponents of natural law, not least because of the church's heretofore unrestricted jurisdiction over marriage. Once marriage was no longer viewed as an institution established by divine commandment, but as a contract between two equal partners, it could only be voluntary, and the contract might be dissolved at any time through divorce. The obligations of spouses, and even parents, were thus conceived of as reciprocal and mutual, since marriage was fundamentally a "community of equals." The supremacy of the husband that was justified in the same breath, the *imperium conjugale*, arose because the wife voluntarily subordinated herself, through the marriage contract, to the authority of the husband. If the woman's subordination to the man's will is legitimized through the marriage contract, however, it should also have followed that unmarried women enjoyed fundamentally equal rights. This would have rendered superfluous the subordination of women in legal transactions, so-called gender tutelage of unmarried women. But this was by no means the case. In fashioning the legal details and putting these principles into practice, convention and the weight of traditional supremacy and authority in gender relations continued to have an impact in customary law. In following the various authors over time, not even a gradual development toward greater freedom and equality for women can be discerned. Hugo Grotius assumed as a matter of course the "natural"—in the sense of innate—supremacy of the husband. He based his views, like his defense of polyandry, on the Bible, both Old and New Testaments, which includes references to the husband as the "head of the wife." This confirms that Grotius was completely unable to distance himself from church doctrine when it came to matrimonial law.[55]

John Locke, on the other hand, distinguished explicitly between the different forms of political and domestic authority, and argued vehemently in his *Two Treatises of Government* against using biblical arguments to justify viewing the monarchical form of government as an example of absolute partriarchy. He especially opposed drawing an analogy between the divine rule of the monarch and Adam's rule over Eve, also based on the story of Genesis: "[T]he Subjection that is due from a Wife to her Husband [is] far enough from that which Subjects owe the Governours of Political Societies."[56] Also, Locke stressed that in marriage, "Rule . . . naturally falls to the Man's share, as the abler and the stronger. But this reach[es] but to the things of their common Interest and Property, . . . being so far from that of an absolute Monarch."[57] As long as the "procreation and the bringing up of children" (§ 83) were not threatened, Locke left all further legal questions, such as the right to divorce, marital property rights, and parental custody, to free contractual agreement between the spouses.

Samuel von Pufendorf (1632–1694) was the first to develop natural law doctrine into a comprehensive system of private law, thus greatly influencing jurisprudence in Germany. Christian Wolff was one of his most notable successors. Pufendorf, too, viewed the right to exercise authority over individuals—including women—as arising solely from either a one-sided act of subordination or a two-way contract. Consequently, in a marriage contract the wife grants her husband conjugal authority, thus obliging herself to obedience; and the man is obligated to protect his wife. There are two noteworthy aspects to this more common than innovative deduction: First, Pufendorf saw a women's subservience to her husband's authority as being compatible with matrimonial love, just as the dominion of a ruler does not prevent the love of a subject. And second, a so-called Amazon marriage can also exist—that is, one which involves not a marriage contract, but a simple contract, such as for the purpose of procreation. This type of marriage would not initiate a long-term relationship or any absolute rights over the woman. An example of a possible reversal of matrimonial authority are the marriages of reigning queens.[58]

Thomasius (1655–1728) was definitely an outsider in his time on questions of women's rights, since his system of family law was based on natural law. In his *Institutionen jurisprudentiae divinae* (1688), he proclaimed astoundingly egalitarian ideas on marriage. As the purpose of marriage he named not only the obligation to procreate but also the husband's obligation "to satisfy the desire of the woman." In his view, the marriage contract did not even require that the partners live together permanently, nor did it grant the husband the right to determine the place of residence.[59] In particular, however, Thomasius rejected the husband's absolute authority, since the purpose of marriage could only be achieved through friendship or "rational love," as he later put it in his ethics: "Where there is coercion there is no love."[60] In a manner quite unusual for German legal theory, he described human nature as being characterized not only by the "instinct of sociability" (as in Pufendorf) or by a "ruthless egotistical wolf nature"[61] (as in Hobbes), but also by the "search for happiness." By including women in this search—something that was not to be taken for granted— Thomasius also acknowledged a woman's ability to preserve her dignity in love.[62]

Following directly from Pufendorf, Christian Wolff's (1679–1754) natural law theory would have practical legal impact as a result of his influence at the universities, and in keeping with the specific Prusso-German form of enlightened absolutism. The authors of the Prussian General Code (Preu-ßisches Allgemeines Landrecht, or ALR) of 1794 had all come from the Wolffian School and were influenced by his understanding of law.[63] According to Wolff, spouses entered into marriage through a contract; marriage is explicitly a "community of equals, and whatever shall take place therein must be determined through mutual agreement." But Wolff's explanation of the fact that this equality is then ended is as typical as it is awkward. The "rule" or authority of the husband can be restored among "equal" partners either by contract or tacitly, by resorting to "custom." "[T]he wife can relinquish her right . . . by tacitly accepting that which is brought by custom; and then the woman is subordinate to the man."[64]

Wolff, like all proponents of natural law, saw the aim and object of marriage to be first and foremost "procreation and the bringing up of children."[65] Legal historian Marianne Weber's 1907 appraisal of Christian Wolff and his benevolently patriarchal teachings on matrimony was devastating, though not only because of this utilitarian, demographic justification. In her view, "these statements on the relationship between the spouses hardly represent a hint of some great and new personality ideals . . . ; it's just the everyday petty bourgeois air of so-called 'common sense,' . . . the familiar, philistine German opinion."[66]

International feminist critiques of individual authors and the specific "gender dialectic of the Enlightenment" have demonstrated that Philistine opinions and patriarchy are typical not only to Germany. This critique has shown that contradictions in equality discourse cannot be reduced to a mere "patriarchal power play." Instead, they must be analyzed within the context of scholarly discourse of the time. With respect to the French Enlightenment in particular, this criticism has succeeded in tracing a path from the "genderless reason" of the early Enlightenment to the anthropological definition of woman as a "natural being" and, finally, as the "moral gender" essential for society. Poulain de la Barre's famous 1673 work *De l'égalité des deux sexes* (The Equality of the Two Sexes) is thought to have opened a new "querelle des femmes" in the rationalistic, Cartesian tradition, concluding that "reason has no gender."[67] The decisive shift to functional gender difference was completed almost a century later with Jean-Jacques Rousseau's concept of femininity and sexual difference.[68]

Participation by women in this discourse is becoming increasingly apparent. The heretofore unacknowledged evidence of female self-reflection no longer allows women to be depicted exclusively as obedient and subservient, but also lets them be shown as participatory, active, and oppositional.[69] But the sociohistorical and political contexts of the very different expressions of gender relations, and especially their legal aspects, have been neglected for too long in the philosophy of gender.[70] Laws are an expression and a part of social reality; though legal practices have experienced cultural delays, they are still a measure of the relations of power and authority between the sexes.

Crawford B. Macpherson's *Political Theory of Possessive Individualism* describes in detail the social premises that have been incorporated into, and appear to prove, the consistency of natural law, without dealing with the gender issue.[71] Conclusion of a contract, either in private law or as a social contract, presupposes recognition of the equality of the participating parties.[72] However, state law doctrine from the sixteenth to the eighteenth centuries assumed that both social contract and state contract were concluded only among men. More precisely, they could only be concluded among male heads of households.[73] That is, in seventeenth- and eighteenth-century society, the only individuals considered equal in a political sense were property owners, "free equal individuals related to each other as proprietors of their own capacities and of what they have acquired by their exercise." "Since the individual is human only in so far as free, and free only in so far as a proprietor of himself, human society can only be a series of relations between sole proprietors, i.e., a series of market relations."[74] This is why Locke could justify the actual social inequality of citizens by stressing that, while "Man [is] born, as has been proved, with a Title to perfect Freedom, and an uncontrouled enjoyment of all the Rights and Priviledges of the Law of Nature," this applied only to those in a position to "provide for themselves."[75]

At first, not only were women, or wives, to be exact, excluded from this society of property owners and market participants, so were those who were not "proprietors of their own capacities" or who lacked "freedom from dependence on the wills of others."[76] This included all wage workers, or, in the terminology of the time, servants, who surrendered, however temporarily, their ownership of their abilities and capacity to work. Locke wrote about the relationship between master and servant: "[A] Free-man makes himself a Servant to another, by selling him for a certain time, the Service he undertakes to do, in exchange for Wages he is to receive: And though this commonly puts him into the Family of his Master, and under the ordinary Discipline thereof; yet it gives the Master but a Temporary Power over him and no greater than what is contained in the Contract between 'em."[77]

Consequently, not only were women and children ruled out as parties to the social contract, so were all other persons living "in the peace of the house," such as servants and workers, as well as "vagabonds and beggars."[78] The gender-specific exclusion of women was thus eclipsed for the time being by the fact that they did not own property, a quality shared by underprivileged men and the lower social classes. Men who were only "temporarily" subjected to the authority of a master in the form of a work contract, and even (male) minors, whom Locke often used as an example of those serving a "Temporary Power," were in a different situation from women to the extent that women were robbed for a lifetime of their capacities and that which they acquired through their work; they had no "freedom from dependence on the wills of others." Women were subject to the authority of either a father or a husband, but in any case a male. The social relations of those subject to the authority of the master of the house remained in the natural state; they were "subordinate Relations."[79] They continued to fit into a class or estates-based order, according to which the status of the home, the "domestic society," was the lowest level in the "societas civilis," at that time a feudal state. In this societal order, "domestic society" was represented and controlled by the master of the house, and "domestic peace" defined the boundaries of authoritarian power. But even when the estates order was abandoned and the emancipation of these masters made them citizens, civil society consisted of "the ties of the families for the purpose of the common good." Ernst Ferdinand Klein, one of the authors of the Prussian General Code, expressed it as follows in 1801 in an attempt to grant historical legitimacy to the rights of the masters of the house: "Domestic society paved the way for the rest; from families grew nations; man and woman joined together before the emergence of a citizen's council; masters of the house issued orders before kings began to rule."[80]

Significant to the later formation of civil society is the fact that the social sphere of the home, the *oikos*, "with all these subordinate Relations of Wife, Children, Servants and Slaves," was excluded from the political sphere, the sphere of rule, and subjected to the special authority of the head of the "domestic society."[81] More than that, *labor*, the everyday economy and housework, was all incorporated into the property of the "Master of the Family." Once appropriated by him, it was excluded from market relations, or, rather, it formed the indispensable foundation upon which these market relations rested.

Civil society as conceived by natural law theorists of the sixteenth to eighteenth centuries thus had a hidden base from the outset. Beneath the newly forming bourgeois public sphere, "the sphere of private people coming together as a public," was a private sphere that preserved and maintained it. This was the family, where gender relations were resolved. In the transition to a capitalist society, this family order was evidently measured by standards other than efficiency and was not subject to universal market principles and equality:

> To the degree to which commodity exchange burst out of the confines of the household economy, the sphere of the conjugal family became differentiated from the sphere of social reproduction. The process of the polarization of state and society was repeated once more within society itself. The status of private man combined the role of owner of commodities with that of head of the family, that of property owner with that of "human being" per se.[82]

Gender—A Political Category: Rousseau and Fichte

As the principle of equality gained social and political importance and as (male) individuals started breaking out of the estates-based order and becoming citizens and owners of capital, or at least of labor, it became impossible to hide the fact that women were excluded. "Gender" consequently emerged as a political category. This social model first became a target of criticism with respect to the features that constituted its antifeudal advances and specifically bourgeois character. The critique came from the proponents of reason—a reason that enables all individuals, not only men, to perceive "total liberty" and their right to equality, provided they are given the chance. It was not possible to completely exclude women as human beings from education and science; in any case, there were exceptions that proved not the rule but the opposite. The extraordinary examples of female scholarship were so obviously impressive, and aristocratic as well as middle-class women showed such an eagerness to learn and to read, that their achievements continued to provoke vehement opposition and polemical responses. Adolf von Knigge's 1788 bestseller *Über den Umgang mit Menschen* (On Human Conduct), for example, can be considered to have captured the male zeitgeist. Von Knigge conceded that "in the company of a lady, . . . who has high standards when it comes to aesthetics or scholarship, . . . [he] always [had] an attack of chills."[83] A special educational effort was necessary to bring such unfeminine endeavors back on track, "to delight the man."[84] The medieval legal institution of "gender tutelage," which applied to unmarried as well as married women, was outdated and had fallen somewhat by the wayside. It is striking that precisely in the century of the "scholarly woman," gender tutelage was revived in jurisprudence, with the new justification that the "weakness" and inferior intelligence of the female sex made it incapable of coping with the complexity of legal transactions.[85]

One of the few women in the eighteenth century who was permitted to participate in male reason and scholarship, in this case thanks to an understanding father, was Dorothea Christine Leporin. In 1742 she wrote a treatise on obstacles that kept women from studying. In it she stated: "I deliberately do not deal with those who do not even include women in the human population figures; for they do not deserve to have others make an effort for their sakes, until they themselves have proven through the use of reason that they are not unworthy of being called human beings."[86] Dorothea Erxleben (Leporin's married name) was indeed forced to deal with the opponents of education and study for women. Only after numerous attempts and the intervention of the King of Prussia was she—"a special female being [*ein weibliches Sonderwesen*]"—permitted to complete her doctorate at the University of Halle in 1754.[87]

Natural law doctrine started crumbling in its very own field, law, without which "domestic societies" and family relations apparently could not survive the development of capitalist production. Whereas classical natural law scholars were able to leave matrimonial law, or the law of the "conjugal society" (that is, the married couple), to traditional custom, the pressure for legitimacy grew toward the end of the eighteenth century. This becomes apparent when comparing the 1754 explanations by Christian Wolff with Johann Gottlieb Fichte's *Grundlage des Naturrechts nach Prinzipien der Wissenschaftslehre* (The Science of

Rights), written in 1796. In making this comparison, it is also necessary to consider Jean-Jacques Rousseau's contribution to gender philosophy.

The claim can still be heard today that "there has seldom been a person with such a strong sense of justice as the philosopher J. G. Fichte" (from the introduction to the 1960 German edition of his work). In his *Science of Rights*, Fichte explicitly derived law and right not from nature but from reason. He stressed that "the fundamental principle of law, as law generally, has been shown to be, not a mechanical law of nature, but a law for freedom."[88] At the same time he justified the "subjec[tion]" of the woman and the husband's "right of compulsion over her" on the basis of reason.[89] His explanation employs the "nature" of woman; that is, everything he attempted to subject to male reason he declared to be woman's nature. From this biased position, he developed a whole network of intellectual contradictions. Fichte's entire "idealistic" philosophy is based on the ego, the self-determining and free subject that is "internally compelled to recognize every other being which has the same form as a rational being, and thus as a possible subject for the Conception of Rights."[90] Nevertheless, according to Fichte the woman "stands one step lower " than the man in the "natural institution" of marriage. She regains the same level "in making herself the means to satisfy man . . . and she receives her whole dignity back again only by thus making herself means to satisfy man from love for a particular one."[91] Thus his starting point was not the original equality of all individuals. Instead, Fichte *imagined* the woman as a "non-ego" that could serve his narcissistic masculinity as an opposite, an object. Here he took idealism to an extreme, comprehending "All Being, that of the Ego as well as that of the Non-Ego" as "a determined modification of consciousness."[92] He declared that: "Since he may confess all to himself, and hence finds in himself the whole fullness of humanity, he is able to overlook his whole relation to woman, as woman herself can never overlook it. He, therefore, sees how an originally free being voluntarily submits itself to him with unlimited confidence."[93]

Fichte then continued consistently; regarding the civil and legal status of the woman, he concluded that since only a self-determined, free subject can realize the concept of right, that is, can restrict its freedom through the possibility of another's freedom, "[woman's] continuous necessary wish . . . to be so subjected" excludes her from all individual rights.[94] "Her husband is, therefore, the administrator of all her rights in consequence of her own necessary will."[95]

The legal framework anchoring this gender-based inequality was the same for Fichte as it had been through the ages: marriage. Although uprightly bourgeois, it was—in a clear dig at natural law theory—more than a contract, which ideally demanded the "free will" of the woman. "Marriage is not merely a legal association like the state, but rather a natural and moral association."[96] The new, "modern" motivation for marriage was significant. Bartering and economic calculation were replaced by love, mutual though unequal. But Fichte's acknowledgment of this thoroughly "modern" emotion by no means signified greater self-esteem, self-realization, and emancipation for women. Instead, it implied consent to subservience and subordination to the will of the man. This was very different from the gender philosophy of early Romanticism, which developed at the same time. For writers like Friedrich Schlegel and Friedrich Schleiermacher, the experience of love, both sensual and intellectual, created the conditions for woman to escape social convention and follow her destiny as a human being.[97]

Fichte did not believe the crux of woman's subordination and lower status lay only in her "nature," whatever that might mean. He saw it much more precisely in the "nature" of marital intercourse, though it is apparent that Fichte's understanding of love and sexuality was narrow and inhibited. For women, only marital love is "moral," since only in marriage is paternity certain. The woman, however, shows greater forgiveness: "It is certainly possible, nay, even honorable, to the wife to pardon her husband in such a case [adultery]."[98] Fichte reduced marital love to genital sexuality, in legal terminology "consummated intercourse." Its aim, however—and in this sense Fichte was "modern" and distinguished himself from classical natural law theorists—was not limited to procreation: "As the moral impulse of woman manifests itself as love, so in man that impulse manifests itself as generosity."[99] But since, "so far as the real act of generation is concerned, the one sex keeps purely active, and the other purely passive," "a woman can not confess that impulse to herself." "This impulse must assume in women the character of an impulse to satisfy the man."[100]

Anthropology, which provides the basis for this analogy between a specific sexual behavior, described as "natural," and the social order governing men and women—and thus the connection between love and state theory—had already been referred to by Rousseau. Though mentioned in a seemingly less obvious manner, it played a central role in his political theory. To be sure, such polarizing characterizations—male/female, active/passive—represent an almost constant pattern of thought in Western philosophy.[101] But it was new to take the gender roles thus defined to such an extreme, assigning women the sphere of love and morality, as opposed to law. This was a response to developments in a society that was unable to function on the basis of its fundamental principles: labor as a commodity, self-interest, competition, and rationality separate from emotion. At the same time, it reflected the insecurity and horror triggered by the mere thought of human equality in relation to the most important social institutions (such as family) and the imposition of organizational norms on the private sphere. Rousseau helped pave the way for the French Revolution and at the same time critiqued the emerging civil society. He clearly recognized the social and moral deficiencies of this new society; he aimed at least to "slow down the progress of our vices," though by no means to initiate a "return to nature."[102] Since he viewed women as the "moral sex" in this society, he assigned them a special social function and a role complementary to that of men.[103] While certainly not the first or only one to do this, he was the most influential.

Rousseau's return to the "nature" of woman was his way of maintaining virtue and morality, because nature endowed "the weaker sex" especially with "modesty," in order to harness women's sexual desire and the "excessive passions" of men. This was a task accomplished by men through "reason." By appealing to "nature," Rousseau also attempted to prove the impossibility of sameness or equality of the sexes: "I grant you this is not the law of love, but it is the law of nature, which is older than love itself."[104] His explanation appears as clearly as this in his great novel on education, *Emile* (1762). Book 5, entitled "Sophy, or Woman," deals with the search for an appropriate wife for the protagonist. She "must possess all those characters of her sex which are required to enable her to play her part in the physical and moral order."[105] Not simply spouse, housewife, and mother, which represented the ideal for his German followers in particular, the "ideal partner" in Rousseau's view was more than a gift of nature. The educational endeavors he considered necessary demonstrated that "gender" must indeed first be socially formed (or, as we say today, constructed) and that it should be viewed as a political category within the framework of a social theory. Many generations of educators of girls subsequently attempted to carry out this political task.[106] Mary Wollstonecraft thus had good reason, during the French Revolution, to declare war on "Rousseau's wild chimeras" in her *A Vindication of the Rights of Women*.[107]

Rousseau also derived the bourgeois argument for the legitimacy of female subordination from a typology of the sexual act: "In the union of the sexes each alike contributes to the common end, but in different ways. From this diversity springs the first difference which may be observed between man and woman in their moral relations. The man should be strong and active; the woman should be weak and passive; the one must have both the power and the will; it is enough that the other should offer little resistance. When this principle is admitted, it follows that woman is specially made for man's delight."[108]

In contrast to Fichte, Rousseau assumed mutuality and a secret power of the women, if the traces of the gender struggle and the motivations for this gender philosophy were to be revealed. For Rousseau, it was not definitively clear which gender is truly stronger in love, and whether "the stronger party seems to be master." "For nature has endowed woman with a power of stimulating man's passions in excess of man's power of satisfying those passions, and has thus made him dependent on her goodwill, and compelled him in his turn to endeavour to please her, so that she may be willing to yield to his superior strength."[109] Whereas Fichte would never have made such a concession, Rousseau granted sexual attackers the same general absolution in his comments on rape that are found in legal practice even today. Supposedly, the man cannot distinguish between woman's "cunning" and her resistance: "This uncertainty constitutes the chief charm of the man's victory, and the woman is usually cunning enough to leave him in doubt."[110]

Both Fichte and Rousseau have since been criticized and analyzed thoroughly from a feminist perspective.[111] What is noteworthy about Fichte's "Deduction of Marriage" in the appendix to his *Science of Rights*, especially for legal theory, are the consequences of his philosophy for women in the theory and practice of family law even today. Well beyond nineteenth-century legal scholarship, Fichte's marriage doctrine offered a justification of marriage that was considered progressive, modern, and "moral" compared with natural law theory, because it involved more than merely a reciprocal civil law contract. The "dignity of marriage as an institution,"[112] still vehemently defended today, sets "a generally valid standard for the cohabitation of the sexes,"[113] even according to today's prevailing legal theory and jurisprudence. Not only has it played a decisive role in the debate on divorce, it also influenced and supported the fact that matrimonial power relations were until recently established as relations of authority by the highest courts.[114]

In contrast to Fichte's unconcealed and "crude" sexism, Rousseau has elicited a more complex feminist response.[115] There is hardly an author, philosopher, or educator whose works and novels (for example, *Julie or The New Heloise*, 1761) have been read with such enthusiasm and zeal, especially by women; Rousseau was able to impress upon women themselves the cultural significance of "femininity" and compassion as a moral strength. It must be noted that his "program of domestication," with which the social character of "woman" would be formed as a complement to that of "man," only makes sense within the overall context of his philosophy of history. Yet from the perspective of legal theory and politics, Rousseau's concept of femininity is neither merely "a literary dramatization"[116] nor "a placement in a theoretical system."[117] The fact that an individual author made some patriarchal slip-ups misses the point, however, since "none of the thoughts taken up by him [Rousseau] were his exclusive property, even if he gave many of them their prettiest attire."[118] What was important from the perspective of legal theory were the practical and political consequences, which were considerable in Rousseau's case—indeed, virtually inestimable—for girls' education and other fields. For more than two hundred years Rousseau's arguments have served bourgeois jurisprudence in justifying legislated inequality for women. Thus Jean Étienne Portalis, co-author of the French Civil Code of 1804, especially its family law section, wrote a commentary that reads like a paraphrase of Rousseau's exposition in *Emile*: "People have long argued over the superiority or inequality of the two sexes. Nothing is more foolish than this argument. . . . What they have in common comes from their species; the ways they are different come from their sex. . . . Nature made them so different in order to bring them together. This difference in their very essence is the basis for their rights and obligations. There can be no doubt that the two spouses share a common goal. But they pursue this goal in different ways. They are the same in certain areas and cannot be compared in others. Strength and boldness are on the side of the man; fearfulness and modesty on that of the woman."[119]

Immanuel Kant's theories of law left indelible traces on the legal history of women. Kant also considered the sex act and the gender traits of men and women in determining legal relations under matrimonial law. His notorious and often cited definition of marriage as "the union of two persons of different sexes for lifelong possession of each other's sexual attributes" is as unsentimental as it is utilitarian. Yet his subsequent discussion showed that he took seriously the contractual nature of marriage as a relationship between equals: "For the natural use that one sex makes of the other's sexual organs is *enjoyment*, for which one gives itself up to the other. In this act a human being makes himself into a thing, which conflicts with the right of humanity in his own person. There is only one condition under which this is possible: that while one person is acquired by the *other as if it were a thing*, the one who is acquired acquires the other in turn; for in this way each reclaims itself and restores its personality."[120] His language is similar to that used by Hugo Grotius, who in turn based his work on Roman law and the corpus juris.[121] As unoriginal as these instructions on the purpose of marriage might sound, reciprocal, egalitarian purpose is central to his concept of "human dignity." Kant's categorical imperative, that "Reason accordingly refers every maxim of the will as giving universal law to every other will and also to every action toward oneself," presupposes "the idea of the dignity of a rational being, who obeys no law other than that which he himself at the same time gives"—that is, "because he could claim *to be an end in himself*, to be accepted as such by all others, and not to be used by anyone else simply as a means to other ends.[122] This . . . is the basis of man's unconditional equality."[123] By not denying the woman equal dignity, even in marriage and the love relationship, but on the contrary viewing devotion as mutual and thus expressly incorporating the woman, Kant's thesis is very different from, for example, Fichte's. Nevertheless, ultimately women are certainly not granted equality in Kantian legal theory. Even in matrimonial law, Kant restricted women's equality by deriving the "authority" of the man, as head of the household, from a "natural superiority." Even his doctrinally unsuccessful attempt to construe the particular personal and material relations in marriage and family law as *"rights to person akin to rights to things"*[124] can hardly be considered an "unmasking" of unjust relations in civil or private matrimonial law.[125] And the early Kant, influenced by Enlightenment thought, can hardly be defended against the later "critic of practical reason."[126] For even in the public law of the state, it was taken for granted that women were only *"passive* citizens," since "an apprentice in the service of a merchant or artisan; a domestic servant (as distinguished from a civil servant); a minor (*naturaliter vel civiliter*); all women and, in general, anyone whose preservation in existence (his being fed and protected) depends not on his management of his own business but on arrangements made by another (except the state) . . . lack civil personality."[127] Thus their lower status here was based—as in classical natural law theory—on the dependence of their modes of production, similar to the situation of other "dependents under protection" in the domestic economy. Their status therefore appears amenable to change once that dependence is ended. This was not the case in the views of theorists such as Rousseau and Fichte.

Even before all feudal chains were broken and estates-based patriarchy entirely lost its legal legitimacy and material base, political theory toward the end of the eighteenth century found an explicitly sexist means of excluding women from the ranks of legal persons and providing for their legal discrimination. It was sexist not only because it was based on gender traits possessing a supposedly immutable biological foundation, but because, in a narrower sense, it made the sexual conduct of women the basis of legal standards, and thus of a new political theory of inequality.[128]

Fichte's "natural law without nature,"[129] as well as Kant's legal insight into practical reason, are all the more astounding because these legal theories were published "at a time when human rights are loudly proclaimed from the rooftops," as Theodor G. von Hippel wrote in his 1792 appeal for the rights of women.[130] At the same time, early Romantic literature and discourse brought to light an understanding that "the renewal and perfection of humankind could not be set in motion without the other half of humankind."[131] Certainly the elimination of gender difference within the main category of "human," as propagated by the Romantics, did not include political and civic emancipation along with gender and cultural emancipation, nor was this demanded by the numerous intellectual women among them. For the German middle classes in particular, this period offered at best "a climate promoting a woman's individuality,"[132] but not her status as a legal person or citizen with equal rights.[133]

Nevertheless, although much remained unfulfilled, some insights would have lasting relevance. Friedrich Schlegel, for example, wrote in his letter "On Philosophy" that "masculinity and femininity, as they are usually taken and pursued, are the most dangerous obstacles to humanity."[134] Friedrich Schleiermacher stated this with equal clarity in his *Katechismus der Vernunft für edle Frauen* (Catechism of Reason for Noble Women, 1798). A century later, activists in the first German women's movement often quoted him: "I believe in the infinite humanity that existed before it took on the shell of masculinity and femininity."[135]

Human Rights for Women as Well as Men

Chapter 3

Olympe de Gouges's Counterproposal

THE FRENCH REVOLUTION represented a dramatic turning point in the history of the concept of equality. The old order in France collapsed under the weight of its own economic and political contradictions. As theories of equality became more radical, especially through the writings of Montesquieu and Rousseau, the theory that all human beings are equal became a legal concept from which concrete demands and a political program of social justice could be derived.

Montesquieu's *The Spirit of the Laws* showed how the equality that had been lost in the state of nature could be regained in civilized society.[1] The only way was "through laws." Rousseau reaffirmed the social contract as a compact of agreement—not one of subjection—in which the free will of the involved parties was not denied, but merged into a general will, a "volonté générale." Not only did this general will justify state sovereignty, but—and this is what made Rousseau's theories revolutionary—this state sovereignty was conceptualized as a sovereignty of the people, "formed wholly of the individuals who composed it." According to Rousseau, the general will was manifested in general laws. He thus described an essential principle of democracy and the state under the rule of law. Because the French Revolution was an example of political practice and not merely theory, however, we must pose the skeptical questions, Who were the people composing the sovereignty, and what was "general"?

"But when the whole people determines for the whole people, it considers only itself," wrote Rousseau in *The Social Contract*. "Then the affair on which they enact is general, as is the will that enacts. It is this act that I call a 'law.' When I say that the object of the laws is always general, I mean that the law views its subjects collectively and their actions abstractly, never a man as individual or an action as private."[2] The new understanding of equality took effect in political practice through the Declaration of the Rights of Man and of the Citizen of 26 August 1789. This declaration, unchanged and unabridged, enjoyed pride of place in the first French constitution of 3 September 1791. "When the ideas of liberty and equality were applied to real conditions, their nature was transformed," commented Lorenz von Stein, in his work on the history of social movements in France, referring to the major change that went hand in hand with the radical new concept of law. "Previously they had been considered purely political principles. Now it had been shown that they are in fact principles of society, and from that point onward the revolution revealed its true nature, the nature of a social reorganization of the entire people, since these principles listed in the Declaration of Rights established the nation's first basic law of society."[3]

Nevertheless, even this first constitution presupposed two fundamental contradictions expressing social consequences that remain problematic for civic equality to this day. The first was the fact that the proclaimed equality drew the line at property; "a certain quantum" of property was even a prerequisite for citizenship and voting rights.[4] "The property qualification," wrote Karl Marx in *On the Jewish Question*, "is the last political form in which private property is recognized. But the political suppression of private property not only does not abolish private property; it actually presupposes its existence."[5] The other contradiction that had far-reaching consequences was the exclusion of women.

Lorenz von Stein analyzed the first contradiction inherent in the voting qualification with extreme thoroughness. "Especially in this point, the germ of the contradiction appeared. And this powerful time, which was freer and more liberal than ever a monarchical period was, would cause this contradiction to have consequences more far-reaching than a new constitution. . . . With what right were active and passive citizens distinguished from one another, while the Declaration of Rights explicitly declared in Article 1: 'les hommes naissent et demeurent égaux en droits.'"[6]

Enfranchisement was based on tax liability, calculated on a basis of a minimum of three workdays. But it is interesting that, despite this, all "wage-earners" employed in the "état de domesticité" were also disqualified as voting citizens. Von Stein was a conservative social reformer and, as such, interested in gaining recognition for what he considered the legitimate concerns of the emerging proletariat, the fourth estate. He also hoped to ward off the dangers of socialism with the help of a "science of society." However, in his three-volume work he neglected entirely to mention women, whose lack of equality, even in his own definition of social movements, was "a persistent contradiction to the concept of man."[7] Von Stein was not alone in his neglect of the other main contradiction; quite the contrary, he was joined by numerous contemporaries and successors. Yet this one-sidedness is noteworthy, especially in the context of the French Revolution, for two reasons. The struggle for equality and parity that united the Third Estate, in collective opposition, into a "complete nation"[8] was directed first and foremost against the patriarchy, the privileged estate of the feudal lords, the power of the church and the aristocracy, and landowners and landed gentry. But the authority of heads of households, the traditional preeminence of heads of families, was not encroached upon. Why this was so remains part of the continuing history of the specifically bourgeois patriarchy.[9]

After the French Revolution, however, it was no longer possible to tacitly ignore the "other half of humankind"—and it is no coincidence that this expression became commonplace at that time.[10] Women helped initiate and carry out the revolutionary uprising. Also, around 1789 women as a group entered the public arena as a social movement for the first time, demanding not only bread but also their rights. That is, they did not merely participate in the march of the "marketwomen" to Versailles; they demanded political participation, organized themselves into political women's clubs, published the first feminist journals (for example, L'Observateur féminin and Le journal de l'Etat et du Citoyën), and flooded the National Assembly with their petitions: "You have just abolished privileges; now eliminate those of the male sex as well."[11]

This marked the beginning of the history of modern feminism, which from this point on was linked with the history of demands for civil rights. But in the historical consciousness and in history written by men, the women of the French Revolution appear at most as clichés or caricatures, as "women turned hyena."[12] Such rejection was in keeping with the political reaction of conservative and revolutionary contemporaries alike, which led as early as 1793 to the prohibition of any political activity whatsoever by women, the disbanding of women's associations, and even the execution of famous—as well as many anonymous—women who had spoken out for the interests of their gender. It was also consistent with the denunciation and abhorrence of the radical demands for equality made by the "men of equality" and their supporters, through which the rising bourgeoisie in France and elsewhere attempted to come to terms with the challenges of the revolution and its subsequent terror.[13]

The Declaration of the Rights of Woman and Citizen

Although it goes beyond the scope of this book to discuss the history of women in the French Revolution in greater detail, I would like to call attention to a historical document that offered a systematic counter-argument to men's narrowing down of the concept of equality. It is typical that this document, *The Declaration of the Rights of Woman and Citizen*, written by Olympe de Gouges in 1791, is missing from most collections and bibliographic sources. The way in which it has been withheld, or only preserved in fragments—that is, the lack of knowledge of this document—suffices in itself to illustrate the depth and diversity of resistance to equal rights for women.[14] The text, not available in its entirety in German translation until 1977 or in English until 1979, demonstrates the full significance of this unique piece of evidence of women asserting their rights.[15]

Aside from a number of political writings, many plays, and ephemeral literature, the Declaration of the Rights of Woman is the principal work of Olympe Marie Aubry, who took the pen name de Gouges. Extant biographical information on her is fragmentary.[16] She assumed her pseudonym around 1770, after moving from the provincial town of Montauban in southern France to Paris to start a new life. She was deliberate and adept in her efforts to enshroud in a veil of mystery both her age and her background (she was supposedly born out of wedlock, yet of aristocratic stock), as well as her status as a young and beautiful widow and mother, in order to break through the prejudices and requirements associated with her standing. It is truly annoying that virtually all historians who wrote anything at all about her wasted their time on such sensational details rather than on her statements and writings. In justification of such disrespect, the well-known historian of the French revolution Jules Michelet offered an appropriate explanation: He characterized Olympe de Gouges as "very uneducated, it was even claimed she could neither read nor write" and as an "outstanding extemporaneous poet . . . , who dictated a tragedy every day. . . . She was born in Montauban in 1755; her mother sold cleaning supplies, her father was a merchant or, others claim, a writer. Many regarded her as an illegitimate child of King Louis XV. This unhappy woman, full of noble ideas, became a plaything and victim of her nervous irritability."[17]

The first serious, detailed biography of de Gouges, written by Olivier Blanc on the basis of many revised sources, was published in 1981.[18] After so much time, it is not surprising that much remained unclear, not only about her mysterious background, but especially concerning the role she played in the turmoil of the revolution as part of the French women's movement, specifically her contacts and political activities. Consequently, her Declaration of the Rights of Woman and Citizen is generally regarded as the work of a lone author; but it can only be understood and interpreted against the background of extensive public activities by women at the time, and the intensive and varied participation of women in political meetings and clubs. Even at the National Assembly women mounted the rostrum to submit and defend their petitions; in other words, they were not silent listeners in the stands. In any case, their style of political action was typically quite "unbourgeois."

Blanc described and confirmed many details of Olympe de Gouges's life, such as her struggle to have her plays performed by the Comédie Française. She experienced particular difficulties when these plays contained such an obvious political message as *D'Esclavage des Noirs*, a tendentious play condemning France's slave trade in its colonies. Blanc mentioned de Gouges's numerous political writings and pamphlets, such as "Lettres au peuple," "Pour sauver la Patrie," and "Le cri du sage par une Femme!," printed and circulated at her own expense; they provided a way for de Gouges to become involved in the events of the revolution. Blanc also commented on her consistent activities against the death penalty, even in the case of King Louis XVI; in the end, it was this that aroused the suspicion of her revolutionary comrades and cost her her head. One of her many political posters, "Les Trois Urnes, ou le Salut de la Patrie," in which she spoke out for a federalist constitution, became the ultimate justification, in Robespierre's reign of terror, for trying de Gouges—a Republican who became suspect because she thought for herself. On 3 November (13 Brumaire) 1793, she was guillotined.[19]

Blanc acknowledged de Gouges's Declaration of the Rights of Woman as an unusual document that postulated civic equality between the sexes clearly and insightfully. But he, too, had to admit that this manifesto went "virtually unnoticed," even by her contemporaries, except for political friends at the Societé Fraternelles des Deux Sexes.[20]

In this declaration of human rights for women as well as men, the Declaration of the Rights of Woman and Citizen (for purposes of simplicity hereinafter referred to as the Declaration of Women's Rights or the "female version" of the declaration), the author held strictly to the form of the 1789 French declaration of "universal" human rights, the Declaration of the Rights of Man and Citizen, altering the wording only to the extent she deemed necessary. But what sometimes appear to be merely subtle nuances open it up to theoretical legal interpretation.[21] Olympe de Gouges did not simply replace the term "man" with "woman"; that is, she did not retaliate with a sexist response. Instead, in all political questions, she stressed the necessary "union of woman and man" (article 3) and demanded "the preservation of the natural and irrevocable rights of Woman and Man" (Article 2). The significance of the "Declaration of the Rights of Woman and Citizen" (de la Femme et de la Citoyenne) lies precisely in its catalogue of rights for all people, including men. Only in the preamble did Olympe de Gouge reverse the situation and paraphrase the existing text. It was clear to her that "the only causes of public misfortune and of governmental corruption . . . [were] the ignorance, disregard of or contempt for the rights of women." That is why the document opens with the most urgent of demands: "The mothers, daughters, and sisters, representatives of the nation demand to be constituted into a national assembly."

It is interesting that the foundation of sovereignty for her was not the "people," as in revolutionary theory following Rousseau; instead, de Gouges used the term "nation," a nation—and this insertion was essential to her—that "is none other than the union of Woman and Man." "Nation" was a modern concept in the French Revolution. It was used by the Third Estate in depicting itself as comprising the "complete nation." This concept was understood especially by the Jacobins as a "crowbar,"[22] a lever against both domestic feudalism and the external enemies of France allied with the ancien régime.[23] Not until the nineteenth century did a nationalistic orientation develop—when the bourgeoisie, in its own interests and in defense against the masses, tried to monopolize the public good by identifying with the fatherland. When Olympe de Gouges gave precedence to the term "nation" throughout her Declaration, it was not because she was opposed to the sovereignty of the people. On the contrary, in her other political writings she always sided "with the people" and saw herself as their advocate. But reference to the "people," especially on the part of her revolutionary comrades, had evidently aroused her suspicion, since fewer than half of the "people" were represented in the National Assembly. For this reason, her wording in Article 16 deviated from that of the male declaration, declaring that "the constitution is invalid if the majority of individuals who compose the Nation have not cooperated in writing it."

Another difference between the male and female versions of the human rights declaration follows along the same line. In Articles 4 and 5, de Gouges does not refer to "the law," since it was an expression of a "volonté générale" that had excluded women. Instead she speaks in both articles of the "laws of nature and reason." Her expression "wise and divine laws" is reminiscent of Antigone in the play by Sophocles. The author thus appealed to a law that claimed to have existed even before men had agreed on the compact of rule; she appealed to natural law, in which reason and nature were still joined and not qualified in any way. Nor were they yet arranged in a hierarchy, as in the scholastic teachings of the Middle Ages ("jus naturale dictat ordinem").[24] In her prologue, Olympe de Gouges therefore referred to the order of creation of human being *and* animal. She still considered nature to be the standard of true law and used it to justify opposition to the presumptions of male reason.[25]

The author of the Declaration of Women's Rights was in agreement with the laws of nature and named the reasons why "man" destroys "harmonious cooperation" and finds himself at odds with the "grandeur of nature" through his "tyrannical empire": "Only man has fashioned himself a principle out of this exception. Bizarre, blind, bloated by science and degenerate, in this century of enlightenment and wisdom, he, in grossest ignorance, wishes to exercise the command of a despot over a sex that has received every intellectual faculty; he claims to rejoice in the Revolution and claims his rights to equality, at the very least."[26] Is it surprising that Olympe de Gouges developed the self-confidence to speak so perceptively and provocatively, especially since she characterized women in her preamble as "the sex that is superior in beauty as well as in courage of maternal suffering"? Her motivation—and this appears to be the basis for all struggles for rights and advocacy of women's rights—was indignation and the very personal experience of injustice. The revolutionary Olympe de Gouges knew what women had contributed to the revolution. Now she strove to prevent men from denying women their fair share and their success, a pattern that repeats itself again and again in women's history.[27]

Different Standards of Liberty and Justice

In articles 2 of both declarations, the basic right to liberty was given pride of place among the enumerated human rights. In contrast, the draft constitution of 1793 listed "equality" first; but it remained a draft and never went into force. In 1789 and 1791, "liberty" was followed by the rights to "property, security, and"—emphasized in the women's rights declaration by the word "especially"—"resistance to oppression."

Liberty was already defined in ancient times as the opposite of slavery.[28] But liberty presupposed the social status, or membership in the class, of "freemen." That is, it was a privilege—reserved solely for male citizens of the *polis* or the state. To that extent, it was political liberty, not limited by the equality of others. Centuries of struggle had been necessary to wring single vested liberties out of the rulers, such as those contained in the Magna Carta Libertatum of 1215 and the 1679 Habeas Corpus Act. Liberty then developed into a subjective defensive right of citizens vis-à-vis the state. Typically, language found its way into

the male Declaration of the Rights of Man that refers to the most essential liberty of the citizen in his position as a private person and property owner. The essence of civil law, ownership of something, was also
defined in the German Civil Code (BGB) as a basic "unrestricted, individual, absolute right."[29] According to § 903 BGB, an owner of something can "make use of said object according to his will, excluding any
intervention by others, in so far as it does not conflict with a law or
the rights of a third party." The wording resembles a definition of liberty in the Corpus Juris, which, according to Helmut Coing, "can still
be used for legal purposes": "Libertas est naturalis facultas eius quod
ciuque facere libet, nisi si quid vi aut iure prohibetur (liberty is the natural ability of an individual to make use of something as he wishes, in so
far as he is not prevented from doing so by force or law).[30]

The continuity is astounding—the traditional meaning, passed
down with the adoption of Roman law, of the conceivable substance
of individual liberty, was expressed with utmost precision in Kant's legal doctrine. "*Freedom* (independence from being constrained by
another's choice)," Kant began generally, "insofar as it can coexist with
the freedom of every other in accordance with a universal law, is the
only original right belonging to every man by virtue of his humanity."[31]
This freedom is subsequently made concrete in that "it is possible for
me to have any external object of my choice as mine. . . . It is therefore an a priori presupposition of practical reason to regard and treat
any object of my choice as something which could objectively be mine
or yours" (§ 2). The concept becomes a "rational conception" (*Gedan-
kending*) if these "objects of my choice" (§ 2) include not only the right
to the possession of a concrete object as a thing, but also the possession of persons, referred to as a "Rights to Person Akin to Rights to
Things" (§ 22). Thus it appears consistent that matrimonial law, according to Kant, speaks of the "use of it as a person" (§ 22) and lists
"wife, child, servant" (§ 7)—as the obvious examples—"as included in
the subject's belongings" (§ 7). In the law of reason a priori, too—which
claims to have nothing to do with empirical reality, but whose concrete
examples are nevertheless revealing—freedom can thus only be defined
using concepts of "power," "choice," and "control."[32] Free will becomes
synonymous with "not merely a capacity but also an act of choice" (§
2), a "claim" or presumption of right, or "powerful will" (§ 8); it is un-

derstood as an "obligation" and must always be "laid upon all others" (§ 7).[33]

The definition of equality remains inconsistent with liberty, and reveals its androcentric nature even in such expressions as "being his own master."[34] Formally, equality appears even in matrimonial law[35] as an important indication of the woman's dignity. It is historically conceived of as "equality with all rational beings, whatever their rank,"[36] but in legal practice this equality is violated again and again by existing inequalities of ownership, citizenship, race, and gender; as such it is only a "rational conception" (noumenon),[37] but not a practical political necessity. Rousseau, however, had already worked out in detail the link between the principles of liberty and equality.[38] Only when the two principles were connected and linked to "general laws" could liberty and equality become concepts of revolutionary struggle perceived as a challenge to the existing order, which was a "society of inequality": "If we examine in what precisely consists the supreme good of all, which ought to be the object of every system of legislation, it will appear to reduce to two principal points: liberty and equality; in liberty, because all private dependence subtracts so much force from the body of the State; in equality, because liberty cannot subsist without it."[39]

In article 4 of her declaration, Olympe de Gouges abandoned the style of her model and all traditional language. For her, "liberty" only made sense when spoken of in the same breath as "justice" rather than with "equality." Whereas equality could conceivably serve to add precision to the form of justice, justice was a more fundamental, though at the same time vague legal postulate for those suffering injustice. This link between liberty and justice can evidently be explained by the fact that claims to liberty asserted by others, especially men, have been perceived by women primarily as injustice. Article 4 of the Declaration of the Rights of Woman and Citizen states that "the exercise of women's natural rights is limited only by the perpetual tyranny with which man opposes her."

It is noteworthy that the author was not concerned with claiming or expanding the realm of freedom for women "to do everything which injures no one else" (article 4, Declaration of the Rights of Man), nor to distinguish between "mine and yours" (Kant). Instead, Olympe de Gouges demanded the "rendering to persons those things that belong

to them . . . according to the laws of nature and reason." Interestingly
enough, here de Gouges employed a concept from canonical law that
serves as a basic rule in legal conflicts over ownership. It provides that
anything obtained through interference and force must be returned before the case can even be considered.[40] Apparently, the author of the
Declaration of the Rights of Woman took as her starting point the assumption that a peaceful legal relationship between the sexes was disrupted by male interference. Therefore, de Gouges's text encourages more
fundamental consideration. De Gouges makes us ask why, in all legal
theory, "liberty" is conceivable only as a right or a space that becomes
smaller when shared with others, especially when everyone else is also
free and equal. Why are others perceived only as limitations—not even
as opposites but as adversaries—instead of their freedom being seen as
expanded agency or potential enrichment? Even individual power and
exercise of will need not rule out the power of another. One can envi-
sion an assertive powerfulness that gains in strength and magnitude
when shared equally by many. "Robinson Crusoe"—a state of nature
with the danger of "warre . . . of every man, against every man"—haunts
even the most rational legal theories. Or, at least, the common reference
to the nature of man represents a view of the human being as a man
controlling everything and wanting everything, whose socialization in
the process of civilization can only be characterized as unfortunate.[41]

Within a Kantian framework or legal theory, such questions are at
most questions of morality and morals that need to be carefully distinguished from those of law. Law, "restrict[ed] through the conception of
the possibility of the freedom of the other," is the necessary foundation
for resolving a dispute; it requires sanctions and means of coercion, and
follows different rules than, for example, love.[42] "Women are the representatives of love, just as men are representatives of law in a general
sense," is the explanation and sharp distinction offered by the *Conversations-Lexicon für gebildete Stände* (Encyclopedia for the Educated
Classes).[43] This was the form and justification by which society in
Olympe de Gouges's time broke off all communication about different
interpretations of law and justice. By differentiating between morality
and law, and abandoning natural law in favor of a law of reason or positive law, legal scholarship—and on this point legal theories are surprisingly agreed—failed entirely to resolve its problem of "material justice."[44]

Rostrum and Guillotine: The Political Rights of Women

Olympe de Gouges became active because she assumed that if women participated in politics and legislation, the criteria for justice would change. Her human rights declaration thus set new "universal" standards and offered an agreement about what could be just for men *as well as* women. This is obvious in many details and in sometimes extremely minor, albeit definitive, nuances and deviations from the male draft she used as a model for her Declaration. For instance, in Article 6, the sentence "Law *is* the expression of the general will" became in the female version: "The law *should be* the expression of the general will." She followed this sentence immediately with an explanation of how this was to be achieved: "All female and male citizens must participate in its elaboration personally or through their representatives; . . . should be equally admitted to all honors, positions, and public services."

Article 7 also deviates from the male version in emphasizing that women have no claim to special rights in criminal prosecution. In addition to adopting the prohibition of laws with retroactive effect (Article 8), it is noteworthy that de Gouges simply omitted the final clause in Article 7 of the male version, according to which resistance to the authorities constitutes an offense. In Article 2, she had already emphasized women's right to resistance through the word "especially"; she obviously had good reason to assert that right against the existing state authorities as well.

The rigor with which Olympe de Gouges insisted on criminal prosecution of women in Articles 7–9 is noteworthy, including her stress on the fact that women have no claim to special rights. This insistence on equal treatment for women in criminal law can only be explained on the basis of French criminal law practice. According to the Senatum Consultum Vellejanum, a legal rule taken from a Roman law of 76 C.E., women were considered to have diminished capacity in certain legal acts, and this could be asserted under criminal law. As a women's rights advocate during the French Revolution, de Gouges had to reject such discriminatory leniency, which was referred to in legal terminology as "imbecillitas sexus," or gender-specific imbecility.

Article 10 of the female version of the Declaration deserves special attention. Here the subject is neither merely freedom of opinion nor specifically freedom of religious views, which is mentioned explicitly in the male version and which Georg Jellinek considered the "most natural human right."[45] Following Jellinek, there was extensive discussion about whether the constitutions passed in the individual states subsequent to the United States' Declaration of Independence in 1776, especially Virginia's Bill of Rights, were more significant for the Declaration of the Rights of Man than the French doctrine of natural law, and Rousseau's theories in particular, had been. In this context, it is interesting to note that the Declaration of the Rights of Woman does not mention freedom of religious conscience at all. For Olympe de Gouges, either this was understood to be included in freedom of thought and opinion or she considered it insignificant. The latter is not merely a remote possibility, since she was a Jacobin and, considering her views on marriage, definitely anticlerical.[46] More importantly to her, since it was a "fundamental right," liberty, "the conscience of the other, was not puritanically conceived, but thought in an ancient way as the *citoyen(ne)*."[47] In other words, at issue was freedom of political expression and, even more, women's participation in politics.

This principle is expressed in an image that anticipated de Gouges's own personal fate and later became a familiar quotation. It is the only sentence in the Declaration of the Rights of Woman and Citizen that is sometimes quoted and repeated without context: "Woman has the right to mount the scaffold; she must equally have the right to mount the rostrum [of the National Assembly; that is, the political arena]."[48] The mere fact that this demand from the list of rights for women managed to survive two centuries of neglect and suppression gives some idea of how lasting, unsettling, and tremendously provocative the demand for the right to political participation must have been.

The wording of article 11 is very specifically geared to women. It evidently touched a nerve in women's lives and their experience of injustice. Olympe de Gouges demanded "free communication of thoughts and opinions" as "one of the most precious rights of woman, since this liberty assures the legitimate paternity of fathers with regard to their children." In justifying this demand, the author apparently lost herself in detail, becoming excessively concrete when she included in her solemn declaration a portrayal of the "barbaric prejudice forcing [women] to conceal the truth." Is this an example of "one's own inherent concreteness"[49] or the "element of particularism"[50] of the early French women's movement? Or is the appropriate language merely lacking—that is, the proper form of law? A reference to Olympe de Gouges's "Model for a Social Contract Between a Man and a Woman" can serve to answer these questions; in it, she used the misery experienced by abandoned and seduced women to attack laws created solely in the interests of men.[51] Throughout the history of women's rights, the struggle for women's reproductive rights continued to be central, yet controversial, focusing in the nineteenth century on the rights of unmarried women and children born out of wedlock.[52]

German legal scholars throughout the nineteenth century showed a special liking for Latin terms and legal constructions in questions of sexuality, morality, and paternity, as a way to avoid personal embarrassment. An example in this context is the reactionary 1850 Prussian law on the introduction of the so-called *exceptio plurium*, the defense of multiple lovers, in paternity actions. This was a very self-interested legal means of avoiding the costs of paternity, with the help of male accomplices. It should be noted that the Napoleonic *Code civil* of 1804—obviously in reaction to early feminist demands—was more misogynist than the Prussian General Code in this respect, prohibiting from the outset any efforts to determine the paternity of children born out of wedlock (Article 340 Cc).[53]

It is therefore far from insignificant that in the article on freedom of opinion, which deals primarily with the recognition of paternity, Olympe de Gouges spoke of women not only as women, but also as citizens (*citoyennes*). Assuming she chose her terminology deliberately in this case, it is an indication that this state intervention in the "private" sphere, specifically with regard to motherhood, has always been "political" for women.

As in articles 12 and 13 of the "universal" Declaration of the Rights of Man, de Gouges assumed that women as well as men would share the costs of "public forces and . . . administrati[on]" (article 13). There is no need to consider whether de Gouges, while approving of "public forces," also supported the repressiveness of a "public military force," since the women of the French Revolution, Olympe de Gouges among them, were notably bold and brave as comrades-in-arms in the revolutionary militia and in defense against external enemies. The National Convention, for example, helped women achieve the dubious glory of having helped raise the "morale" of the troops.[54] Still, Olympe de Gouges and other leading women continually took up the cause of victims of the guillotine; de Gouges attempted to end this atrocity by circulating flyers and sending letters to the Convention calling upon the people of Paris to resist Robespierre, whom she called "that animal" and the "disgrace of the Revolution": "Le peuple Français, devenu Républicain, ne deviendra pas un peuple d'assassins."[55] In any case, from the perspective and experience of women, liberties and rights were seldom assured by the existence of public forces, whether military or police, since state authorities generally did not prevent direct force, under the pretext of protecting the private sphere. This is still the case today, despite all the progress made in establishing the rule of law. This is why, in article 12, Olympe de Gouges referred to a higher good, or "major benefit," that was necessary for the "guarantee . . . [of] the rights of women and female citizens . . . for the advantage of everyone." To this extent, her wording was distinct from the male version, which declared the need, not for a "major benefit" but for a "public force" (see appendix).

"Property in One's Own Person"

Article 17 of the Declaration of the Rights of Woman and Citizen also defends the right of property as "inviolable and sacred," "the true patrimony of nature." Does this mean that even the human rights demanded by a woman reflected the narrow horizon of bourgeois law? Does the criticism of the ideology of human rights developed by Marx in "On the Jewish Question" apply here? In that essay, Marx declared that "the so-called rights of man, as distinct from the rights of the citizen, are simply the rights of a member of civil society, that is, of egoistic man, of man separated from other men and from the community . . . [who] see[s] in other men, not the realization, but rather the limitation of his own liberty."[56]

Does this criticism apply? Yes and no. On the one hand, it must be kept in mind that when women demanded the right to property around 1800, they were totally dependent economically as mothers, daughters, and wives. They were completely without assets, owning neither property nor the earnings of their labor nor—and this is the main point—property in their own persons. Their demand for property was in fact a demand for an autonomous existence. Thus Locke's concept of property, oriented toward a simple, precapitalist economy, is appropriate here: "Yet every Man has a Property in his own Person. This no Body has any Right to but himself. The Labour of his Body, and the *Work* of his Hands, we may say, are properly his."[57]

In all of Olympe de Gouges's political writings, lack of property was the basic evil through which she explained the "shame," "servility," and dependence of women. Thus in the "social contract" that she viewed as necessary to regulate the unequal relations between man and woman, she demanded that property be shared, though not, as Marx believed, "to enjoy one's fortune and to dispose of it as one will; without regard for other men and independently of society."[58] Instead, her motivation was to make it possible for women finally to be able to raise their children without disadvantage and to share their property with them. The contract she drafted reads like a private law or marriage contract, although it was intended by its author also to be a social or state contract in the natural law tradition; it demonstrated that the separation of public and private did not correspond to women's experience and was in fact detrimental to women. The contract provided for the following:

> We, N and N, of our own free will, unite ourselves for the remainder of our lives and for the duration of our mutual inclinations, according to the following conditions: We intend and desire to pool our fortunes as community property, while nevertheless preserving the right to divide them on behalf of our own children and those we might have with someone else, mutually recognizing that our fortune belongs directly to our children, from whatever bed they might spring, and that all of them have the right to carry the name of the fathers and mothers who have acknowledged them, and we obligate ourselves to subscribe to the law that punishes the renunciation of one's own flesh and blood. We obligate ourselves equally, in case of separation, to divide our fortune, and to set apart the portion belonging to our children as indicated by the law. . . . Once a law is passed that will authorize the rich man to adopt the poor woman's children, the bonds of society will be strengthened and its morals purified. . . .
>
> I should like a law that protects widows and maidens

deceived by the false promises of a man to whom they were attached.

Finally, she offered in this draft "an invincible means of elevating the soul of women; it is for them to join in all the activities of men[.]"[59] One must consider the boldness it required, at that time, to demand "free love," a marriage that could be dissolved at any time, and the support of concubinage! De Gouges suggested that the "critics of rational philosophy [should] therefore cease to protest against primitive morals or else go bury themselves in the sources they cite"; that is, they should examine the causes of the misery.

This is the social background to women's demand for property. It also justifies something else: Women's "destiny" and their social practices go beyond those of "the egoistic man, the man [who] is a member of civil society."[60] The Marxian utopia of human emancipation is very similar to what had been described in such detail as women's nature and mission in society: "Human emancipation will only be complete when the real, individual man has absorbed into himself the abstract citizen; when as an individual man, in his everyday life, in his work, and in his relationships, he has become a species-being."[61] In this respect, also, Rousseau's criticism of bourgeois society hit the nail on the head, but he was wrong in assigning concern for morality, morals, and humanity exclusively to the female sex, thus costing its members their self-determination.

And what is actually meant by Marx's "species-being"? Since the question will concern us further, a definition by Ludwig Feuerbach is both helpful and general enough to capture the controversial essence of woman: "What, then, *is* the nature of man, of which he is conscious, or what constitutes the specific distinction, the proper humanity of man? Reason, Will, Affection. . . . Reason, love, force of will, are perfections— the perfections of the human being—nay, more, they are absolute perfections of being. To will, to love, to think, are the highest powers, are the absolute nature of man as man, and the basis of his existence. Man exists to think, to love, to will."[62]

This is why, for at least two hundred years, the categories for men and women have obviously meant different things. Ever since the male subject has "[found] in himself the whole fullness of humanity,"[63] there has been a "dissociation of gender characters,"[64] as a result of which the search for the "nature of [generic] man" has led to different answers for men and women. In a socialist utopia according to Marx, the man's essence involves recognizing his societal strengths and absorbing into himself the "abstract citizen," "the individual with political rights."[65] For the woman, on the other hand, feminist proposals up to now have given priority to individuality and to emancipating women from the very gender-specific limitation of their "nature" as a "species-being." The path taken by this feminist agenda shall be discussed in subsequent chapters against the background of human rights. It is not as simple as Rousseau made it seem when he wrote, "All we know for certain is that where man and woman are alike we have to do with the characteristics of the species; where they are unlike, we have to do with the characteristics of sex.[66]

For now it is sufficient to note that men and women experience different treatment in law and society, and the way of realizing basic human rights or perceiving humanity depends upon one's starting point and perspective. It is apparent from the "dialectic of Enlightenment" (Horkheimer and Adorno) and our everyday political reality how questionable and vague any assignments to reason, nature, or progress can be. Are human rights illusory from the outset, because they take as their starting point a concept of commonality and humanity in which, up to now, the necessary share of femaleness has been suppressed? In Olympe de Gouges's writings, it is possible to find an answer appropriate to her time. I would like to summarize it below.

A Legacy Worthy of Consideration

There is no need to make the "Declaration of the Rights of Woman and Citizen" of 1791 into a creed and Olympe de Gouges into a "laurel-crowned statue."[67] It is, however, worthwhile finally to accept her legacy and administer it seriously and critically. Drafted on the threshold of the development of civil equality, the declaration is a unique legal document that summarized women's problems with this equality and illuminated its focal points on the basis of women's experience. It is a mirror of historical contradictions, containing some inconsistencies of its own, yet remaining a political and feminist manifesto whose demands are still valid today; in fact, they are decidedly modern.

The women's rights declaration contains many similar demands; it demands equal rights for women and men. This is significant because it shows that de Gouges, though a women's rights activist, did not limit herself solely to women's concerns and was not content with them alone. At the same time, Olympe de Gouges's list of rights contained important differences.

The demands for women were more than merely up-to-date; they expressed a rebellious consciousness. Thus the Declaration turned human rights into a "revolutionary instrument" for women. It was radical in every aspect of its critique—anticlerical, antifeudal, and opposed to the patriarchy of greater and lesser masters, and consistent in its demand for an inalienable right to resistance. On the other hand, Olympe de Gouges's list of rights did not fit into the scheme of contemporary social theory and practice. It challenged the male legal theory of her time, which had abandoned nature as a "category of social opposition" in favor of the extremely questionable category of reason. De Gouges did not accept the legitimacy of the social contract, grounded as it was in less than half of humanity.[68] She did not, however, entirely reject the idea of a contractual agreement among members of society; instead, she drafted and demanded a new one between men and women.

Her understanding of politics was fundamentally different. All the demands she made that dealt with women's participation in politics and the public sphere were introduced within the context of women's reproductive tasks—that is, the private sphere assigned to women. In article 11, de Gouges clearly indicated that even in her capacity as a citizen, she had no intention of relinquishing the rights and obligations of motherhood. Yet she was no less vigorous in demanding that fathers also take on their share of the reproductive tasks of the species, thus questioning a gender-specific division of labor as well as the separation of public and private spheres that was characteristic of the developing civil society.

She took to its logical conclusion the idea that equality laid down in law need not simply imply making women the same as men. On the contrary, such equality creates opportunities for new forms of relationships between men and women, beyond those typical of patriarchal society. Thus the Declaration of the Rights of Woman and Citizen—which up to now has been erroneously regarded as a simple expansion of universal human rights to include women—was in fact even more radical. It pointed out the other basic inconsistency in the liberal concept of law; that is, the contradiction between authority harnessed through the state's monopoly of power and authority in the relationships between men and women—under the cloak of matrimonial law or in the "unlegislated sphere" of intimacy.

Because civil law, despite all its progress, has not yet been able to resolve this contradiction, the governing principles of reason—which change over the course of history—must continually be questioned. And human rights as a proclamation of the "freedom of the will against historically preexisting law" cannot help us on our way until we take into account the corrections and additions provided by the Declaration of the Rights of Woman and Citizen.[69] A liberty that is not necessarily limited by the liberty of others but can be made compatible between men and women sets new standards for its "realization" and represents a piece of concrete utopia.[70] All of positive law has had to measure up to this declaration of human rights for all human beings since its writing, and it is apparent how rarely its standards have been upheld, especially with respect to women.

Ernst Bloch analyzed, more thoroughly than anyone, the "side [of human rights] that was never honored," their socialist potential, and their political relevance for social liberation in practice. Nonetheless, one wonders why his "orthopedia of the upright carriage," which benefits women as well as men, had to be accompanied by "masculine pride" [although translated into English as "human pride," Bloch's original German referred to *Männerstolz*, which is specifically and deliberately male—Trans.]. Bloch wrote, for example:

> [T]he bourgeois revolution was unquestionably more bourgeois
> than revolution, but as the abolition of class privileges, it
> instituted a powerful cleansing process; it still contains that
> promise and that concrete, utopian form of a promise which the
> real revolution can hold onto. This is the stipend of human
> rights, and if it has the taste for more, then there is very little of
> it in history up to this point, which by virtue of its basis was so

limited and obstructed, and which by virtue of its postulates
was also so anticipatory of humanity. Freedom, equality,
fraternity, the orthopedia of the upright carriage, of human
pride [Männerstolz], and of human dignity point far beyond the
horizon of the bourgeois world.[71]

In my view, the fact that "fraternity" forms the third part of the rally-
ing cry of the French Revolution, after "liberty and equality," does not
justify neglecting the role played by women in the French Revolution
and eliminating their legacy.[72] Fraternity, or brotherhood, does not mean
an old boys' network; it means solidarity. The word originally came from
the Christian tradition,[73] and its inclusion with liberty and equality in
the revolutionary slogan traces back to an expression used in the lodges
of the freemasons.[74] Was it indeed a slogan of strictly male solidarity?
Male solidarity had as little chance in the chaos of the revolution as
the "civic improvement" of women.[75] Yet women have no problems as-
sociating "sorority," or "sisterhood," with "fraternity."[76] Brotherhood
practiced openly and equally, which "must manifest itself concretely"
in the family, in love "of one's neighbor," is dependent on sisterhood.[77]
The problem is that the brothers keep forgetting that.

	Equal Rights
	or Women's
Chapter 4	Distinctiveness

The Program of the
First Women's Movement

THE PREVIOUS CHAPTERS dealt with vanished footprints and a forgotten program of human rights for women as well as men. Not until the advent of an organized women's movement in Germany did the "other half of humankind" begin to make legal history by demanding equality. German women's long, difficult journey began in the mid-nineteenth century, in the period prior to the March Revolution of 1848, and had by no means attained its goals with the achievement of active and passive suffrage in 1918. Leaving aside the history of the first women's movement and its legal struggles, I will focus on the debate over the role of law in women's emancipation—something the first women's movement debated quite vehemently at times.[1] This discussion is not yet over, as evidenced by the women's movement's forgotten history and its subsequent reemergence in the late 1960s.

No discourse common to men and women has yet been established in jurisprudence, nor has a foundation been laid in legal theory for analyzing the problem of gender and law. The women's movement's sources and literature provide evidence of the struggles for, goals of, and especially the resistance to legal equality for women; yet the authors were not involved in contemporary debates on legal policy and scholarship—indeed, as women, they were excluded from them. Thus the emancipatory writings and literature of the women's movement dealt with either injustice and inequality in general or the question of how to deal socially and practically with concrete, day-to-day existential problems. In legal scholarship the problem of women's rights, up to the law's formal recognition of equal rights, has been one large blind spot. Except for a few practical and political supporters, including some from the ranks of jurists, not one of the "great legal minds" of nineteenth- and twentieth-century Germany took up the special problems of legal equality for women, let alone defended such equality or saw it as a challenge to be considered further.[2] The bulk of legal acumen has been employed again and again to deflect women's demands, quibble over scholarly details, or sacrifice women on the altar of doctrine, thus shutting them out of a firmly established system of male privilege and interests.

Because law, especially bourgeois law, has so often been used against women by men, it is hardly surprising that women harbor reservations about it, especially about so-called positive law. The approaches developed and the groundwork laid by scholars connected with the first wave of the women's movement, so-called *Frauenrechtlerinnen* ("women's righters")—Marianne Weber[3] and Emma Oekinghaus[4] come to mind— have, with few exceptions, been barely acknowledged or reviewed in legal scholarship thus far. One of the exceptions was the sociologist Georg Simmel, who, in dialogue with members of the turn-of-the-century women's movement, especially Marianne Weber, characterized law in his philosophy of culture and gender as part of the "objective culture," and thus as "thoroughly male." He wrote, "The 'legal alienness' of women is frequently emphasized, their opposition in regard to legal norms and judgments. This alone need by no means signify an alienness in regard to law in general, but only to male law, which is all we have, and which therefore seems to us to be law per se. In much the same way, we possess a historically determined morality, individualized through time and place, which seems to fulfill the concept of morality in general. Women's sense of justice, which often deviates from men's, would also lead to a different concept of law."[5]

Only recently has women's theoretical and systemic critique of the maleness of law been acknowledged as feminist legal theory.[6] Thus, my attempt to incorporate women's legal issues into legal history cannot be concerned with adapting the history of women's legal struggles and their experience of injustice to the standard of "general" legal theory. Rather, the question arises, again and again, whether any understanding at all is possible between male-created laws and those things that women hold to be just or important—the primal conflict between Antigone and Creon. Human rights remains the common thread running through my examination of whether equality can coexist with an acknowledgment of female distinctiveness. Human rights, especially since having been expanded and supplemented by Olympe de Gouges, provides a standard for examining the prevailing norms—perhaps only a lowest common denominator to resolve the unequal relationship between men and women into a concept of justice and rights that includes both men and women.

The "Forty-Eighters": A Step toward Indivisible Freedom

The single, unchanging goal of all women's movements of the nineteenth and early twentieth centuries was the chance for women to share in the enjoyment of human rights; this was a programmatic reference point even at a time when positivism had emerged victorious in the science of law and the state and, in the words of Bernhard Windscheid, "the dream of Natural Law has been dissipated, [and the titanic attempts of modern philosophy . . . have not stormed Heaven.]"[7] There was good reason for this continuity—namely the stubborn reference to a problem that continued unresolved. At the turn of the century, the uniformity of the demand threatened to turn it into an empty formula that could hold a variety of meanings, or even none at all.[8] Differing views of natural law and human rights played a significant implicit and explicit role in the debate on legal issues among the various currents of the first women's movement. The position on human rights of Louise Otto and other "forty-eighters" was plain, and it harmonized with that of the democrats of the pre-1848 period. "We women are merely demanding our rights, our human rights," wrote Otto in 1849 in the *Frauen-Zeitung*, the newspaper she published. "We want to be not dolls, but human beings; human beings possessing specific rights and duties, like all thinking beings."[9] There is no indication that Otto was familiar with Olympe de Gouges's declaration of human rights.[10]

Nonetheless, the women who joined together in women's associations to organize their interests for the first time in pre-1848 Germany were part of the social and democratic movement of the period, and they fought to catch up with the civic freedoms that had been on the agenda since the French Revolution, as well as for democratization and German unity.[11] They described themselves as "social democrats" or "socialist republicans" and called for a "state in which the people know no higher rule than that of a law that it has given itself," and in which "the disparity between capital and labor is eliminated and labor is organized."[12] Like the members of the earlier workers' movement, these politically active women saw the social, democratic, and national movements as a single movement; indeed, the goal of national unification had played an important role in their political activity, exercising an integrative influence.

These women were more radical, however, than many of their democratic friends in two respects: in the persistence with which they discussed the social question as a problem of female workers,[13] and in their realization that male freedom fighters or revolutionaries were "bad democrats" because, "in all their endless striving, [they] thought only of half of humankind, only of the men."[14]

The following excerpt from an article, signed "Georgine," in the *Frauen-Zeitung* summarizes their position on politics and human rights. "What ideas you, who call yourself the stronger sex, must have of *human rights* and human obligations, if such injustice can be excused or even called right. You want to help improve social conditions and cannot even overcome the source of all social disparities and abuse—self-interest. You demand organization of labor, that is, liberation of the same from capital, and yet you aim only to grab the power taken from capital for yourself and to use it to oppress the weak! Then we will merely have changed masters, and indeed gained *nothing* from that exchange. You speak of brotherhood and make no bones about not only excluding your sisters from your association, but even systematically depriving them of work and thus of their means of livelihood. . . . I say to you: you are sinning against the laws of religion, nature, and society by working hard for your own self-interest, toward the demoralization of women, and thus toward the demoralization of all of human society; by not recognizing, for the same reason, the equal rights of the woman who is equal to you; by finally, for the same reason, oppressing those with lesser physical strength rather than protecting them. You are sinning, in a word, against the sacred laws of humanity, and your work, which you view with such pride, must and will come to nothing if you do not take as its basic principle the single law of the future—humanity."[15]

The women's grievance against law was triggered by their experience of injustice, their disappointment at being excluded from organized labor and deceived by their "brothers," who harvested the first fruits of the revolution; at the Frankfurt Parliament there was no mention of basic rights or suffrage for women. Like Olympe de Gouges, "Georgine" based her complaint on law that transcended positive law, "sacred laws" or, in the same breath, "the laws of religion, nature, and society"—that is, a natural law that allowed an "upright carriage," though in a new variation in which "society" had taken the place of reason.[16]

In addition to human rights, the key concept in the texts of the forty-eighters was "liberty," an "indivisible liberty" for men and women. After the long period of restoration, the issue was first of all one of catching up with the civic freedoms: freedom of opinion and press, freedom of assembly and organization, freedom of trade, and the right of political participation. For women to dare to break new political ground required that every single one of them should also experience a very personal liberation from convention and custom, an emancipation from narrow, bourgeois family relationships or the constraints of a marriage of convenience. The biographies of so-called emancipated women such as Louise Aston, Mathilde Franziska Anneke, and Malwida von Meysenbug are examples of emancipation achieved through personal struggle. They were caricatured or portrayed unfavorably in a defensive response to their lived equality, which is why even Louise Otto felt the need to dissociate herself from them for the sake of the political cause.[17]

It is noteworthy that even in texts written by women around 1848 there is no longer talk of "liberty and equality." Did the "concept of equality," as Otto Dann claimed, "play only a subordinate role in the debates in these years?"[18] It may be noted that "liberty" was frequently linked with "humanity," "which basically," according to Louise Otto, "are two words with the same meaning." "Equality" did appear with some frequency, for example in demands for "equal work" or "equality before the law," but it referred as a rule to concrete details of equality or special entitlements.[19] From then on the relevant texts increasingly used the phrase "equal rights."[20]

"Equality before the law," however, was also the formula that allowed social inequality to remain unremarked. It was a legal abstraction from reality that, after Kant, became the basis of nineteenth-century legal doctrine, and for which a conceptual distinction between the "formal" and the "substantive" equality of law sufficed.[21]

For the women caught up in the 1848 revolution, equal rights, or "equal status" [Gleichstellung], certainly referred to the totality of societal relationships, encompassing "all people." This is plain in all their statements and demands for greater justice, for "equal rights" to enable them to "have the right to act freely and independently" and "satisfy their motherly duties fully and manage them with dignity," or for the "right of mature participation and autonomy in the state." "Because nature created two different sexes, . . . it created them with *equal rights* to work, be educated, enjoy—in a word, to *live*."[22]

Muzzling Political Women: The Press and Association Laws

After the failure of the revolution, the seriousness with which the governing authorities of the German Confederation had taken women's political involvement in the press and associations became clear in the harshness of their political repression.[23] This was manifested by new press and association laws[24] directed expressly against the political activities of women and the women's movement.[25] A press law was first enacted in Saxony in 1851 targeting Louise Otto's *Frauen-Zeitung* (the "*Lex Otto*"); in addition to other restrictions, the law explicitly prohibited women from editing and publishing newspapers and magazines. Under the law, "the managing editors of a newspaper shall hire or continue to employ only those male persons with primary residence in the Kingdom of Saxony who are at least twenty-five years of age, of full legal capacity, and in possession of political rights."[26] In the next-to-last issue of her newspaper before it was temporarily discontinued, Louise Otto sarcastically praised the "specificity" of this section, a characteristic normally lacking in most legislation; those laws "dealing with 'citizens' in general" underwent "highly arbitrary interpretation . . . where female citizens [were] concerned."[27]

Looking back at the long period of restoration from 1815 until the revolution, it becomes clear that freedom of the press was the decisive achievement of the 1848 revolution. Censorship had prevailed for nearly thirty years on the basis of the Karlsbad Resolutions of 1819, alongside persecution of so-called demagogues and surveillance of universities, fraternities (*Burschenschaften*), gymnastics clubs, and all those striving for freedom. The Metternich system had attempted, with varying success, to prevent and gag the formation of public opinion through censorship of the press and all printed matter. Thus guarantees of freedom of the press and opinion—along with the freedom of teaching and research, religious freedom, and freedom of association and assembly—were among the most important democratic freedoms and defensive rights adopted by the Frankfurt Parliament at the outset as "fundamental rights of the German people" and enacted into law at the end of 1848. Article 4 states, inter alia, "Freedom of the press shall not be restricted under any circumstances or in any way by preventive rules, including censorship, licensing, security orders, restrictions on printers [etc.]."[28] This federal law was never acknowledged as binding by the separate states; after the failure of the revolution and the nonimplementation of the Frankfurt constitution, it was repealed first by various state laws and then, in 1854, by federal decision. Individual states had relaxed these provisions by the 1860s, however, and the German Reich press law of 7 May 1874 required only the managing editors of periodicals to possess rights of disposal and civic rights. Otherwise, by this time commentators and prevailing doctrine assumed that these provisions included women—equal rights for women were acknowledged to this extent.[29]

In contrast, repression under the association laws after 1850 was significantly more rigid and enduring and had a particularly strong effect on the history of the German women's movement. Since the late eighteenth century, clubs, societies, and associations had represented a "new type of social organization" in which civil society—at first still in a largely estates-based, corporative environment—created a space for sociability, for literary and, ultimately, political discourse. Within a few decades, these clubs and associations would become "one of the forces that organize and influence people's social relationships."[30] This new bourgeois public sphere,[31] identified by Jürgen Habermas in its ideal form as the "sphere of private people come together as a public," thus emerged as a counter-world to the courtly or representative public; yet at the same time it was historically quite heterogeneous, with various arenas and competing publics.[32] Contemporaries themselves repeatedly conjured up the image of the "powerful spirit of the association" through which the individual, guided by his or her interests and in form freely agreed upon, liberated him- or herself from dependencies, outside of any corporation or estate.[33]

The significant, socially mediated role of individual women in the salons stood out in both Germany and France not only as part of this transitional period between the old regime and the modern era but also in regard to the social interstices between estate, class, and gender and between bourgeois and parvenu.[34] There was nothing to be gained politically for the female sex as a whole, however, beyond the involvement in so-called patriotic women's clubs that had been desired during the "wars of liberation" against Napoleon. Rahel Levin-Varnhagen described with great clarity her social position as a Jew, a woman, and a "pariah": "Certainly, 'one is not free when one must represent something in respectable society, a married woman, an official's wife, etc.' If one had freedom one was, in the eyes of that society, always in 'wretched situations.' . . . After all, the much-praised freedom of the outcast as against society was rarely more than complete freedom to feel despair over being nothing . . . not a sister, not a sweetheart, not a wife, not even a citizen."[35] It is hardly surprising that the old regime and the authorities responded to the new forms of social organization and "magnification of the power of the individual" with skepticism and suspicion, as well as repeated prohibitions and restrictions.[36] The tightening of the law of associations through the Karlsbad Resolutions of 1819 for the entire German Confederation thus reflected general distrust, as well as the political defensiveness of the state in repeatedly prohibiting "associations with political tendencies in all confederated states" (as in the federal decision [Bundesbeschluss] of 1832).[37] As a consequence of the revolutionary uprising before March 1848, complete freedom of association and assembly were granted for the first time in a series of German states and, on 2 April 1848, through a federal resolution. But this freedom, like the other fundamental rights negotiated by the Frankfurt Parliament, remained merely an isolated episode. At the same time, there began a history of association laws whose political significance for legal and constitutional history has so far been underestimated.

The failure of this revolution revealed more than the class contra-dictions in bourgeois society that would later determine the policies of Prussian Germany under Bismarck's leadership. The exclusion of the female sex from the public political sphere, too, was now plainly estab-lished, not only implicitly, through increasingly bourgeois-patriarchal marriage laws and noninclusion in public laws such as those granting the right to vote, but also explicitly, even earlier, through the public association laws.

The creation of dual fronts in the reaction of state and bourgeoisie to the proletarian class and the female sex is directly evident in the prohibition and persecution of all workers' and women's associations. But even after the temporary liberalization of the 1860s, when work-ers' associations were able to coalesce into a movement and then a po-litical party (the Social Democratic Party), and even beyond the period of the Socialist Laws, women in Germany were prohibited until 1908 from participating in any political activity or organization of their own political interests. The "Decree on Protection Against Abuse of the Right to Assembly and Association that Threatens Legal Freedom and Order," proclaimed in 1850, contained an innocuous-sounding § 8 for-bidding "females [*Frauenspersonen*]" and "students and apprentices" from joining associations "for the purpose of discussing political subjects in assemblies." Women were not even permitted to participate in the as-semblies and meetings of such political associations; their mere pres-ence was cause for the authorities or police officers to shut down the assembly, levy a fine, or, depending on the "seriousness of the circum-stances," even disband the organization. The only organizations ex-empted from the restrictions of § 8 were the so-called electoral clubs created before the Reichstag elections.[38] This regulation remained in force until the final enactment of a Reich Association Law in 1908 and was applied, with slight variation, in the state laws of Prussia, as well as Bavaria, Braunschweig (Brunswick), Saxony-Anhalt, both Mecklen-burgs, Reuss, and Lippe.[39] It was noteworthy because, like the political philosophy of the social contract doctrine, it placed the female sex on a par with minors, students, and the economically dependent category of "apprentices," whose status was bound to patriarchal authority.

During the nearly fifty-year history of the association laws, the courts frequently had to decide what qualified as "political subjects."

The labor movement and its associations, in particular, were subjected again and again to arbitrary application of the association laws, even though the freedom to form coalitions was actually guaranteed by § 152 of the trading regulations of the North German Confederation, and later in the German Empire. In a precedential decision in 1887, the Reich Supreme Court therefore once again clarified this issue: "Political subjects" included "all matters that encompass the constitution, administration, government legislation, civic rights of subjects and the international relations of states to one another."[40] This meant that any time women attempted to improve their legal and social position by legislative means, their action could, or even had to, be interpreted as political.

There is no doubt that this political muzzle hindered the German women's movement, or at least forced it to adapt.[41] When the women's movement reorganized in 1865, it found itself forced into a politics of "small" and very modest steps; all desire for social change was trimmed down to isolated, laboriously attained rights. The General German Women's Association (Allgemeine Deutsche Frauenverein) was formed in 1865 at the initiative of Louise Otto (married name Peters) and Auguste Schmidt. Its goal was to secure the right to work "as a duty and honor of the female sex," as well as the right to education and training. Bourgeois women had recognized "Women's Right to Earn"—as the title of an 1866 piece by Otto termed it—as a prerequisite for economic independence, and they demanded it, along with the "right to free self-determination," the "most sacred and inalienable right of any rational being."[42] However, public opinion at the time saw the "woman question" as at most a labor question; although there were also a large number of unmarried middle-class women not supported by their families, it was specifically interpreted to refer only to the women from the proletariat, who were forced to earn their living in any case. Therefore, it was in the interests of conservative advocates of better jobs for women to emphasize that conceding such means of earning a living by no means implied equal rights, let alone the political emancipation of women.[43]

In the subsequent period, the Women's Association, along with a steadily increasing number of sister organizations, petitioned for many necessary rights, such as admission of women to the post office and telegraph services, freedom of trade and movement, improvement of women's status in family law, equal pay for equal work, admission of women to medical school, and others.[44] "The insect work of the local organizations went busily on," mocked Gertrud Bäumer in 1901 in her historical review of the years 1870 to 1880,[45] but industriousness and the laborious "proof" that women were "suited" to take on the same "rights and duties"[46] were not enough to break down the wall of male resistance.

Gender Tutelage—But "Human Rights Have No Gender"

Between the failure of the 1848 revolution and the creation of the German Reich in 1871, the patriarchal front in Germany regrouped.[47] The united force of male scholarship produced a flood of antifeminist and anti-emancipatory treatises, speeches, and essays that seemed to expressed the true feelings of an entire generation of men, while also socializing the next one ex cathedra.[48] Male professors such as Theodor von Bischoff, Heinrich von Treitschke, and Heinrich von Sybel apparently found themselves challenged by their English colleague John Stuart Mill, more so even than by women's legal demands. Mill's 1869 book, *The Subjection of Women*, a call for women's emancipation, was widely distributed in Germany. The result was a new naturalism whose alliance with the natural sciences failed to make its recourse to "nature" any more convincing or scientific. In fact, the zeal and fervor of the response betrayed the object of its defense. Von Sybel called it "the great law of division of labor," and, as we know today, he was pointing to the pivotal element of female subordination. In his opinion, "for spouses . . . the division of labor, and thus, essentially, their legal status, is determined once and for all by nature, and neither human will nor personal talent nor the progress of the times could change that."[49]

One of the first people to counter these scientific fools and "attack the sacred institutions of the male Prussian state—first the Protestant pastors, then the German philosophers and the gynecologists," was Hedwig Dohm, whose consistency and radicalism far surpassed that of the women's associations of her day.[50] Only later would turn-of-the-century radicals catch up with her and honor her as a model and a pioneer in their struggle. In her book *Der Frauen Natur und Recht* (Women's Nature and Privilege), published in 1876, she demanded equal voting rights for women as a necessary and urgent step on the "path to independence and equality, women's freedom and happiness."[51] Dohm's pen was sharp; she refuted all the reservations and inconsistencies put forward by those opposed to women's right to vote with harsh polemics, basing its necessity on the requirements of reason and justice, as a question of morality. She was realistic enough to assume that men "hold fast the prerogative of their sex," unwilling to surrender their privileges voluntarily. But she was just as cutting toward some women: "Every proud woman must . . . be indignant with those of her sex, who hold their peace for fear, while one generation after another goes by and pushes them aside—with those who are satisfied with their freedom for cooking and sewing, who allow such a miserable being as Griselda to be upheld to them as a pattern of perfect womanliness; who allow themselves to be used and thrown aside."[52]

Hedwig Dohm has often enough been praised for her masterly polemics and argumentative skill.[53] Yet the explosiveness of her statements sometimes threatens to be overshadowed by the brilliance of her formulations, as in her provocative conclusion, "Human rights have no gender." Critics have accused her of negating or leveling gender differences with her demands for human rights and "unconditional" equality, or of aiming merely for women to share in male rights.[54] Precisely because of her radicalism on the issue, there is a danger of misreading Dohm's position, substantively and therefore as a matter of legal theory, as a merely egalitarian one. Hedwig Dohm was fully aware of the "labor of Sisyphus" required to repudiate men's arguments against political participation by women and against their liberty and equality. For the single person and lone fighter that she was, such repudiation was a bold undertaking, and her polemics are a thoroughly fitting response to the male zeitgeist and to injustice toward women based on sex differences. The insistent demand for human rights irrespective of sex—this is indeed the meaning of "human rights have no gender"—was not intended to deny sex differences; it was a challenge, a slogan against a patriarchy that had again, in the second half of the nineteenth century, accommodated itself to the contradiction between recognizing legal equality in principle and preventing it through "gender tutelage" of women.

Neither in politics nor in jurisprudence did human rights have any currency in this period. Prevailing opinion held it to be unnecessary to anchor them in the 1871 constitution of the German Reich, either because they had already been incorporated into most of the individual constitutions of the states in the German Confederation or because their principles had been integrated into most important Reich legislation. "In truth, however," said Georg Jellinek, "in the German Reich, the extent of public rights of the individual was much greater than in many countries with a catalogue of basic rights in its constitution."[55]

The bourgeoisie, the champion of political liberalism, had been abandoning its democratic goals since the failed revolution of 1848; it now viewed basic rights as the product of "doctrinarism."[56] For primarily economic reasons it had adapted to the authoritarian Prussian state on the Bismarckian model. These economic interests were guaranteed by the specifically German form of the *Rechtsstaat* (state based on the rule of law), and bourgeois legal scholars and government bureaucrats had a significant influence upon the development and expansion of this *Rechtsstaat*. Franz L. Neumann named as its constitutive principles the primacy and universality of law (that is, interference with the freedom and property of the citizen was possible only on the basis of law); neutrality toward the form of government, in this case the monarchy; and independence of judges, whose social status and recruitment from the upper classes, or at least from the educated middle classes, ensured the maintenance of the structures of power.[57] In the alliance "between crown, army, bureaucracy, property, and the bourgeoisie," the "German bourgeoisie was satisfied with its relationship to the state. Judges and legal theoreticians no longer needed to call upon natural law to fight hostile positive law. Both natural law and legal philosophy vanished. Positivism had emerged victorious."[58] What this positivism meant for law is most clearly summarized in a definition by Friedrich Julius Stahl, a scholar of the law of the state: "Law and positive law are . . . identical concepts. There is no law but positive law."[59]

In public law, concerned with the relationship between the citizen and the state, a theory of reflexive law replaced the concept of vested basic rights predating the state. Later, a system of subjective public law was developed in administrative law; it provided no legal rights, but at most delineated limits on state power.[60] In private law, however, before adoption of uniform law and the codification of the German Civil Code (BGB) in 1900, a legal science prevailed that had tailored for itself a doctrinal system of concepts and precepts for the study of pandects. Given the fragmentation of law, this fulfilled a veritable "national po- litical mission."[61] These political conditions would have drastic conse- quences for the legal status of women in the German Empire.

By the end of the nineteenth century, women had failed to gain equality under either public or private law. Under private law, married women were covered by special laws in marriage and family law and thus excluded from "universal" developments toward civic freedom and equality. Not even unmarried women, widows, and women emancipated from their fathers' authority were seen as equal citizens. German women in the nineteenth century possessed none of the important public rights that would have made political participation possible—neither the right to vote for the Reichstag or for city or village councils nor rights to participate in other public representative bodies such as chambers of commerce, commercial courts, or parish councils.[62] Even when women who owned property and thus paid high taxes possessed a formal right to vote in some village communities, they could only exercise it through a male proxy.[63] Only the kingdom of Saxony granted women voting rights for local assemblies, but even here wives could only vote by proxy through their husbands.[64] It was self-evident that wherever individual rights of citizens were concerned, from the freedom of establishment (by way of the husband's right to determine residence) to citizenship rights, wives followed their husbands. It was just as natural that none of these legal issues was ever discussed, let alone clarified, in the contempo- rary legal literature.[65]

Toward the end of the nineteenth century, the contradiction be- tween "universal" norms and the particular exclusion of women became increasingly dubious, too obviously open to attack, thanks to the new consciousness of injustice nourished by the women's movement. Around the turn of the century, the women's suffrage organizations, which had gained political strength together, ultimately refused to accept this lack of legal clarity and began exploiting the "forgetfulness" or silence of the legislators. Because the Hamburg association law made no explicit men- tion of women, Anita Augspurg and Lida Gustava Heymann decided quite spontaneously in 1901 to found the first German women's suffrage organization in Hamburg.[66] Nevertheless, the association laws remained in force in most of Germany—specifically Prussia and Bavaria—until

the adoption of a unified Reich association law in 1908, and they decisively influenced and hindered the politics, language, and practices of
the first women's movement for more than half a century—in contrast
to women's movements elsewhere in Europe and in the United States.
Only women's right to petition, as an individual and collective public
right, was never disputed even in the German Empire, probably because
that right contained no political or legal guarantees and thus could easily
be turned to women's disadvantage. Nevertheless, women's associations
made very active use of it.

The anchoring of male, patriarchal prerogative in the private
sphere, in private law, was regulated in the family in a specifically bourgeois manner. The traditional means of preventing women from speaking for themselves on any legal matters, so-called gender tutelage of
women—a sort of legal incapacity—had outlived its time even in the
opinion of nineteenth-century legal scholars and was finally formally
repealed. "Male authority," however, the principle of the power of husbands and fathers, remained legally valid and practiced, supported by
the united force of all legal reasoning.[67] Precisely because of the very
varied and unclear legal situation that prevailed before enactment of
the Civil Code in 1900, legal doctrine, with the support of the Reich
Supreme Court's case law, was able to institutionalize the husband's authority in marriage and family law, despite all the differences in the various family laws of the nineteenth century. Literally, the Court said that
"[g]uardianship in marriage is characterized even today as the authority of the husband, the right of the husband to the person and property
of the woman, even where gender tutelage had been eliminated by
law."[68] Liberal as well as bourgeois philosophy and family law theory
(above all that of Fichte) had laid the ideological groundwork for this
specific form of speaking for and "subjugating" wives. The restoration
of male authority in the home, beginning in the mid-nineteenth century, ran parallel to the reinforcement of a specific bourgeois patriarchy in all areas of life, and justifies reference to a "patriarchal backlash"
precisely because of the challenge posed by equality as a human right.[69]
Essential elements of gender tutelage as a structural principle of patriarchal authority even made inroads into the Civil Code (BGB), despite
the loud and united protest of all segments of the women's movement.
Accordingly, although wives were basically recognized as legal persons

capable of legal action (§ 1 and § 2 BGB), under §§ 1353 ff. BGB they remained subject—along with their labor, property, bodies, and sexuality—to the will of their husbands; de jure and de facto, they were subordinated to male authority.[70]

In explaining their motives and in adopting the Civil Code in 1896, the legislators openly admitted that the "restrictions on the rights of disposal (for women under matrimonial law) merely serve to protect the interests of the husband."[71] Revealing naked interests even conformed with the scholarly trend of the times; the prevailing school of interest jurisprudence made no secret of the idea that, in the "struggle for right," the law of the stronger prevails: "in the struggle of nations, of state authority, of estates, of individuals . . . (for) without struggle there is no right, as without labor there is no property."[72] Economic interests, above all, were accepted as "universal." He who allowed his rights to be taken from him was a "cowardly fellow and at the same time a man who did not fulfill his moral duty toward the community."[73]

There were also scattered opposing views among jurists that should not be ignored. An example was Emil Preetorius, whose dissertation on "conjugal tutelage and the Civil Code" subjected gender tutelage in historical and contemporary law to detailed scrutiny, and simultaneously provided a good overview of the reactionary and contradictory attempts to justify the prevailing scholarly view. Plainly influenced by the "seething . . . sociopolitical currents" of the women's movement in his period, which was now "loudly demanding its rights," Preetorius wrote, "One need neither desire the supremacy of women nor demand the elimination of marriage in order to support full equal rights for men and women. It is not a mechanical sameness that is sought, not an equal valuing of things of unequal worth, but merely the same opportunities for each to develop in his own way, in accordance with his predisposition, to show these to best advantage and thus make best use of them for the good of the whole."[74]

Moderate or Radical—Or, How "Human Rights Were Brought to the Masses"

The failure of the struggle against the Civil Code was the signal to all segments of the women's movement to approach the women's issue above all as a legal issue.[75] The social grievances, the disparities between the sexes in all areas of life, "the heaviness of those chains," were now felt by "many" to be a disgrace that degraded an entire sex.[76] Women began to withhold their traditional "obedience" and were no longer willing to be appeased by exceptional permissions or individual entitlements. The issue now was the "rules," the principles of law that professed to be "universal," yet obviously served only male interests.

Women in the labor movement, too, became involved in the struggle against the Civil Code, taking a leading role on the suffrage issue through the Social Democratic Party's early (since 1891) support for women's right to vote. Nevertheless, women's rights took second place to the resolution of the main disparity, the one between labor and capital; Clara Zetkin, in particular, used the term *"Frauenrechtlerei"* [women's rights mongering] with a pejorative connotation in distancing herself from the so-called bourgeois suffragettes.[77] The result was that specific women's rights problems were underestimated and chances for alliances among women on these issues missed and lost, despite the fact that equal rights for women were taken for granted in socialist theory.[78] Yet even in the proletarian women's movement at the turn of the century, vigorous debates flared up on the relationship between class and sex; there were socialists such as Johanna Loewenherz who, unlike Zetkin, declared war on "male socialism." In answer to the question "Can Social Democrats and Bourgeois Women's Righters [*Frauenrechtlerinnen*] Work Together Toward Common Goals?" Loewenherz wrote in the journal *Sozialistische Monatshefte*: "Every woman is a member of two classes: one completely without rights, the lowest class—the class of women; and the other, more or less privileged or disadvantaged, that she belongs to through the medium of husband or father. Or the woman herself is a member of two classes: one through her sex, the other through her property. May the class of women emphasize their demands by not letting themselves be confused by the interests of the other class to which they also happen to belong. Then the woman worker and the women's rights advocate will be able to struggle together to achieve their common goals."[79]

Among the varied new initiatives that had emerged since the beginning of the 1890s, the bourgeois women's movement organized the protest against the legal incapacity prescribed for women. Women's emergence as human beings still required incredible courage in a society that was not only male and nationalist, not only a class society with remnants of feudalism pursuing ever more imperialist policies, but one that also prided itself on the irrationality of male chauvinism as a special quality of the "German spirit." "As long as there are Germans, there is nothing to fear from feminism," announced university instructor Karl Joël in a "philosophical" lecture in 1896 in which he extolled the Enlightenment as the dawn of a "masculine era" because during it, "the German spirit awakened."[80]

The Enlightenment was also a starting point for women, as in Immanuel Kant's programmatic response to the question "What is Enlightenment?": "Enlightenment is the human being's emergence from his self-incurred minority. Minority is inability to make use of one's own understanding without direction from another. This minority is self-incurred when its cause lies not in lack of understanding but in lack of resolution and courage to use it without direction from another."[81] Despite Kant's inconsistency with regard to women, references can be found for the rights of woman as an individual, her dignity as a human being, a member of the species and not merely a gendered being: "The human being and in general every rational being exists as an end in itself, not merely as a means to be used by this or that will at its discretion."[82] By returning to these rights of human beings with a new, provocative understanding of the "woman question" as a "question of humanity," women in Germany finally caught up, through collective action, with the ideal goals of the Enlightenment.[83] They reclaimed their subjectivity, their own rights as human beings, and their right to criticize, for "the principle of the modern world requires that what anyone is to recognize shall reveal itself to him as something entitled to recognition."[84]

But how were they to achieve individuality, self-discovery, and self-determination when this "self" had thus far been structured and defined only as an "object," a means to an end? How could "the free development of all their abilities" and equal participation in society's wealth be possible if all concepts and positions were already taken up by men and defended as such?[85] It was not only "liberty" (as legal philosophy teaches) and subjectivity that were burdened with certain preconceptions and prejudices. All "objectification" of the intellect, "objective values," as Georg Simmel himself critically described them in his debate with the women's movement, political power and culture—especially law—as well as material resources, the market, and money were defined by men and given meaning in such a way that they could not accommodate women's modes of production, their learned orientations, or their values.[86] One of the leaders of the women's movement wrote, "A woman who wished to put her intellectual strength into a major enterprise, developed thoroughly down to the last detail by a thousand-fold division of labor, entered a world that to an extent obeyed different laws from those which she felt lived within herself. We can only guess what this meant for her productivity."[87]

Women in the first women's movement were aware from the start of the particular difficulties they faced and the dilemma of either adapting to or attacking and changing the existing situation. They knew it was not merely a problem of coming late to modernity, but a more fundamental issue—a task that required at least a cultural revolution. The forty-eighters had already emphasized that they were interested not in "imitating men's brutality" but in sharing the "cultural tasks of humanity."[88] In the same way, all the legal struggles of the 1890s, whether for the right to vote, the right to education, civil equality in family law, or the fight against double standards and for liberated sexuality, were based on equality as a human right. This meant, however, an equality that recognized the diversity of the human experience, not an understanding of human rights as male rights.[89] The common justification was very simple: "German women are socially thinking, socially struggling human beings who demand human rights because they carry out human duties."[90]

Differences even among women emerged during the practical transformation of this very general demand into policies guided by women's interests, since the question was not merely how and how quickly to proceed.[91] At issue were the substance and goals of women's politics—ultimately, a question of the "essence of the human being."

"Within the women's movement," wrote Emma Oekinghaus in a 1925 overview, "complete agreement prevailed in rejecting the norms that had heretofore applied to women. But as the women's movement develops, two clear currents are emerging in regard to the psychological explanation of this attitude; one assumes a psychological opposition between the sexes, focusing on the question of the nature of woman;

women's tasks and their position in society are determined based on this nature. Advocates of the other current, too, fight . . . for a strong female influence on society . . . (;) the supporters of this second current are guided solely by the desire to allow women to come into their own purely as human beings."[92]

Behind the current that took the "nature of woman" as its standard for political action stood the moderate majority of the Federation of German Women's Organizations [Bund Deutscher Frauenvereine], the umbrella organization of the bourgeois women's movement. It should not be labeled conservative or reactionary simply because, in its defense of "female distinctiveness" and the resulting concept of "organized motherliness," it expressed a desire for preservation of and a commitment to traditional roles. The concept of "motherliness" as "organized mother love"[93] or "motherliness transferred to the world"[94] was more an attempt to overcome precisely those limitations of traditional femininity and—according to its program—"to bring the [specific] cultural influence of women to complete inner development and free effectiveness in society."[95] It was the attempt at a self-confident "renunciation of nonautonomous imitation of the man"[96]—a female proposal for "humanization of labor, humanization of science, humanization of interactions among human beings"[97] to counter the "rationalism of the modern capitalist world, which is alien to and neglectful of nature."[98]

It was always stressed that this concept meant not only biological or physical motherhood but also motherhood as "a prospect even for childless women,"[99] a social "quality,"[100] what today we would call a specific labor capacity that, in addition to women's first and primary disposition for the "profession of mother," "sends [them] not only to day care centers, preschools, and schools, but also to ministries and parliaments."[101] How was this specific labor capacity explained? Through the "natural disposition" of women, which, according to Helene Lange, "is based not on an anatomically provable difference in brain structure, but on a difference of interests and emotions. . . . The woman is meant for motherhood; this disposition determines her distinctive physical and psychological characteristics."[102] This was an extremely risky justification, as it legitimized a special "cultural mission" of women through the very distinctiveness of woman as a gendered being, a concept that had always been the cause and purpose of her oppression in the political theory of patriarchy. Thus the crucial question is what alternative the political theory of "motherliness" offered to a legitimation of male dominance in the private, most intimate relations between men and women. How did it intend to escape the "sexist" designation of the woman as a gendered being, and thus necessarily subservient, passive, and unequal (as portrayed by Rousseau and Fichte)?

The liberation of woman as a person, a subject with equal rights, was—especially in the view of the bourgeois moderates—more than just an economic problem; it presupposed the free development of the personality and the "development of all her abilities, in order to make them available to their full extent to serve humankind."[103] That is, liberation of women was above all a question of women's education—in the sense of the old liberal belief that "knowledge is power"—and of fundamental improvement and change in how girls were raised. The original aim of the bourgeois women's movement was to emphasize the "intellectual driving forces of the women's movement" over the economic causes and to see them as a special quality and a political task. In education the movement was on its own terrain, mainly as a movement of teachers at first, because of the lack of other educational opportunities.[104] Here it enjoyed its decisive, most lasting successes. That women should "be educated for their own sake as human beings, and to be human beings per se" was also a basic premise for Helene Lange. She created a stir in 1887 with her "Yellow Brochure," an explication of a petition for the improvement of higher education for girls, in which she aimed her sharp pen at the "very problematic views in Germany, following Rousseau, with respect to women's education."[105] In the nineteenth century, the field of girls' education was dominated by men. It put into practice Rousseau's philosophy of the sexes, including his dominance theory; but in fact very little of that philosophy was left but an unconcealed "sex egoism" and an unquestioned "interest in male convenience."[106] Lange, an expert on education policy (and along with Gertrud Bäumer, the authoritative thinker and spokesperson of the moderates), doubtless had the better arguments, compared to the petty bourgeois demands of a Weimar memorandum by the "Leaders and Teachers in the Higher Girls' Schools." This 1872 memorandum culminated in the statement that "women should be permitted equal education so that the German man is not bored by the intellectual shortsightedness and

narrowness of his wife at the domestic hearth, thus crippling his devotion to higher interests."[107] With the creation of basic and preparatory
high school courses for girls, and ultimately with universal admissions
of women to universities after 1908, Lange was proved right on this issue at least.

By then, however, her program of cultural opposition had tightened
into a neat philosophy of gender difference that found broad support
even among opponents of women's emancipation—and is suspect, I believe, for this very reason. Human beings, or human rights, had now
been abandoned in favor of women's "natural disposition" as the decisive norm in women's demands. In her 1908 "Theoretical Foundation,"
Lange explained that "[h]uman rights had been 'brought to the
masses.'"[108] Her supporters distanced themselves in particular from the
terribly radical (that is, democratic) demands for suffrage and argued
that this demand belonged "on old-fashioned liberalism's junk heap."[109]

The new reference points were marked off in an 1897 essay titled
"Intellectual Boundaries between Man and Woman." The "intellectual
difference" between men and women, which was even empirically
proven here, by no means served to strike "women from the ranks of
rational beings." Rather, it was the condition that makes them "so per-
fectly suited to mutually complement each other," not only at home
but also in the professional sphere. Helene Lange defended a necessary
division of labor with this differentiation, but she hoped to replace the
mechanical division of labor, under which "the woman was given the
house and the man, the world," with an organic one, in accordance with
nature, that gave "the unique characteristics of both sexes complete
space, side by side, in all cultural arenas."

She clarified what this was supposed to mean in practice, using law
as a model: "There is a yawning rift between written law and law that
is born with us. If the woman of today . . . becomes the woman of the
future, and she is not denied spiritual culture, like the man, her lively
feeling for the personal, for the concrete, will undoubtedly form a welcome complement in the areas of law and administration to the different views of the man. The one-sided 'fiat justitia, pereat mundus' of
the man, and the equally one-sided 'fiat misericordia, pereat justitia' of
the woman that is often contrasted to it, would then be able to tone
each other down."[110]

The question that concerns feminism even today is whether a "female law" suited to women should be based on sex differences or the postulate of equality as a human right.[111] Helene Lange had decided solidly in favor of difference, combined with a demand for "complementary harmony" of the sexes. She apparently also imagined that in this "dream of human happiness," which accompanies the history of the notion of equality in the form of the rebellious Antigone, the dialectic between reasons of state and humanity as compassion would resolve itself.

The direction in which this philosophy of the sexes drove the practical policies of the first women's movement, with its moderate majority opinion, was addressed in a 1908 review of the "Literature of the Woman Question" by Alice Salomon. In it, she also summarized the principal differences of opinion within the women's movement. Distancing herself from the "left wing," the radicals and their policy of equal rights—of "levelling" [*Gleichmacherei*], as she put it—Salomon defended the moderates, the conservative majority, because of their "new," truly female politics. Apparently, political labels were reversed: the older current of the women's movement, the first generation of women's rights advocates—Louise Otto and others—were accused of having reached out to "male rights" in their "one-sided emphasis on women's humanity," while the "more recent current, certainly more conservative in its position on family . . . bases its demands for equal rights on the equal worth of the female contribution." Salomon concluded that "professional work by the married woman should not be seen as a universal postulate," and was obviously aware "that the fulfillment of women's sexual nature once more comes to the fore as determinative of destiny."[112]

With these arguments, the goal of women to become liberated, self-determined, self-realized beings thus once again faced an unshakable barrier: women's sexual disposition, their (capacity for) motherhood. Motherhood as destiny, as the purpose of the species, for Gertrud Bäumer even as a "cosmic constraint"[113]—it sounds like a satire of patriarchy, in which the concept of the human being is reduced, for women alone, to sex. Yet these women apparently knew what they were doing; the conflict between "ties to nature and freedom, between individual and general disposition" and, in practical terms, between family and career were discussed in ever-new variations, weighed and declared to be "consequences of a rationalism that is alien to and neglectful of nature . . . pernicious outgrowths of the freedom that began with the rationalism of antiquity." In this return to antiquity, Antigone was once again put on the spot: "On a great mission . . . no longer from instinctive, indissoluble, natural attachment, but from spiritual belief, to help cosmic law regain its rightful place, reveal its meaning, and once again subjugate life to it, to make it fruitful."[114] Poor Antigone—subjugation even here; a reactionary philosophy!

Gertrud Bäumer conjured "the tragedy" of women's lives like no one else and thereby mystified existing power relations. It is instructive that it was Bäumer who gained high office and honors as a representative of the women's movement and whose name, in contrast to many others, remains known. At most, allowances can be made for this cult of motherhood in that, at the turn of the century and beyond, motherhood was in fact an inescapable fate for the majority of women and only rarely an act of freedom or liberation. This was because of the absence of birth control and the relations of power and authority legitimized by positive law (not only in the abortion law, § 218 of the Penal Code, but also in matrimonial law), and because of the usual forms of interaction between men and women in marriage, in prostitution, and in economic dependence. The politics of motherhood should thus be interpreted as an attempt to provide an antithesis to the all-powerful patriarchy. But in this vehement defense of marriage as an institution that "serves not the comfort of the individual, not the fulfillment of a personal need for happiness, but primarily the species,"[115] the newly awakened individuality of women was sacrificed to a "higher purpose" in the vague hope of thereby gaining protection and care while being able to "demand greater self-control from the man" and influence "the ongoing process between the sexes" through the ideals of love and fidelity and the higher standards of women.[116]

In fierce debates with the radical wing of the women's movement, which Lange accused of "anarchical feminist thought," such ideas evaporated into an elite consciousness, even a bourgeois class view, as, for example, when marriage was defended with the following argument: "As soon as we speak of marriage as an institution, we are speaking of Hans and Greta . . . a matter of the masses . . . (;) the masses simply can do nothing but cling to the fulfillment of the form."[117] Such polemics were revealing; they were aimed at the radicals, who around 1905 had organized a League for the Protection of Mothers [Bund für Mutterschutz] and who supported a "new ethics" in relations between the sexes, freed of bourgeois morality—that is, free love, as long as it was based on freedom, equality, and the love of the partners.

The most prominent representative of the "new ethics" in Germany was the philosopher Helene Stöcker, founder of the League for the Protection of Mothers and later an active pacifist. "Stöcker was interested in the power relations between the sexes as the center of the power issue."[118] She attacked them precisely at the point at which modern political theory legitimated the subjugation of women as love and as part and parcel of marriage. "Perhaps nowhere is the full brutality of the human condition as clearly demonstrated as in the sexual sphere," wrote Stöcker, explaining the goals of the movement to protect mothers-to-be and, especially, single mothers.[119] Once again, motherhood was at the center of feminist politics, but the premise was different. Motherhood could no longer be the biological fate of women, but became instead a privilege, "a chance to be a human being." For this reason, one consequence of Stöcker's philosophy was practical social work for the protection of expectant and single mothers, aimed especially at securing equal status for children born out of wedlock, sex education, free access to contraceptives, and the abolition of §218, the prohibition on abortion. Stöcker broke the taboo on talking about sexuality and encouraged women to "reclaim their sexuality."[120] In her view, the admonition "be who you are," which she saw as the start of the process of female emancipation, meant "the entire person"; this included sensuality and women's own—perhaps different—sexual needs. It also meant establishing women's human dignity in precisely the area in which bourgeois theories of law and the state, aided by a double standard of morality, had denied it—that is, in love, including the sex act. In showing devotion to a man, according to Stöcker, woman regained her dignity not by doing it "for the one man" (as Fichte claimed), or by becoming a mother—in both cases she was merely a means to an end—but rather "through the precious joy of mutual respect."[121] Consequently, Stöcker demanded a "revaluation of values," a "new ethics," "to develop all the strength within us; to have the courage of ourselves, of our own female human nature; to learn to give ourselves our own laws; to determine the hierarchy of values by and for ourselves. This is liberation from the spell of ascetic morality of dead or dying cultures and traditions, and also liberation from the male worldview, which we accepted unresistingly without asking ourselves whether it was the one that was important to us and without establishing our own values."[122]

This program was as provocative then as it is now; it led to enmity and condemnation, and ultimately to persecution by the Nazis. But it also helped bring clarity to the debate on the many issues and strategic differences within the women's movement. Thus the "morality issue," for example the women's movement's struggle against government-regulated prostitution, was more than simply part of a social program out of pity for "fallen sisters"; it touched upon a pivotal aspect of women's subjugation. Thus the struggle for equal rights for women became the demand for a "fundamental change in the existing order."[123] "No, no, not to want to be a man, or to be like a man, or to be able to be mistaken for him; what good would that do us!" wrote Helene Stöcker in defense against the common misunderstanding, "and what we want, we in the young, striving generation of women, is more than the philistines over there can imagine. Not only the opportunity to be dentists and lawyers, . . . we demand everything and much more, a new humankind." [124]

The recognition of women as subjects with equal rights also implies a different understanding of state and politics. It naturally assumes a democratic system of suffrage,[125] and, in its consistent support of law instead of force—in the "struggle for the force of law instead of the law of force"—it leads to rejection of war as a political tool.[126] Unlike some of their radical partners in the struggle, such as Anita Augspurg and Lida Gustava Heymann, Helene Stöcker and Rosa Mayreder did not believe in a specific "female pacifism.[127] They considered femininity and masculinity to be "cultural products," and in their hopes for the day "when women finally sit in parliament" they were realistic enough to expect the consequences of "millennia of women's subjugation by men."[128] The moderates Helene Lange and Gertrud Bäumer immediately offered the female individual—still stooping her slave morality and unused to "upright carriage"—as a sacrifice to family and state, supporting their view with an organicist understanding of the state[129] in which, "in the end, it did not matter . . . whether this state is parliamentary, democratic, or fascist."[130] For the radicals, in contrast, human rights remained the guiding principle of political activity. Human rights as a part of women's rights was the radicals' "concrete Utopia"[131] for connecting justice and freedom, socialism and feminism.

The conservative majority's politics of "organized motherliness" hit a dead end, not only as a political theory but also in practice, because the moderates failed to pursue the causes of women's subjugation "to the roots of the evil." At most they practiced "rebellious adaptation,"[132] leaving the structures of power and the institutions of patriarchy untouched and even accommodating themselves to "complementary harmony with the man," to "equal worth" rather than "equal rights."[133]

The "motherliness" project in the state and the community was doomed to failure. On the pretext of "political neutrality," it failed to call into question the form of the relationship between men and women—a political, generalizable, and universal relationship based on rules and rights; instead, it ignored the issue in its politics. Nor could this lack of a democratic form be overcome by "social acts," commendable as they might have been as social policies that transcended class.[134] The attempt, even here and there in the second-wave women's movement, to rehabilitate this feminist self-limitation falls short, while demonstrating how pertinent the issue remains and how unresolved the dilemma of a feminist politics that excludes from its political perspective the male and patriarchal nature of law and the state. By increasingly limiting their politics to specifically women's issues, the moderate, bourgeois women's movement fell short of the goals and conceivable possibilities of a human rights tradition. As Olympe de Gouges's declaration shows, this by no means implies merely a formal extension of the catalogue of rights to women; it would radicalize the relationship between the sexes by eliminating private authority and subordination, and would fundamentally change the form of politics and social relationships in general. Particularly where there is a consciousness of cultural difference—the different history and experiences of women—the issue becomes one of "finding a form of relations between people (men and women) that can be generalized and at the same time preserves special qualities; in short, a different 'political model.'"[135]

Chapter 5   Interim Remarks

Equal and Different

GRADUAL LEGAL IMPROVEMENTS followed once women attained the right to vote. Despite all obstacles and resistance, this was a substantial step; in Germany, equal rights of citizenship came first (1919), followed by equal civil rights (1949). In both cases, Germany's defeat in a war served as a catalyst for women's emancipation. These newly won rights for women were a "victory of principle"; the principle was equality, clearly winning out over the principle of legal incapacity and authority—hallmarks of patriarchy that had subjugated women. From then on, the law was on the side of women, all disadvantages and power imbalances notwithstanding. Anyone countering equal rights with a reference to force of habit or entrenched conditions—whether in terms of legal doctrine, prejudice, or the "nature of things"—was missing the point of the legal concept of equality, and violating positive law. To this extent, since 1949 the legal situation in the Federal Republic of Germany has differed from that in the United States, where the Equal Rights Amendment failed to be ratified.

What good do laws do us? asked women, who had become more impatient than ever and sensitized toward age-old and seemingly "natural" injustices. Factual discrimination contradicted legal principle; once women had achieved equal rights at least formally, in principle, they became increasingly disillusioned at the realization that formal, equal rights were not the same as social justice.

After 1919, women were not able to achieve very much with their new citizenship rights, especially because men's patriarchal privileges in the family and society remained essentially untouched. The laws, in particular family law, that assured husbands authority over the productive and reproductive capacities of their wives remained in force until 1957; in that year, the German Civil Code was changed, through passage of an equal rights law, to conform to the equal rights guarantee in Art. 3 of the West German 1949 constitution. Matrimonial and family law were similarly reformed in 1977. The abortion law, § 218 of the penal code (StGB), which has been in force, with minor modifications, since its adoption in 1871, has been a decisive challenge to women's right to self-determination. Family patriarchalism and structural disadvantages on the labor market thus undermined from the outset the formal possibility for women to participate politically and take a definite, active role in forming the first parliamentary democracy in Germany. "Never in history," wrote Otto Kirchheimer in his 1930 analysis of conditions in the Weimar Republic, "has the aim of voting rights been specifically to change social conditions and their political forms. . . . None of the many possible voting systems has ever been implemented by those in power in order to destroy the foundation of an existing social order."[1] Anita Augspurg and Lida Gustava Heymann, two women's rights activists who were also involved in consistent, pacifist, international work for women's issues, tried to implement feminist goals politically—in vain. After emigrating from Nazi Germany in 1933, they wrote, "Equal rights for women . . . was in the constitution, was laid down in black and white, but that was the extent of it. The economy, finances, administration, the entire state apparatus that is a decisive factor in revolutions and during periods of radical change, were all exclusively in the hands of men. Not even through voting did women have the same chance to exercise influence as the men. For men alone controlled the party apparatus and the party coffers, and thus the propaganda."[2]

At the same time, in the embattled legal and political discourse of the Weimar Republic prevailing theory interpreted the equality clause in a new, restrictive way. Only the parliament rose in status to become the sole legislative body. And although there was a chance for democratic interests to succeed, the standard once again became only "proportional, relative equality," in the Aristotelian sense of equality, which assures "to each" only "his own." The equality clause was thereby turned on its head. "Adjusting socially underprivileged living conditions, or even changing them entirely, [was] . . . of necessity ruled out by this relative concept of equality. Relative equality [remains] . . . an instrument by which inequality is stabilized."[3] Thus it was only a small step from the abandonment of the principle of formal legal equality to a juridical assessment of "essential differentiation . . . within the body of the people," and to the Nazis' "differential treatment of those belonging to the species and those foreign to the species."[4]

Compared to this, it was a notable achievement that women were granted equal rights under the constitution. This directly applicable legal rule, Art. 3, Sec. 2 of the Basic Law, West Germany's constitution, was cleansed of the word "basically" that had appeared in Art. 109 of the Weimar constitution. Ultimately, it succeeded against considerable resistance only because of the special commitment of the four "mothers of the Basic Law" and the support of an extraparliamentary protest by women's associations and unions. The parliamentary discussion once again brought up the concept of treating only likes alike and unalikes according to their unalikeness; the simple word "basically," which is generally included to allow exceptions to the rule, was heavily contested, but finally rejected.[5] Under a landmark 1953 decision by the Federal Constitutional Court, all these achievements were nearly lost; the court again confirmed that "in the area of family law," not only "objective biological" but also "functional [that is, related to the division of labor] differences allow or even necessitate a special regulation, relative to the nature of the respective living situation."[6] This decision created new and unnecessary obstacles to equal treatment and the establishment of equality under law, because, until its hard-won revisions in the 1970s, it continued to allow and maintain the existing conventional division of labor between men and women, the cause of so much unequal treatment, as sufficient grounds for legal distinctions—that is, discrimination.[7]

The history of Article 3 of the Basic Law again demonstrates, however, that rights, especially when they are directed against tradition and customs, must not only be fought for again and again; they must be defended. After 1949, established women's organizations should have been able to reap the benefits of the harvest sown by the women's movement of the 1920s and the first feminist lawyers trained in that spirit. But they were far too few in number, and they basked too long in the deceptive sunshine of equal opportunities and rights. In the 1960s these women still assumed there was "no more 'woman question,' . . . just individual women's issues" that could be resolved by making corrections in the legal system through reforms.[8] The second-wave women's movement finally exposed the unfulfilled promise of equal rights. However, its members based the justification of their efforts not on the claim for equality as a human right but on their own everyday experiences of social discrimination as well as private and structural violence. Even though the movement initially mobilized around a legal demand—elimination of § 218 StGB—it could not be regarded as a rights movement continuing the legal campaigns of the turn-of-the-century suffragists.

On the contrary, isolated from the experiences of the first women's movement and unaware of its radical tradition, second-wave feminists at first dissociated themselves from the "old" politics that sought "only" equal rights, in the moderate sense of "equal worth." That was the only women's rights tradition that had been passed down by the established women's associations, and it was perceived by equal rights advocates as a "specific historical" understanding of equality.[9] The new women's movement, rejecting formal, universal rules and opposed to the politics of the established women's organizations, and with an unorganized and spontaneous manner of networking, shared a great deal of common ground with other new social movements. In fact, the feminist movement was a fundamental part of them. Yet its raison d'être and its aim—to claim equal liberty and, especially, autonomy for women as well as men—was farther-reaching than the other movements.

Based on past as well as present-day experiences, there are many reasons for women and the women's movement to deeply mistrust "the discursive power of law."[10] I contend, however, that because women are "half of humankind" and yet underprivileged, it is more imperative that they claim their rights than it is for those who are traditionally privileged; women cannot afford to ignore injustices. It is impossible for women to continue to dissociate themselves from legal issues and practice nonintervention when they are among those hardest hit by cuts in social benefits, and when their hard-won rights to participate in society are about to be lost again. In the course of the worldwide debate on globalization, many countries have been seeking since the 1990s to decrease public expenditure, thereby legitimizing the welfare state's retreat from public responsibilities and public services. Women are the first to suffer from these cuts and from the new economy. There is also considerable resistance to the growth of the "legislated sphere," meaning an expanding bureaucracy and greater legislation of our social relationships; and the left and the right are debating the issue—using different lines of reasoning but exhibiting "odd agreement."[11] Such resistance and debate reveal themselves to be one-sided as long as the emphatically defended "private sphere," especially the family, continues to be a potential site of violence, not only between men and women, but also between parents and children.

When injustice occurs daily, and in view of the growing contradictions between social wealth and social disadvantage, second-wave feminism could not afford to "[lie] down in the field at the point where injustice is to be fought. Political indifference is the price it pays for the premature insight that the state which would be best is the one which exists the least."[12] This is why more and more women in legal professions have become involved in the everyday legal concerns of women, and this is why the problem of violence against women has been brought out of hiding in the private sphere into the public eye and the criminalization of rape within marriage has become a subject of legal reform.[13] The growing interest shown by women as voters has also caused the "woman question" to make its way into the institutions; again, it is treated there within the scope of demands for an anti-discrimination law and for quotas. The difficulty that the existing liberal, capitalist, and (still) patriarchal order has with the concept of, and demand for, the human right of equality is not eliminated through these changes; nor is the persistent resistance to equality. In its radical and oppositional sense as a human right, equality, as the epitome of justice, promises interpersonal relationships based not on subordination and subjection but on equal freedom of action, on a "dynamic of interdependence," and on acknowledgment of differences.[14] Even for women today, I believe there is a long way to go before equality, in the sense of "equality without adapting to the status of men" or "equal but different," is achieved, or even becomes irrelevant.

These historical and theoretical reflections were intended to reclaim a legal history of women (with special attention to the German case) that has been heretofore ignored. It can certainly only offer the beginnings of a general theory of law that incorporates the legal concerns of women. I would like to make a very provisional appraisal by naming what I see as three obstacles to the realization of greater equality for women:

- Conventions and factual power relations stand in the way of achieving equal rights. The resistance these represent, ranging from subjective factors (behavioral roles, routines, convenience, and power interests) to the material basis of our property relationships, can hardly be emphasized enough. The fact that women have entered the structures of power in economics and politics has so far changed virtually nothing. At most, women have become a topic of discussion on the labor market and in the area of education; but they are rarely found in higher positions that would lead to influence and make possible a reversal of priorities. If women wish to succeed, to become truly involved and change existing conditions, they must be prepared to struggle long and hard for greater equality, without accepting or adapting to the status quo. This is a difficult task, and it reveals a dilemma: the necessity of demanding equality and rights of citizenship for women while at the same time relying on women's "specific capacities, talents, needs and concerns, so that the expression of their citizenship will be differentiated from that of men."[15] But how else can this task be accomplished, if not by force, than by using the law, legal agreements, and rules that make coexistence possible?
- Equal rights also means recognition of difference. However, in a gender comparison this does not only entail taking gender into account through special regulations or protection to compensate for disadvantages. Instead, it means recognizing differences and providing equal opportunities and life choices for all people, male and female. Since in a liberal market economy the only things that count are those that bring in money, law registers people only from the point of view of their labor—that is, labor that carries a price. Indispensable tasks such as housework, child rearing, and caring for others have no calculable value and lead to actual legal

inequality, since the substance of the laws does not correspond to female production modes. This social ill can only be eliminated by abolishing the gender-specific division of labor. Our family and social laws are built upon compensations that cannot help the situation; they merely extend the two-tiered division of the social welfare state.

- The maintenance of male authority over women's bodies and their special capacity—the ability to raise children—is like a thread running through all of women's legal history. This has been the point of departure of all attempts by women to liberate themselves. In 1920, the following appeared in the journal *Die Frau im Staat* (The Woman in the State): "The fact that, even today, women do not have full control over their bodies is a shocking sign of the male fist in today's concept of the state." Today, women are still feeling the man's fist, or at least are still under his thumb.

Part II

<table>
<tr><td>Chapter 6</td><td>"Getting at the
Root of the Evil"</td></tr>
</table>

Legal Struggles and Legal Critique by Radicals in the First German Women's Movement

IN THE INAUGURAL ISSUE of the journal *Die Frauenbewegung* on 1 January 1895, Anita Augspurg, the radicals' leading legal expert, wrote, "The woman question may be in great part a question of food, but perhaps to an even greater extent a question of culture. . . . Above all, however, it is a legal question, because a definite solution can only be imagined on the basis of guaranteed rights. . . . Whatever an individual woman may achieve and gain in art, science, industry, general respect, and influence, it is something private, personal, momentary, isolated; it will always have the character of something exceptional, and thus tolerated. But it is not a matter of entitlement and thus cannot become the rule, cannot gain influence on the general public."[1]

Understanding the "woman question" as a primarily legal question was not just the program of one single, active suffragist. Rather, this view was typical of the later current of the "first" women's movement; for this reason, its proponents from then on made a name for themselves as "radical." Certainly women in Germany had made legal demands long before this, as individuals or organized into women's groups; with Louise Otto, an active participant in the 1848 Revolution, foremost among them, they had criticized and fought against wrongs and injustice toward women. What was new in the radicals' efforts after 1895 was the primacy given legal questions in the overall struggle for the emancipation of women. Legal equality, the "complete recognition of women as equal legal subjects with equal rights," was now no longer considered a final goal but was instead a prerequisite to any possible solution of the woman question—"the foundation on which the German woman must build her entire structure of freedom, the roots from which her tree of freedom shall spring."[2]

The rejection that "women's righters" [*Frauenrechtlerinnen*] experienced and the disrepute into which their efforts have fallen has caused a part of women's history to be lost. Thus this chapter will be devoted to the legal struggles of radical women's rights activists. They are not yet found in our textbooks and history books, and even modern feminists know far too little about them. Underlying this discussion is the question of how radical this women's legal movement around 1900 really was and whether it might be worthwhile to reconsider the delicate and complex relationship between women's legal rights and feminism.

Women's Suffrage: Crown or Roots?

The demand for equal rights of citizens, and thus for women's suffrage, was, as we have seen, one that had already been made during the French Revolution; it is necessary to distinguish here between the history of the demand itself and that of the suffrage movement. The German suffragists of the late nineteenth century[3] based their campaign on "great forerunners and bearers of the idea." Notable among these were Olympe de Gouges's *Declaration of the Rights of Woman and Citizen* of 1791,[4] Theodor G. von Hippel's essay *On the Civic Improvement of Women*,[5] and Mary Wollstonecraft's *A Vindication of the Rights of Women*[6]—writings of the Enlightenment and the French Revolution. Louise Otto's programmatic intervention in the democratic debates preceding the 1848 revolution was also quoted repeatedly—including her first article in the *Sächsische Vaterlandsblätter* of 1843 on "the participation of the female world in state affairs," not only "as a right, but as a duty" of women, as well as the *Frauen-Zeitung* she published under the motto, "I am recruiting women citizens for the realm of freedom."[7] Other pioneers in the fight for women's rights included Malwida Meysenbug, whose *Memoirs of an Idealist* went to forty-three editions by 1927;[8] John Stuart Mill and his *The Subjection of Women*;[9] and Hedwig Dohm, whose polemical *Women's Nature and Privilege* became the credo of the

German suffrage movement. Her polemics are just as pertinent today as they were then: "Wake, women of Germany . . . if you have spirit enough to feel your degradation, and intellect enough to see the source of your misery. Demand the suffrage!"[10] Suffrage, she continued, is the road to women's independence and equality, freedom and happiness. Not to be underestimated, finally, even for the bourgeois women's movement, is the significance of August Bebel's *Women under Socialism*.[11]

While the representatives of the German women's movement were united in their assessment of their pioneering forebears, as well as in the goal of seeking "complete social, legal and political equality," a deep divide separated the radicals and the moderates in the paths they chose. Marie Stritt, a women's rights activist in the ranks of the radicals, though she would from 1899 to 1910 head the Federation of German Women's Organizations [Bund Deutscher Frauenvereine], based her explanation of the differences on the views of Louise Otto, "the mother of the German women's movement and a classic witness." In 1876, Otto had already criticized "the tactics of the women's organizations fighting for female progress": "They too have consistently failed to place the [suffrage] issue on the agenda, so as not to disconcert women working for less distant goals, in order, on the other hand, to first promote education, self-reliance, and independence among women, so that they are suited to take on these duties and rights. . . ." Stritt continued, "Even in 1897, there are still differences of opinion within our movement on the suffrage issue, but only insofar as some feel the moment has not yet arrived to demand public and political rights for the female sex, because the great mass of women do not yet seem ready for it; others, in contrast . . . view this right as the necessary basis for the material and moral liberation of women, and as the best means of educating them in social and political self-reliance."[12]

The delay in the German suffrage movement, compared, for example, with its American counterpart, resulted not only from tactical considerations or backwardness; an important factor was also the reactionary policies that followed the 1848 revolution. The consequences of these policies, especially for women, were long-lasting and dire, because reactionary press and association laws prohibited them from pursuing any political activity. In most of the states of the German Confederation, especially Prussia and Bavaria, women were expressly

prohibited until 1908 from joining political associations or even attending political gatherings. In this way, women were denied any political
voice—they were silenced—and women's organizations that dealt with
"political subjects" risked being fined and broken up by the police.[13]
The only remaining legal means by which women could express their
political will was the petition, the use of which was already dismissed
by Clara Zetkin as "petition heroics."[14] Petitioning was made possible
by § 23 of the Reich Constitution but was left to the rather arbitrary
handling of a Reichstag petition commission.

Only in this context does it become clear what boldness was required, and what a new style was heralded, by the convening of a public "people's assembly" in Berlin on 2 December 1894 on the subject of
"Women's Duties as Citizens." The first public gathering of bourgeois
women, let alone one with a political theme, it was organized by Minna
Cauer, chair of the Berlin Women's Welfare Organization [Frauenwohl-
Berlin], and the speaker was Lily von Gizycki (married name, Lily
Braun).[15] The gathering attracted considerable attention. It is true that
"some newspapers took only derisive notice of some ridiculous fact,"
while others completely ignored it,"[16] but witnesses wrote of a "storm
of enthusiasm" in the audience. That Sunday morning, the concert hall
on Leipziger Strasse was packed.[17] "Many members of the organization
[Frauenwohl] saw this as so alarming and threatening that a number
canceled their membership."[18]

Lily Braun's speech, subsequently repeated in Dresden and Breslau
and printed as an agitation pamphlet, is a rousing summary of the arguments for women's suffrage, a refutation of fearful prejudices, and an
appeal to women to assume responsibilities in the state, the community, and the institutions of social work that they were striving to take
over as their domain. Braun spoke of her great models—Jean Antoine
de Condorcet, Olympe de Gouges, and others, but she had also studied
the development and successes of the American and English suffrage
movements, and she argued that the typically German emphasis on a
woman's duties as housewife and mother did not release her from her
civic duties. "I cannot accept that a woman who casts her vote at the
ballot box risks losing her 'womanliness' any more than another who
carts stones. And I cannot comprehend that the sight of a woman with
child should be more scandalous in the polling places than in the lead

foundries." She dismissed the objection that the female sex was not yet ready for freedom with a reference to Kant: [19] "'We cannot ripen to this freedom if we are not first of all placed therein.' And thus we demand free rein for our development for our own sakes and for the sake of suffering humanity. We demand thoroughgoing reform of the association laws, which in no other country but Germany place such fetters on women. We demand application of the principles of the modern state—universal human rights—to the other half of humankind, to women. We, an army of millions upon millions of women, who place our strength in the service of the public as much as men, demand our right to participate in forming the public sphere."[20]

The new topic of women had thus been placed on the agenda and the controversy delineated. No suffrage organization had yet been created because of the association laws, but the radicals now developed a lively program of agitation, organizing lecture tours to smaller towns and to other women's organizations. In addition to Lily Braun and Minna Cauer, others who took to the road in the suffragist cause were Marie Raschke, Anita Augspurg, Lida Gustava Heymann, and Käthe Schirmacher. Starting in 1895, the journal *Die Frauenbewegung* became a forum primarily for legal issues. Space was also provided to opposing views, but actually only for them to be refuted with hair-splitting and polemical arguments. It was convenient that the Social Democratic Party, which had made women's suffrage part of its platform in 1891, introduced the demand for suffrage in the Reichstag for the first time in 1895. Women thoroughly appreciated the motion, and the Social Democrats' explanation.[21]

To its advocates, suffrage was not only a principle of justice but a prerequisite for equal rights in all spheres of life—in the family, on the job, and in public life. For the radicals, therefore, it was not the "final goal" that would be the solution to all women's problems but, on the contrary, the "foundation" upon which equality in public and private life could first be established. "The difference in principle can be expressed as follows: The radicals see women's suffrage as the roots of the women's movement, while the moderates view it as a distant goal, as the crown of the tree of the women's movement, which women must first earn through work in the public interest, community activity, and better education and training. . . . Lengthy agitation and petitioning by women is necessary for even the smallest step forward, as long as they do not have access to the handle to legislation, the right to vote."[22]

Not "satisfied by halfway measures and palliatives," they saw the lack of suffrage as "the root of the evil."[23] Our reference today to our negative experience with the ineffectiveness of formal law seems to be little more than a self-righteous objection. The right to participate in legislation to change social conditions and policies is one that must not only be fought for but also, as German history has shown, constantly defended, and even rewon.

The Struggle Against the German Civil Code: Women's New Legal Consciousness

A vivid example of legislation guided only by male interests actually emerged in the course of the suffrage movement: the Civil Code. This huge Reich-wide codification effort was begun in 1873 to standardize German private law, fragmented as it was among many areas and sources of law. It came up for a second and third reading in the Reichstag in early 1896. In the course of putting together a petition in 1876, Louise Otto and her General German Women's Association in Leipzig had already diligently collected all legal provisions regarding women in a paper titled *Some Sections of German Law on the Status of Women* [Einige deutsche Gesetz-Paragraphen über die Stellung der Frau]. The authors demanded "that the rights of women, especially as regards marriage and guardianship, be taken into account when amending the Civil Code."[24] In the early nineties, this collection was expanded and revised on the basis of a new second draft of the Civil Code; along with other recommendations by these women, now experts, it was attached to a petition from the Federation of German Women's Organizations.[25] As always, these efforts received little notice, and it was almost too late by the time women came together in a massive women's campaign [Frauenlandsturm] protesting the Civil Code. The mobilization, which the contemporary press both ridiculed and focused upon, was once again initiated by the radicals, the Berlin Women's Welfare Organization. Unlike other initiatives, however, in this case all currents of the women's movement opposed the renewed legal entrenchment of female subordination to "conjugal authority," and all participated in protests, mass rallies, and petition-signing campaigns.[26] It is not true that this indignation was merely typical bourgeois activism by "women's righters" concerned only with the marital property rights of the propertied classes, as antifeminists liked to maintain as a way of dividing the women.[27] Even Clara Zetkin, spokeswoman of the proletarian women's movement, supported the struggle against the Civil Code, despite the polemics against women's rights activists dictated by the party line. "Considering that the complete liberation of the great mass of women can only be achieved by socialist society; that, however, legal equality of the sexes is possible even within bourgeois society and the ground laid by economic developments is not merely a requirement of justice and fairness, but an economic necessity for millions of women; further considering that the equality of the sexes raises proletarian women to a higher social plane, lending them greater freedom of movement, but also a greater ability to fight and defend themselves against bourgeois society," she called on her fellow party members, and especially the Social Democratic Party in the Reichstag, to give "unqualified support to full legal equality of the sexes."[28]

The main points of criticism of the Civil Code (BGB), those which particularly inflamed the legal consciousness of women, were:

- The husband's right to make decisions "on all matters concerning married life" under § 1354, an "obedience section" that limited every married woman's ability to act and make transactions and continued in force until 1953. The equal rights law was not passed until 1957.

- The husband's exclusive right to administer and use his wife's property; this placed women on a worse footing than minors with regard to property brought into marriage or acquired during it and thus sealed their subordination and economic dependence upon their husbands. Only property acquired through independent or wage labor, not from working in the husband's business or trade, remained at a woman's full disposal, as so-called reserved property. This was a legal accomplishment for working women, but because of the low wages women earned and the fact that husbands were permitted to terminate wives' work contracts "without prior notice." (§1358 BGB), it had little practical significance.

However, in the final version, husbands' rights to terminate work contracts were made dependent on authorization by a guardianship court.[29] This was a result not of women's protests but of intervention by employers and their interest in "greater independence of the women among industrial workers."

- Authority over children, described as "parental," but nevertheless only paternal, because the father was the final arbiter in all questions of child care and child rearing. Even after adoption of the 1957 equal rights law in the Federal Republic of Germany, a constitutional court decision was necessary before this legal imbalance was finally eliminated.

- The "flagrant injustice" in the legal status of unmarried mothers and their out-of-wedlock children, which "blamed the weaker half, the woman, for any consequences of a mistake, while letting the stronger, more blameworthy half, the man, off virtually scot-free. [It] not only once again sanctions the traditional double standard, but also makes a mockery of humanity."[30] According to civil law as it existed until 1969, children born out of wedlock were unrelated to the father. The "progenitor" could escape his duty to pay support by claiming the possible participation of other men, the so-called multiple-partners defense.

This reference to injustices that continue into the present makes it apparent that the protests, despite the unusual mobilization of women, had no immediate success. With only a small concession allowing women to serve as guardians—wives, of course, only with the husband's permission—the Civil Code passed the Reichstag in 1896, the opposition of the Social Democrats notwithstanding. Although "the greater part of the nation at the time" rejected its family law provisions as undignified, anachronistic, and culturally inhibiting,[31] legal scholars and politicians hailed it as a "manifesto of liberal legal culture," with which "the German nation [guaranteed] not only formal legal uniformity in private-law relationships, but also justice and welfare."[32]

Despite their disappointment, the legal activists did not allow this defeat to be the last word on the subject. Further protest meetings were organized, to great public attention. The realization that the legal question concerned, and had to concern, all women inspired them to daring hopes that they might achieve more very soon, perhaps even in the next legislative session.[33] "A thousand years of injustice are not an hour of justice," wrote Marie Stritt in summary. "This truth was never placed before German women with such urgency as now, with the new Civil Code. The legal questions that were formerly considered mainly from a theoretical and abstract perspective were brought home to them for the first time in definite, concrete demands. They became questions of eminent, immediate significance, . . . and will remain so until a solution is found that satisfies all women."[34]

All legal progress that has since been achieved for women in private law, from the first equal rights law in 1957 to the matrimonial and family law reform of 1977, are in this sense only "partial payments" on the demands of the radical women's movement at the turn of the last century.

Legal Aid Associations: Assistance by Women for Women

Realizing that women's legal interests would not be represented by men, women's organizations accepted the consequences and founded legal aid offices by and for women. The Dresden Legal Aid Association [Dresdener Rechtsschutzverein], which had already emerged from the local chapter of the General German Women's Association in 1894, took the lead. The idea was promoted by the association's president, Marie Stritt, and quickly spread after the defeat in the struggle against the Civil Code. In 1900, eight organizations from various cities joined together to form the German Legal Aid Center for Women [Zentrale deutscher Rechtsschutzstellen für Frauen], headed by Marie Raschke, D.J. By 1901, eighteen legal aid offices had joined, and by 1918, the women's legal protection association had 101 member organizations.[35]

Like other initiatives by charitable organizations, professional associations, and, especially, unions—which were at the time organizing legal information offices and legal support services for their members in the form of "workers' secretariats"—the legal aid offices for women saw their task to be "offering women and girls of all classes the opportunity to obtain legal advice free of charge," to help with briefs or even letters, and to support those seeking assistance in conflicts with employers or landlords by pursuing settlements. Only in difficult cases did they call upon a lawyer with experience in women's affairs. It is noteworthy that the women providing the legal advice, unlike the increasingly professionalized workers' secretariats, remained legal laypersons; even if they possessed law degrees, they were excluded until 1922 from positions administrating justice or in the judiciary. Unlike today, the provision of legal counseling was not yet licensed: it did not require an official permit, and public administration of justice was not restricted to lawyers. The founders of the first legal aid office for women saw their lay status as a strength rather than a shortcoming. They assumed that "the knowledge of the law acquired through diligent independent study and the rich practical experience of the women providing service" generally sufficed to calm the clients' "shyness and excitement." In fact, it was important to them, "for practical and ethical reasons," to place "the main emphasis of their work on direct contact with the women desiring their help." In their opinion, "complete, unqualified trust [was] the basis of a sense of solidarity that has been rare among women, and thus an extraordinarily important educational factor for those seeking help as well as for those helping them."[36]

There was a political and legal goal behind this. The bourgeois women who offered their private homes to the legal advice offices often learned for the first time during office hours about the extent of social want and injustice. This could encourage them to make legal demands beyond their own class-bound experience. For "only the thorough knowledge of all legal provisions that disadvantage women, in detail and in context, gives certain guidance for the future standardization of law in accordance with women's legal awareness."[37]

This was the idea; in practice, however, opinions split into moderate and radical. The experiences of the legal aid offices indicated that, as a rule, a letter was enough to help clients assert their rights against husbands or employers. Increasingly, however, the role of the legal aid offices as "justices of the peace" was emphasized, because they shielded women from legal disputes and thus ensured legal peace and reconciliation—a double-edged result. This becomes clear in a tribute in 1922 on the occasion of the twenty-fifth anniversary of the Munich legal advice office, which was run by Sophia Goudstikker, a former associate of Anita Augspurg. It is ironic to read what Gertrud Bäumer, a moderate, wrote about the achievements of these "radicals." On the one hand, she described their activities quite vividly; on the other, she emphasized the "human side," in contrast to the legal, to such an extent that only the charity aspect of their legal aid activities remained. "In this period, more than 60,000 women were advised by the legal aid office. But numbers alone do not tell us everything. In fact, they tell us very little. For it makes a difference whether I tell a women about a section of law or give her a referral, or whether I help her. And not only legally, but humanly—not only formally, but prudently and effectively help her. . . . Sophia Goudstikker was a complete autodidact. What she achieved was based just as much on an intelligent, insightful, warm-hearted understanding of actual situations as on the legal knowledge she had acquired. She had a fabulous, natural talent for taking up the cause of the unprotected. She proved it—layperson that she was—even as a defense counsel. She was the first woman admitted as a defender in Munich, and stood up for women in the courtroom long before the first woman lawyer appeared. Incidentally, these words can characterize her and her work only very imperfectly. The original vitality of the women's movement is in her and her work—all the fresh energy of the early period of this movement, all its fire, and all its adventurousness."[38]

Marriage Boycott: Propaganda of Deeds

An important aspect of the propaganda by the legal aid offices consisted of drafting and distributing marriage contracts that would prevent the negative consequences of divorce law by drawing up different marital property arrangements. Some radicals went further; they refused to marry and discouraged others from doing so, given the existing injustice in the legal status of marriage. Anita Augspurg's call for such a marriage boycott in a 1905 letter to the weekly *Europa* unleashed a storm of indignation. The cause of the criticism, in particular, was her conclusion that "legitimate marriage means, for woman, the legal sacrifice of her legal existence; it includes not only the renunciation of her name and her right of self-determination, which is degrading to an independent individual, but also, in most cases, complete pecuniary dependence and, in all cases, complete lack of rights with regard to her children. For a woman with self-respect who knows the legal effects of civil marriage, it is impossible, I am convinced, to enter a legitimate marriage; her drive for self-preservation, her self-respect, and her claim to respect from her husband leave only the option of a free marriage. . . . It seems to me that only such propaganda of deeds can lead our legislature to make the urgently needed reforms."[39]

The subsequent controversy, published only in excerpted form in the journal *Die Frauenbewegung*, separated the wheat from the chaff; a flood of publications, some of them reactionary, followed.[40] Many of those who considered themselves progressive found themselves unable to approve of this attack on the pillars of the bourgeois order, marriage and the family, or to agree with what they characterized as its "whore morality." Typically, in the midst of this indignation, many were unable to distinguish between the "free marriage" propagated by Augspurg— which in today's legal jargon is known as "extramarital cohabitation"— and free love, or even libertinism. Minna Cauer defended Augspurg in a number of editorials; she also defended—critically but in solidarity— Helene Stöcker. Stöcker's "new ethics" were advanced at the same time by the League for the Protection of Mothers [Bund für Mutterschutz], which led her to be condemned and "disowned."[41] At a meeting of the Alliance of Progressive Women's Organizations [Verband fortschrittlicher Frauenvereine] that same year, 1905, Augspurg and Stöcker had a chance to present their critiques and views in foundational speeches; this was reason enough for Minna Cauer to call the discussions at this conference on the "reform of marriage"—held with "dignity" and on a high moral level—a "milestone of the women's movement."[42]

Flip Sides: The Double Standard

The flip side of this discussion of bourgeois marriage—the sexual double standard—was the focus of the morality campaign's attacks. Campaigns for moral reforms were certainly a double-edged sword. In other countries, women's organizations in this period owed significant legal successes to their involvement in morality or temperance movements, through which they proved their "respectability." In Australia, New Zealand, and the state of Wyoming they even attained the right to vote.[43] Without a doubt, moral indignation at immoral conditions was itself an aspect of bourgeois Victorian narrow-mindedness, and not only a sign of protest. One must ask whether the enormous attention that the German public, scientific publications, and gazettes paid to prostitution, procuring, and sexual waywardness before the turn of the century was a function of the actual situation or simply a reflection of social repression and contradictions. The disproportion is obvious if we compare the great sympathy among all sectors of the public for reforms—that is, tightening of sex-crimes law (triggered by the murder trial of a pimp named Heinze, and thus dubbed the "Lex Heinze"), which ultimately led the Reichstag to "block" the law—with the lack of attention paid to women's protests against the Civil Code.[44] In any case, women in particular were affected by the standardization of sex-crimes law, because it was one-sided and thus sexist; because it blamed and punished the female victim alone; and because state power and the male judicial system acted as pimps in the exploitation and humiliation of women as sexual entities.

The most obvious expression of the double standard was state-regulated prostitution. Under § 180 and § 361 of the German criminal code (StGB) of 1870, prostitution was prohibited, especially brothel keeping, which was considered procuring and prohibited by § 180 StGB.[45] However, the so-called French system, introduced to Europe by Napoleon, had spread, abetted by state vice regulations. This system tacitly tolerated brothels and every other practice of prostitution, and even taxed them, as long as prostitutes remained subject to police supervision and health checks. Only "female persons" could be fined or forced to undergo health examinations under § 361, no. 6 of the criminal code, while male participants remained untouched, and in fact could even feel safe from the danger of infection due to the increasing numbers of health checks.

The international women's movement to eliminate state-regulated prostitution, in conjunction with the International Abolitionist Federation, had a varied and difficult history in Germany.[46] Once again it was the radicals who, in the 1890s, forced a public discussion of the scandals. After Gertrud Guillaume-Schack was expelled from the country in 1886 for her bold abolitionist and socialist activities, it was Hanna Bieber-Böhm, the stubborn, hardworking "women's rights rebel" and founder of the Youth Protection Organization [Verein Jugendschutz] in 1889, who continued the fight for the elevation of morality, placing

"embarrassing things" on the agenda of the women's organizations.[47]
One of her in-depth reports and a petition against state-tolerated prostitution were permitted to be read at the general assembly of the Federation of German Women's Organizations as the result of energetic
intervention by the radical opposition, which constituted itself as a "left
wing" for the first time at this assembly. Lily von Gizycki (Braun) reported in Die Frauenbewegung, "Pale, in a voice soft at first, but ever
clearer, Frau Hanna Bieber-Böhm read her petition aloud. Even those
who had so much feared the 'indecent ones' listened with breathless
excitement. . . . I will never forget how an elderly lady, personally unknown to me, said to me in a trembling voice, wringing her hands, 'And
I have two grown sons and knew nothing of all this.'"[48]

Though united in indignation, the women in the women's movement soon went their separate ways in the legal conclusions they drew.
In 1898, Minna Cauer was invited to the federation's international congress in London by Josephine Butler and returned with abolitionist
plans; this resulted in a major altercation in the Berlin Women's Welfare
Organization between Cauer and Hanna Bieber-Böhm.[49] Bieber-Böhm
and her faction, represented by the Youth Protection Organization, advocated the elimination of state-regulated prostitution, increased penalties, punishment of both women and men for prostitution, and forcible
commitment to reformatories. The representatives of the new, German
chapters of the Abolitionist Federation, however, considered prostitution "not a crime in the penal sense, but a vice that concerns only the
conscience."[50] In the opinion of the radicals, more law and justice did
not have to mean higher penalties and greater repression.

"Not from a lax view of morality," wrote Anna Papritz, head of the
Berlin organization, "but for moral reasons of justice, the Federation supports decriminalization of prostitution. . . . It expects clear success neither from punishment of prostitution nor from rescue work; it is instead
searching for the root of the evil. Two factors make up the main causes
of prostitution: first, demand on the part of men, and second, women's
economic and legal dependency. Here it is necessary to tackle the problem through education, information, and social reforms of all sorts."[51]

The radicals' practices, too, were unconventional in this matter:
in addition to mass protests, a complaint to the Hamburg Senate concerning illegal brothel keeping, critiques, and attendance at Reichstag

debates on the issue, they also gained a sense of the situation through "participatory observation."[52] Lida Gustava Heymann, head of the Hamburg Abolitionist Organization, described how one night, together with a dock worker and a district nurse, "dressed shabbily and unobtrusively . . . [she wandered] through the bars and dance halls of the port." "Deep sympathy with these unfortunate souls gripped us, disgust, fury, and revulsion at a state which allowed such 'pleasure places' for a class of its citizens, in order to satisfy the desire for happiness that dwells within every person. We did not regret this nighttime excursion; we had enriched our store of knowledge. We lost the last shred of respect for this male state and its undignified institutions."[53]

Sex-Based Justice

Female solidarity and concern for the welfare of "fallen" sisters were not all that motivated women in the international campaign against state-regulated prostitution. The morality movement was in fact the focal point of their social criticism; they saw in it the connection between sexual life or gender relations and the organization and exercise of patriarchal power. Furthermore, discrimination on the basis of sex by the state and its institutions directly affected all women, including bourgeois wives—first, because marriage and sex crimes laws could not prevent the danger of infection being carried into the marital bedroom, and second, because no woman appearing in public was apparently safe from "vice squads," forced examination, and arrest. Turn-of-the-century periodicals reported on countless incidents in which the police mistakenly or intentionally arrested unaccompanied women as prostitutes and forced them to undergo physical examinations. "Neither poor nor rich, high nor low, women in the most luxurious attire nor those in plain garments, neither the slowly ambling nor the hurriedly rushing, long nor short haired, and so, ad infinitum" could avoid arbitrary police action.[54] *Die Frauenbewegung* published examples: "In both cases, very young, inexperienced, and vulnerable girls were arrested in a brutal manner by police officers, without the least attempt having been made to determine their identity and reputation. They were taken to the police station, treated in the same dishonorable way in which low- and high-level police organs enjoy treating registered prostitutes, held in police

custody until the next day and the next, then given a physical examination, found completely healthy and untouched, and then released and
left to their fate, without compensation or apology, but probably with
some rude remarks by the honorable Mr. Police Officer."[55]

Given this drastic portrayal, it is understandable that even the hir-
ing of women—police matrons—by the police was praised as a legal
achievement. In the same year that radical women's organizations went
to the public with protests throughout the country against "police errors," "glaring sex-based justice," and "exceptional laws," a police officer in Weimar, the capital and royal residence of the Grand Duchy of
Saxony, managed to accidentally arrest Anita Augspurg on suspicion
of violating § 361 no. 6 of the penal code.[56] "Doctor juris Anita," as
she was called in a satirical poem about this embarrassing incident, knew
what to do.[57] Reading her complaint brief and her replies in the press
and at protest and solidarity rallies, one cannot avoid the impression
that it was the defender of law and order who was ultimately dragged
to the station house, rather than the suffragist suspected of "curious conduct."[58] Sexism in the legal system could not be more clearly illustrated
than by such police "errors," especially since women at the time had
more than police officers to worry about. They demanded "unrestricted
freedom of movement for women citizens at night as well as by day." It
was clear to them, however, that "women's absolute lack of rights on
the streets and in public spaces, as soon as the dark of night covers every insult against them on the part of cowardly men, is so deeply rooted
in popular consciousness, and so strongly supported by our social conditions, that decades shall pass before people will have become accus-
tomed to letting female taxpayers have unrestricted use of public streets,
even at night."[59]

Thus, attention to everyday violence against women has a history.
Not even feminist legal criticism of rape trials and the familiar acquit-
tal of men by men is new. In any case, the fact that such criticism continues to be necessary exposes social conditions in which male power
defends traditional bastions, using law as a pretext. The radicals' critique and arguments could have been made today.

A typical example was the 1905 case of the gang rape of a fifteen-
year-old servant girl. The four rapists were acquitted by an Altona court;
the girl was labeled "disreputable" because "she didn't resist." Because

the public was excluded from the trial, women themselves researched the case and came to a different conclusion. To their complaints, the rapists' defenders answered, "What girl wouldn't resist?" Thus the victim became the guilty party; violence and resistance were measured by two different standards. The women's press sharply criticized this male collusion, which "brands the entirety of German women as without rights and fair game. . . . —a class judgment, though in a different sense; that is, a judgment of the ruling class of men against women, who lack rights."[60]

Only the Social Democratic women's organizations joined the radicals' public protests and their criticism of the judgment. The local Hamburg chapter of the General German Women's Association [Allgemeiner Deutscher Frauenverein] expressly defended the ruling. The liberals and the liberal press, as the radicals bitterly noted, were not prepared "to defend objective law standing shoulder to shoulder with the Social Democrats, instead of drawing a veil, against their better judgment, over serious damage to the bourgeois legal order."[61] By taking up this scandal and making it a central object of their politics and propaganda, the radicals were fighting not only male justice, "male morality," and customary injustice; they were also attacking indifference, subservience, and the "silence of women." Over and over again, the avant garde found that their demands remained "more or less academic statements" as long as no "actual event" affecting everyone "formed the background for protest against the unbearable disregard for the personality of the woman."[62]

Note on the History of § 218 of the Penal Code

The radicals were also ahead of their time in their political and legal demands regarding § 218 of the Penal Code. When a revision of the Penal Code came up for consideration in 1910—at the time, self-abortion was punishable by up to five years' imprisonment, a provision unchanged since 1870—the radicals demanded that § 218 be repealed, referring to the "right to self-determination, the right over oneself, over one's own body." Empirical data for their fight was provided by a survey of six hundred well-known figures conducted by Helene Stöcker for the League for the Protection of Mothers. More than half the respondents supported the League for the Protection of Mothers' demands, including Gustav Radbruch, who later became the Social Democratic Minister of Justice, Hedwig Dohm, and the criminal lawyer Franz von Liszt. "We want to help women to better perform their maternal duties. But no woman should be coerced if she has become a mother against her will, for example through rape, or if an infectious disease is involved, or if she can expect to experience deep, life-destroying harm to herself or her family as a result. As long as society leaves motherhood almost without protection, and in some cases even punishes motherhood with shame, it has no right to consider avoidance of undesired motherhood as a crime deserving of imprisonment."[63]

The legal commission of the Federation of German Women's Organizations, which was entirely in the hands of the radicals when it was founded in 1896, was very progressive under the leadership of Marie Stritt and the overall charge of Camilla Jellinek; it called for complete elimination of § 218 but was outvoted at the federation's general meeting. In a petition submitted to the Reichstag in 1909, among other demands concerning vice laws, the Federation called only for reduced penalties for abortion and for exemption from punishment only on medical, eugenic, and ethical grounds.[64] Not until 1926, after a mass movement developed against § 218 during the Weimar Republic, were the penalties reduced to regular prison terms, only to revert to the more severe penitentiary term in 1943.

The radicals' progressiveness in advocating complete elimination of the abortion law becomes evident if we compare their attitude with the blindness and prejudice of labor movement leaders on questions of sexual morality. During the "birth-strike debate" within the Social Democratic Party in 1913, Clara Zetkin condemned birth control—which was indispensable to female workers—and the workers' popular demand for a birth strike, saying it would reduce "the number of soldiers for the revolution."[65]

The Rights of Mothers

No chronicle of legal struggles would be complete without the petitions and legal achievements of the League for the Protection of Mothers, even if it seems absurd that Helen Stöcker, a pacifist, scored a success in this regard just at the outbreak of World War I. "Under the thunder of the world war, some seeds that we had sown in a decade of laborious work matured with surprising speed."[66]

The League for the Protection of Mothers had been fighting since 1905 for new ethical standards and for sexual reform. By combining practical social work with a reevaluation of false concepts of morality, it had attempted in particular to achieve equal rights for single mothers and their children. In August 1914, the petition signed by Helene Stöcker enjoyed immediate success. The Reichstag decided to pay support to wives of soldiers and to extend this to cover mothers of out-of-wedlock children. Payment of survivors' benefits was also taken under advisement. This was but a minuscule legal step, it is true, and the main issue was "to keep the generation born now as complete as possible" because of "the enormous loss of human material."[67] But wasn't it a "victory of principle," even if it would not be recognized completely until out-of-wedlock children were granted legal equality in 1969?

In addition to these ambivalent wartime achievements, mention and admiration are due the alternative proposals for improving the situation of mothers that were prepared by the League for the Protection of Mothers through careful legal research and directed to the "high Reichstag" in 1907. Aside from the urgent extension of labor protection laws to all female employees, including agricultural workers, home workers, and domestic servants, these proposals also called for comprehensive maternity insurance, which was to be financed with the help of government subsidies and would be facilitated by a carefully calculated rise in social security payments from both men and women. The succinct explanation pointed out that, "since men and women are equal participants in the formation of a child, maternity insurance is not the concern of women alone."[68]

Women today are again, rightly, complaining of reductions in maternity benefits and the lack of legal recognition of their child rearing and household labor. This historical example demonstrates how little has been achieved to this day, and perhaps also how necessary it would be to examine, apart from the larger issues of equality in family and labor law, the niches of systematic social disadvantage in public benefits, social security, and pension laws.

One peculiarity of the German women's movement should be noted in regard to labor laws protecting women. Women's rights activists in Anglo-Saxon and Scandinavian countries were already agitating at the turn of the last century, and certainly by the 1920s in the so-called open door movement, against special protection for female workers; they felt it put women at a disadvantage in the labor market and reduced their wages. But German radicals, like moderates and Social Democrats, surprisingly enough always unanimously advocated legislation for the protection of women, because it could "easily be transferred to men" and thus was a "pioneering act," setting an example for the humanization of working life.[69] The contradiction between women's liberation and women's protection was less significant in their minds, given the consideration that equality here could only be illusory. Else Lüders, the radicals' expert on protection for female workers, therefore quoted Helene Simon's famous address[70] to the Society for Social Reform [Gesellschaft für soziale Reform] in 1901 (but even Clara Zetkin might have expressed herself very similarly): "If women are to be forged weapons for the struggle for existence, they must be protected from overburdening, from undermining their physical strength; they must bring healthy children into the world without impairing their employment opportunities. Only expanded, knowledgeable protection of female workers in general, extended protection for mothers before and after the birth of their children, with corresponding benefits . . . will gradually create a system of division of labor in which women no longer find employment because of the low wages they receive, their obedience, and their powerlessness, but because of their performance."[71]

Women's Suffrage Once Again: Factional Struggles

In order to understand the suffrage movement in Germany, it is important first to briefly consider its complicated organizational history.[72] The first women's suffrage organization in Germany, the German Association for Women's Suffrage [Deutsche Verein für Frauenstimmrecht], was not formed until 1902, in Hamburg. What was prohibited to "female persons" in Prussia and Bavaria, the two largest states in the Reich, was made possible in Hamburg by a loophole in Hamburg's association laws. The 1894 Association Law for the Hanseatic City of Hamburg [Vereins-Recht für die Hansastadt Hamburg] failed to mention women at all; presumably, they had been forgotten. The initiators of the suffrage organization were Augspurg, Heymann, and Cauer, and members were drawn from throughout Germany; there were contact women in several German cities. Besides the right to vote for the Reichstag, they also demanded the right of representation in communities, schools, churches, and especially in professional organizations, chambers, and courts. Among the many goals the association identified as necessary to "achieve political equality in all areas," a primary objective was a free, uniform association and assembly law; many protest rallies and petitions addressed this issue.[73] It was not least because of the association's newly won strength and propaganda efforts that, in 1902, the Federation of German Women's Organizations could not avoid incorporating women's suffrage into its platform.[74]

The 1904 inaugural conference of the International Alliance of Women's Suffrage (IAW) was a glorious event and a great success. It brought to Berlin everyone of note in the international suffrage movement and provided the public with impressive evidence of female solidarity and "political maturity." As its membership increased, the Association for Women's Suffrage was renamed the German Federation for Women's Suffrage [Deutscher Verband für Frauenstimmrecht] in 1904, in order to make it possible to establish suffrage organizations in German states that had not yet formed any.

"The year 1908 should be inscribed in golden letters in the history of the suffrage movement," wrote Frieda Ledermann in her reflections.[75] But this is, in fact, open to question. On the one hand, it is true that in 1908, the restriction on women's political participation fell after more than half a century, as state association laws were replaced by a Reich association law that no longer treated women as minors. On the other hand, once women were allowed to participate in party work, political differences that had heretofore been hidden beneath a cloak of common oppression emerged even more forcefully. On the suffrage issue, dissension emerged over what type of voting rights was meant—universal, equal suffrage by secret ballot or the three-class suffrage that continued in the Prussian state parliament until 1918 and was mocked by Clara Zetkin as "limited, ladies' suffrage."[76] Not until 1907 did the radicals in the German Federation for Women's Suffrage, defending themselves against the right and left wings, write what they considered the obvious demand for "universal suffrage as a binding principle" into §3 of their statute. Because only the Social Democrats clearly supported democratic suffrage for women at the time, this was interpreted as a party affiliation, and within the federation an opposition formed that was satisfied with a demand for suffrage "under the same conditions that men have and will have."[77] This opposition came together in 1911 as the German Union for Women's Suffrage [Deutsche Vereinigung für Frauenstimmrecht]. As if this were not enough, even among those who remained in the federation unity was more apparent than real. To win the hesitant female masses and preserve neutrality at any price, the "reform party," headed by Maria Lischnewska, developed a compromise proposal that retreated into a pure women's rights standpoint. The demand for democratic suffrage for men was eliminated. What remained was language such as "The Federation strives for equal, personally exercised suffrage for all women" and "full rights of citizens for all women,"[78] as though the general political conditions of class-based law were irrelevant to the exercise of women's rights—an apolitical, feminist, self-imposed restriction.

Additional splintering followed. After Minna Cauer and Tony Breitscheid resigned from the Federation,[79] the remaining "supporters of an open profession of support for universal equal suffrage for women and men" also left to form the German League for Women's Suffrage [Deutscher Bund für Frauenstimmrecht].[80] In addition to the old leaders Augspurg and Heymann, and Cauer, also a dedicated activist, this small but steadfast group of radicals also attracted new recruits from local groups in Baden, Hessen, Berlin, and Bremen (such as Auguste Kirchhoff and Rita Bardenheuer), as well as many unaffiliated individuals.[81]

Thus three suffrage organizations existed in Germany at the outbreak of World War I. An attempt to form a loose "alliance" failed. Not until December 1917, shaken by the war and recognized for service to the nation and the fatherland, did women of all persuasions join in a forward thrust, a "Declaration on the Suffrage Issue," signed by Marie Juchacz for the Social Democratic women, Marie Stritt for the German Federation for Women's Suffrage, and Minna Cauer for the German League for Women's Suffrage.[82] This was preceded by an invitation from the radical suffragists to all other suffrage organizations to take part in a public rally in Berlin protesting the fact that the women's suffrage issue had been ignored by the constitutional committee. The gathering was banned by the Supreme Command of the German army and the police headquarters, something that starkly illuminates how political work, especially for suffragists, was made more difficult, and even prevented, by martial law and censorship.[83]

Fundamental issues underlay these factional struggles and disputes over which form of suffrage was the correct one. On the one hand, it had become clear that women's legal demands should not only be guided by the more or less limited legal status of men. Merely adapting or aspiring to the status of men was insufficient to establish democratic equality. Demanding women's rights made sense only if these rights served to call into question the existing power relations—that is, if they would dismantle privileges based on sex *and* class advantages, and thus change the status quo of men's *and* women's rights. On the other hand, the apparently very "feminist" restriction of the struggle to women's rights alone, the reformers' compromise, was also a dead end—a concession of unsuccessful, even narrow-minded policies. Minna Cauer harshly judged these supporters of "only women's rights," who had given up being citizens: "It is my conviction that such support [of three-class suffrage] is a betrayal of the basic rights of the people, upon which the German Reich is based. But it is also a betrayal of the women's movement itself, because it should never find itself encouraging any reactionary measure or reactionary law whatsoever. True citizens of the state and true women's rights advocates do not come into conflict over such issues—only those with blinders, seeking *only* women's rights, who are unaccustomed to looking at the larger, general picture."[84]

The difference between the "bourgeois" and the "citizen" marked another divide during the war, one that separated the majority participating in national women's service from the radical pacifist minority.

Peace Work and Women's Rights, or the Relationship between Law and Force

The fact that the radical suffragists were among the anti-war minority at the outbreak of World War I and that they were practicing pacifists is no coincidence; it was a quite consistent reflection of their understanding of law. Their idea of a different kind of law, of equal and just conditions, was the only imaginable alternative to force; and they saw war as the most violent form of force and lawlessness. The International Congress of Women held in the Hague in 1915, in which twenty-eight women from Germany took part, was a doomed but bold attempt to defeat war with the tools of law, through agreements, arbitration, conciliation, and democratic control.[85] One of its principles, which all participants had accepted in advance, was a demand they considered essential to ensure peace—equal political rights, granting the "parliamentary franchise to women." Suffrage and the peace movement—one was a prerequisite for the goals of the other. "Only when women are in the parliaments of all nations, only when women have a political voice and vote, will they have the power effectively to demand that international disputes shall be solved as they ought to be, by a court of arbitration or conciliation. Therefore on a program of conditions in which wars in future may be avoided, the question of woman suffrage should not be lacking, on the contrary, it should have the foremost place."[86]

This vision of a more peaceful world brought about through the political responsibility of women was controversial even then, and was soberly considered to be a long-term task.[87] The "struggle for the force of law versus the law of force," a slogan coined in 1899 at the beginning of the pacifist women's initiative in Germany by Margarete L. Selenka, itself demonstrates the dialectic of law through its inherent contradiction.[88] Both historically and in the present, law has always been part of a coercive apparatus that can be used, in alliance with the ruling power, in the service of class and sex interests. At the same time, the Enlightenment's and the revolutionaries' promise of liberty and equality for all *people*, to which the radicals and pacifists always referred, provided a "measure for examining prevailing norms"—in order to criticize existing, unjust conditions.[89] At best, law lies at the intersection of force and emancipation; that is, it points the way toward more humane, peaceful, and just conditions.

To this extent, the radicals had the right idea, but they were too few. To influence and change the substance and form of politics, it was not enough to admit a few individuals as tokens. Those who today self-righteously point out that the women's suffrage gained in 1918 failed to prevent the subsequent political catastrophe should not forget how little power and how few opportunities for involvement had been opened to women's rights activists, despite formal equality. No radical feminists had a seat even in the first Reichstag of the Weimar Republic. Places on a party's list of candidates were reserved for women who had subordinated their interest in women's issues to party interests, or who were explicitly antifeminist and had opposed women's suffrage, such as Paula Mueller, head of the German-Protestant Women's Union [Deutsch-Evangelischer Frauenbund]. Lists of women candidates, or a women's party, though repeatedly proposed, were always controversial and never stood a chance.[90]

Nevertheless, the radicals had by no means given up. The journal *Die Frau im Staat* provides evidence of the unwavering insight with which the failure of the Weimar Republic as a social democracy was recognized and criticized. Some of the most upright ones, joined by new members, were active in the Women's International League for Peace and Freedom (WILPF), which until 1933 did propaganda and educational work for increasingly lost causes—for peace, disarmament, and minority issues, especially for German-Polish understanding, and against anti-Semitism. Their program of social, political, and economic equality and international cooperation continues to be relevant today.[91] So does a reply by L. Wäldin-Kobe (her first name is unknown), who in 1913, in the periodical *Frauenstimmrecht* [Women's Suffrage], responded to the increasingly nationalist and bellicose Käthe Schirmacher, "On both sides of all the borders, no one tires of insisting, 'We do not want war! But we must be armed in case we are attacked.' But who should these attackers be, if everyone wants peace? This is the error in the calculations—the mutual distrust. Each takes the other for a cheat, and thus we are all making ourselves into cheated cheaters of ourselves. Let us not hide from ourselves any longer the fact that this senseless arms craze can only lead to ruin."[92]

Connections to Today's Legal Discussion

Today, the "prevailing opinion" in male legal scholarship, expressly following from a "specific historic starting point," takes equal rights to mean "attaining the status of men"; but this only repeats a misunderstanding of history.[93] This misunderstanding stubbornly persists because radical, and especially feminist, traditions have yet to find a place in legal history.

The legal struggles and critiques of the radicals in the first women's movement made it clear that these radicals were not interested in adaptation or imitation, or in functioning merely as "a harmonious supplement to the man"—these were the words of the moderates.[94] The radicals wanted a fundamental change in legal and political conditions. They criticized the central pillars of the patriarchal, capitalist system: the legal basis of immorality and coercion in gender relations; women's material inequality and dependency, and their exclusion from politics; and the belligerent way in which international conflicts were addressed. They strove for changes that would call into question existing property relations, the traditional legal system, and everyday customs, right down to the most intimate relationships. Was their belief in law therefore anachronistic?

Legal scholarship had aged in the course of the nineteenth-century conflict among schools; it was unable to resolve its "value problems" with the doctrine of the national spirit, or through concept or so-called interest jurisprudence, or with the help of an empty legal positivism.[95] In contrast, the radicals took the natural-law model of a possible, more just order at its word. In so doing, they were not all that anachronistic; in 1918, Germany had its first chance ever to establish a parliamentary, even a social democracy. But in contrast also to the "old liberalism," which "had failed in regard to the women's movement as much as it did in regard to the labor movement" ("shamefully," as the radicals often pointed out), the women's rights advocates represented the "freest and most consistent" standpoint.[96] The continuing resistance from all sides to the implementation of women's rights shows how threatening this standpoint was, and still is, felt to be.

To demand legal equality, and yet mean different conditions from those that already exist, appears inconsistent. But could it not be that, "by demanding, fighting for, and ultimately achieving equality, [we are already] changing the conditions" under which "people," that is, men and women, live?[97] Why do we accept the limitations of male legal discourse, instead of taking up the tradition of our radical forbears in order to transcend today's narrow legal horizons?

Sometimes, when this legal history makes me despondent and impatient, I wish I had the élan and radicalism of the old suffragists: "Give us content for the empty basket that is our demand for suffrage—sexual reform, pacifism, all the specific women's issues; into the working program with them, with flags unfurled, so the world can see what is to come: room for feminism, not just as an empty formula, a scrap of paper in the ballot box, but as a new purpose in life."[98]

Chapter 7   Gender Tutelage

"In every true marriage, the woman is under the tutelage of her husband."
—Wilhelm T. Kraut, 1835

Women in Nineteenth-Century Legal Doctrine

It is DIFFICULT to find nineteenth-century legal literature in which women were regarded as legal persons; the concept of "women's rights" did not yet exist. Wherever we might expect them to be mentioned, even if the result would exclude them or deny their rights, women do not appear—not in the debate over the right to vote and the basic rights of Germans in the Frankfurt Parliament, nor in the constitutions of the individual states (for example, the Prussian Constitution of 1850), nor in the new freedoms of trade and business.[1] Even in present-day constitutional history, the fact that the words "universal, equal" suffrage referred only to male Germans is never discussed, except perhaps as an aside.[2]

Only if we take into account this complete neglect or "forgetting" of women's rights can we understand why Louise Otto praised the Saxon press law of 1850, which permitted only male editors to engage in working for the press, for its "specificity." In the next-to-last issue of the newspaper she published, *Die Frauen-Zeitung*, before it was temporarily discontinued, she wrote, "We know that equality of men and women under law does not yet exist, whatever one may pretend; we know that the laws dealing with 'citizens' in general undergo highly arbitrary interpretation in regard to female citizens, and that in one case (tax liability) they are acknowledged as such and are counted, while in other cases, on the contrary, they are viewed as nonexistent, all as a result of an unspoken agreement."[3]

Because legal scholarship and legal history have hitherto neglected the treatment of women's rights, I will attempt here to give at least a rough overview of the state of private law relating to women in the nineteenth century. Only against the background of these quite concrete legal problems, taking account of the "weight of the chains" and the lack of legal certainty, does it become clear what obstacles women and the women's movements had to overcome on the road to greater and equal rights—an effort we can barely appreciate today. The legal pathos that speaks from this early evidence demonstrates the degree of courage necessary to fight this legal battle against preconceptions and gender role assignments—for example, when we read in a call to a women's protest of the adoption of the German Civil Code, around 1900: "All you women, if you see your lifelong legal incapacity as an affront to your sex—even if a more fortunate lot has perhaps protected you from feeling the full weight of the chains that this law forges for you—think of those other women who are rubbed raw and pressed to the earth by them . . . (;) raise your voices too for the human rights and dignity of German women."[4] Law, especially private law, is the specific form by which civil society expresses its organizing principles, values, and dominant interests, which "may thus be reconstructed through the medium of law."[5] Its constitutive, guiding principles—freedom, equality, and universal laws—were revolutionary as long as they were aimed against the hierarchy of privilege in an estates-based society, but they remained particularist and patriarchal to the extent that equality before the law, freedom of acquisition, and the guarantee of property were gender-specific, guaranteed to male citizens alone.

The separation of public and private in civil law was "substantively uncertain and controversial," yet it was "omnipresent" and constitutive.[6] In the language of jurists, this distinction reflected the historic process of differentiation or separation of state and society, a separation secured by legal guarantees of property, private autonomy, and freedom of contract, in order to develop a societal sphere free of state intervention. The sphere of public law thus encompasses relations characterized by the public interest, the presence of the state as a legal partner, and expressions of state authority, and thus also relations of subordination or domination. Private law, in contrast, regulates relationships among private parties—as legal relationships among "equals." This contrast between two legal spheres has been familiar since Roman law, as a "conceptual abstraction" that typifies "the duality of human existence—as a single person and member of the species, and as an individual and 'part of community life.'"[7] In the definition of the *corpus juris*, "public law is that which is related to the state; private law, that which serves the individual." (*Publicum ius est quoad ad statum rei Romanae spectat, privatum quoad ad singulorum utilitate pertinet*).[8] Nevertheless, in neither legal doctrine nor legal practice can one simply assume the continuity of this duality; instead, there is constant emphasis on the "historical nature of the fundamental dichotomy" that dominates civil law doctrine and practice.[9] Not until the nineteenth century did the confrontation between "bourgeois (i.e., a member of civil society)" and "citoyen (i.e., the individual with political rights)" become an issue for legal theory and politics.[10] A monopoly on state sovereignty did not emerge until the complex, multilayered structure of authority in an estates-based society was dismantled and the separation of state and society completed. This monopoly was claimed at first by absolutist rulers and later by representatives of the people, legitimized by a social contract, a process which created a direct relationship between the sovereign and the subject or citizen.[11] The dual structure of civil society and its law was assumed in Enlightenment philosophies of law and the state, especially in the doctrine of the social contract, as we saw in chapter 2, "In the Footsteps of the Philosophers." At the same time, this structure justified women's exclusion from the public and political spheres and their inclusion in the private sphere, in responsibility for the family. In the contrast between state and family, between public good and private interest, reason and emotion, culture and nature, sex-specific "assignment" of roles and hierarchical establishment of sex differences were repeated as variations on a theme. This chapter will show how private law went along with, facilitated, and preformed this exclusion of women from the public sphere.[12] In addition to a survey of the various private laws that determined the legal status of women in nineteenth-century Germany, attention will be paid especially to a comparison between the Prussian General Code (Preußisches Allgemeines Landrecht, ALR) of 1794 and the French *Code civil* (Cc) of 1804, first because the French code was also in force until 1900 in large sections of what became the German Reich, and second because the French code was considered a particularly progressive civil code. The extent to which this characterization also applies to women's rights will be examined. This aspect of legal history deserves our particular attention, not least because of the pioneering role of women in the French Revolution and Olympe de Gouges's declaration of women's rights.

The Patchwork of Women's Rights: Diverse Legal Sources and Systems

It is difficult to assess the legal status of women in nineteenth-century Germany, because private law relationships were multifaceted, complex, and fragmented into many jurisdictions and systems of law before being standardized in the Civil Code (BGB) of 1900. Comparative legal studies as a rule examine private law codes and compare the major codifications of natural law and the Enlightenment, specifically the Prussian General Code (ALR) of 1794 and the French *Code civil* of 1804, as well as the Austrian General Civil Code (Allgemeines Bürgerliches Gesetzbuch) of 1811.[13] Others deal initially with the Prussian General Code in trying to characterize German law.[14] This places the German situation in an unduly favorable light, since it makes it appear relatively women-friendly. Aside from this, however important the Prussian General Code might have been to the development of law, until the Civil Code went into force around 1900 legal routine and the practice of private law in Germany were characterized by variety and complexity. The particularism of small states, with their constantly changing borders and regimes, caused the law to be fragmented into various legal sources, individual laws and codifications. This was especially the case in family and marital property law, made up of local statutes, special municipal laws, customs, and particularist laws still organized by traditional estates. This variety made the "thankless, painstaking work" of standardizing the laws in the Civil Code into a national task—the hundred different systems of marital property law alone that had to be considered became legendary.[15] In addition, the absence of legal uniformity was criticized as an absence of "national culture,"[16] and it caused a deficiency in the rule of law that contemporaries experienced as a lack of legal clarity, even legal certainty: "Until now, in nearly every German state, different laws [on the legal status of German women] have rightly existed.

With the flexibility and the antiquated language of the same, their treatment is very varied and thus their implementation can depend on the views and insight of the respective judges involved. This is one of the main reasons that knowing the law is so difficult, not only for the individual in the state, but also for those of us who would like to gain and provide an overview."[17] These words were written by Louise Otto in the foreword to a petition by the General German Women's Association to the first preliminary commission charged with drafting a new Civil Code, appointed in 1874, in which the association requested "that the rights of women, especially as regards marriage and tutelage, be taken into account when amending the Civil Code."[18] Otto addressed a problem that also plagues researchers on legal history. One must imagine the legal map of Germany before 1900 as a colorful patchwork of varied legal sources, some of whose patterns had already faded, but which were nevertheless closely interwoven. The validity of the individual rules was often controversial, as is common among jurists; a preliminary procedure was frequently required to determine which laws and legal norms were applicable. The deciding factor was the place of residence of the complaining party—for married couples, the marital residence, that is, the man's residence. This created a situation that the parties to the conflict could often only experience as arbitrary.[19]

My survey is limited to the four most important legal systems, among which the German population was distributed, according to an 1896 map of law and jurisdictions more or less as follows: 42.6 percent were subject to the jurisdiction of the Prussian General Code,[20] 29.2 percent to so-called common (Roman) law, 16.6 percent to the law of the French *Code civil*, and 10.9 percent to Saxon law.[21]

- The Prussian General Code of 1794 is considered a "model of enlightened government planning" and the art of codification.[22] Yet due to its exhaustiveness and complexity, and its authoritarian presumption in regulating even minute details in order to rule out judges' discretion, legal scholars at first boycotted it and often criticized it. "The basic tone of well-meant paternalism"[23] to "ensure and promote the private happiness of every inhabitant of the country"[24] was also beneficial to women. In fact, some provisions, such as those concerning married women's capacity to

own property and unwed mothers' right to support, were so
unabashedly woman-friendly that one commentator voiced the
fear even before its passage that the code would "soon make the
Prussian state a true paradise for women."[25]

- So-called common law was general Germanic customary law,
  which developed from the gradual adoption of Roman law in
  Germany, representing a *"jus commune,"* a lowest common
  denominator invoked wherever it had not been supplanted by
  specific laws or codifications. Its formal validity and substantive
  provisions were complicated by the fact that these customs had
  developed very differently in different places. In any case, the
  revival of Roman legal sources in the so-called study of pandects
  [*Pandektenwissenschaft*] in the nineteenth century gave legal
  consistency precedence over fidelity to historical sources. German
  private common law was thus based on a combination of this law,
  adopted in many steps, and Germanic legal traditions, and it
  separated jurisprudence into two camps, Germanists and Roman-
  ists, depending on the preferred form of historical justification. In
  matrimonial law, the Roman-law wing was more favorable to
  women, as marriage had no influence on their legal status. In
  contrast, common law in the Roman tradition was harsh in regard
  to child custody law. The territory to which common law applied
  was especially confusing. The states in which common law applied
  included many former free Reich cities such as Lübeck, Bremen,
  Hamburg, and Frankfurt and the duchies of Oldenburg and
  Brunswick, as well as Hanover, Hesse, and Württemberg.[26]
- Saxon law, which held sway in the Kingdom of Saxony, in
  Thuringia, and in Schleswig-Holstein (although it was part of
  Prussia), most staunchly preserved Germanic legal traditions. Its
  principal sources were medieval legal texts, particularly the code
  known as the *Sachsenspiegel*.[27] The civil code of the Kingdom of
  Saxony, adopted "at a late hour" in 1863, was a determined
  attempt to replace law that was developed only by scholars with
  state legislation.[28] As the history of the Civil Code for the
  German Reich would soon demonstrate, however, not even
  parliamentary legislation was able to break the legal scholars'
  monopoly on the development of law.[29] Typical of Saxon law were

its religiously based marriage laws, unencumbered by any natural law or Enlightenment marriage doctrines, and the fact that it declared married women legally incompetent and subject to tutelage, on the basis of Germanic legal convictions.[30]

• Finally, many parts of Germany were subject to the French *Code civil*; under Napoleonic rule it applied to the left bank of the Rhine (in the Rhineland and Palatinate), the Kingdom of West-phalia, and the Grand Duchy of Berg, as well as to Frankfurt and the tiny states of Aremberg and Anhalt-Köthen, both ruled by admirers of Napoleon. In German translation, with modifications and many supplements, the *Code civil* was also proclaimed the "General Law of Baden" in the Grand Duchy of Baden in 1810.[31] Here, as in left-bank Prussia and Berg, it remained in force until 1900.[32] It is interesting to note which aspects of this foreign law required adaptation and modification, especially in matrimonial and marital property law, "given their deep significance for civic life."[33]

In light of this pre-modern, particularist legal situation, France's first civil code, the unifying, systematizing, clearly formulated *Code civil* of 1804, appears quite brilliant. Despite many (albeit minor) changes, it has remained in force to this day and is still described in commentary literature as "the legislative embodiment of the commendable ideas of the French Revolution and the victory of the citizenry."[34] The Napoleonic Code was, from the time of its enactment, not only a significant component of national integration, but, for Napoleon himself, a "propaganda instrument" of imperial conquest; as he wrote on the occasion of the Code's introduction to Westphalia in 1808, it "meant more for the expansion and consolidation of his system in Europe than the greatest victory of his weapons."[35]

The *Code civil* is generally considered a "masterful achievement of legislative skill;"[36] it is universally admired for its uniformity and system, clear diction, and elegance of language. The novelist Stendhal is said to have read the *Code civil* every morning before sitting down to write, "pour prendre le ton" (to capture the tone). The section frequently offered as an illustration of this is precisely the one that reflects all the contradictions of women's rights under civil law (Art. 213 of the old version).[37] Until 1938, it read, "The man owes his wife protection, the wife owes her husband obedience." Here the Code is revealed to be "Janus-faced."[38] We must consider whether Marianne Weber's devastating critique is accurate: that where the rights of women are concerned, the French code represented "essentially a systematization of the legal customs of medieval France" and "preserved the traits of medieval patriarchy the longest and in the purest form of all the laws in force [at the time]."[39]

Patriarchal Legal Scholarship

As a result of this diversity and lack of legal clarity, legal scholarship and jurisprudence played a very important role in the nineteenth century. The so-called historical school of law took it upon itself to "interpret the entire stuff of German law in its historical and scientific context"[40] in a "program for the revival of the science of positive law"[41]—that is, to systematize its Roman and Germanic sources, adopted common law, particular and state laws, and so on and organize them into general concepts. Women's rights, however, were largely excluded from this development, or subsumed as pre-modern law under the heading "special cases."

A typical example of this inconsistency is Carl Friedrich von Gerber and his standard textbook on private law, *System des Deutschen Privatrechts*, which went into many editions. In his introduction Gerber criticized the restrictions on "free will" and the particularization of "individual circumstances" in German law as "imperfections" lacking legal abstraction; yet he justified the limited legal competence of women with the "influence of special circumstances on the legal relations of individuals," calling them "natural circumstances." Against his own call for systematization and abstraction from particulars, he continued,

> Section 35: The difference between the sexes appears in
> German law with more perceptible effect than in Roman law,
> because the explanations in domestic private law are largely
> borrowed from public life, in which woman, due to her nature,
> did not participate. The more private law has now escaped this
> influence of public law, the more there has been a gradual
> disappearance of the private-law effects of sex difference, the
> last important traces of which are the neglect of women that

often occurs under certain circumstances in inheritance law; their incapacity to enter into a position of vassalage; and gender tutelage, which has become more or less obsolete.[42]

Apart from the complicated legal jargon, this sounds as if the author preferred not to take a definite stand. His historical facts were imprecise; he failed to discuss the consequences of the "more or less obsolete gender tutelage" for the "legal capacity" of the human being, as defined in preceding sections, and the "personality—including that of women—in the legal sense." Indeed, except for the idea of "special circumstances," the legal consequences of gender are not treated at all. Anyone wishing to learn more about the legal status of women must look under other, sometimes obscure, headings; for example in matrimonial law, under "Mismarriages" (marriages between persons of different social standing) or—something that appears in great detail in all civil codes—under "Influence of marriage on property." Only here do we find an introductory mention of the "different basis" of matrimonial law:

> Section 22: The special character of parents' and children's rights, paternal authority, marital relations and the man's domination in today's law is still based to a great degree on that more profound conception of the family and the special moral force which the German spirit attributes to this natural union.[43]

Gerber is not alone in his frank assumption that the man dominates in the home; on the contrary, with his special involvement in family law issues, he represented the entire branch of Germanists, or the Germanic law tradition. Again and again, a "dignified view of marriage among our people in particular" served to justify systemic inconsistencies. Thus Georg Beseler maintained in his *System des gemeinen deutschen Privatrechts* (System of German Common Private Law, first published in 1847):

> [M]arriage is not consolidated into one legal person in the technical sense, but remains a legal community borne by the individuality of the participants; for these, however, it is based on such a profound union that in joint matters it appears to the outside and acts in name as a unit. . . . This task was fulfilled by

German matrimonial law in that it recognizes the *equal status of the spouses* in essential relationships, but grants *the man a prevailing influence* [emphasis added]. Thus the man appears as head of the household and the marriage. His authority arises from various legal titles, the precise differentiation of which in detail is often difficult.[44]

The increasing pressure to justify this view and the inability to see this particular legal issue in the abstract are apparent. They cannot be explained simply as a belated response or as a result of feudal remnants in family and community rights, in contrast to the needs of commercial and property law. Wilhelm Theodor Kraut's multivolume work on guardianship according to the principles of German law [45] instead highlighted the importance that sex difference still possessed in the nineteenth century, aided by a conception of law brought forward from the Middle Ages. Kraut hedged the patriarchal legal tradition about with much historical evidence in his work on gender tutelage, also called "conjugal authority or court guardianship [*Ehe- oder Kriegsvogtei*]" in earlier law, and prepared the necessary arguments for his increasingly insecure contemporaries.

Gender tutelage—a form of guardianship on the basis of sex, known as *Munt-Gewalt* in old German, describes a legal relationship, or more precisely a power relationship, in the Germanic law tradition.[46] It was a particular form of legal incapacity that applied to all women, at first even the unmarried. Kraut described the *Mundium,* or the obligation of protection (guardianship), identical to the Roman *Manus* or Germanic *munt,* as one of the most important institutions of German law, forming the basis for all of family law. Despite its variety of forms, "gender tutelage" as a rule meant that women could not undertake certain— actually, almost any—legal actions without a male guardian:

1. Women were not permitted to take any kind of independent legal action, except on purely personal matters such as marital or criminal issues, and their guardian's consent was required for them to become engaged or to marry—"an action that determines a woman's entire happiness in life."[47]
2. For any type of action in court, alienation or attachment of real estate, or legal transactions involving their entire assets, as well as all testamentary instructions, women required a male advisor;

their independent legal actions were invalid, and not even construed in their favor, as they were for minors.

3. Women were prohibited from undertaking certain obligations; they were entirely prohibited from standing surety or issuing obligations or promissory notes. Exceptions were made, traditionally, for merchants and for transactions involved in keeping up the marital household—so-called *Schlüsselgewalt* (literally, "power of the keys").

The need for tutelage was justified in Germanic law by the fact that women were not permitted to bear arms or carry on feuds. Because this justification could not be sustained once disturbances of legal peace were no longer dealt with through private feuds, but instead through state authority using the tools of penal law, jurists found another justification for controlling the female sex. Kraut cited the so-called common law theory that became widespread in the seventeenth century, was repeated in all commentaries and judicial decisions, and supposedly was "hardly lacking in practical interest" even in the mid-nineteenth century.[48] Under this theory, there was no doubt "that in part because of the inexperience of women with commerce in general, in part because of their typical compliance and pliant natures, it must often appear desirable that they not conclude important transactions without consulting an experienced, trustworthy male advisor."[49]

It made no difference that this outdated legal institution had been expressly repealed by numerous separate laws in the respective German states—for example, in Anhalt-Dessau in 1822, in the Kingdom of Württemberg in 1828, in the Grand Duchy of Baden in 1835, in the Kingdom of Saxony in 1838, and in the Grand Duchy of Saxon-Weimar-Eisenach in 1839.[50] These were later joined by New West Pomerania in 1855, some Swabian imperial cities in 1861, and Prussia in 1869. Legal scholars now argued that even though tutelage of unmarried women had to be abandoned because of the great disadvantage it posed for the "security of commerce"—a reason already offered for the relatively early independence of merchant women—there was no reason to relax "household authority." Thus some laws—for example, the Saxon law of 1838—while repealing gender tutelage, already expressly declared that conjugal authority would continue. The lack of clarity that followed enactment of the guardianship regulation for the German Reich of 5 July 1875 was then addressed by the Reich Supreme

Court to the effect that "even where gender tutelage was eliminated in law, conjugal authority was maintained."[51] The Court thus followed the now-prevalent opinion among legal scholars, and it matters little who is cited—Beseler, Kraut, Gerber, or Carl J. A. Mittermaier: "Independent of the continuation of the *Mundium,* the status of married women in Germanic law deviates from the Roman view. It is a moral view of marriage and equality of spouses, still valid and confirmed by canon law, and it is determined more specifically only through the authority of the masters of households and the status of the husband as master of the household community."[52] "Equality of spouses . . . through the authority of the masters of households"—the contradictions could not be more clearly formulated. Meanwhile the main scholarly battleground on the subject of women's rights in the nineteenth century has so far been ignored: marital property law. It is important to realize that the question of married women's legal capacity and ability to conduct business was, in practice, never decided by the courts in principle, but only in connection with property disputes.[53] It is noteworthy that even the Reich Supreme Court argued inconsistently in the cases before it, depending on the respective marital property law—that is, it never attempted to reconcile the different laws. Christina Damm attributed this caution to the fact that standardization could have worked to the advantage of women, an outcome the Supreme Court sought to avoid at all costs.[54]

Specific Legal Issues: Women's Competence to Transact Business

The rules in Saxon private law were traditional and upheld an unbroken patriarchy. Once married, a woman was the ward of her husband; that is, she could not appear in court without him as her guardian and required his consent for any legal transactions "by which she is not merely making an acquisition" (§ 1640 Saxon BGB). Thus the Germanic-law institution of gender tutelage was preserved almost unaltered in Saxon law. The law justified male prerogatives with women's need for protection, "their ignorance and weakness," but in reality it protected the man's interest in the woman's property and labor. Even when the Saxon state parliament recognized this legal institution as "outdated" and abolished it in 1838 for single women, under pressure from, and

with the participation of, the new bourgeois public, it was expressly reaffirmed for married women.[55] To preclude any doubt about the power
relations in marriage, a new section 1634 was added to the Saxon civil
code providing that "the husband has the right to demand from his wife
obedience, as well as services for his household and business." This
"marital guardianship" or "conjugal authority [*Ehevogtei*]" accorded with
marital property laws that granted women property rights, but in any
case ensured the husband the administration and use even of the wife's
assets.

The Prussian General Code (ALR) took a transitional or interme-
diate position. There is much evidence of the influence of the Enlightenment, especially Christian Johannes Wolff's school of natural law, on
the legislators.[56] Paragraph 24 I.1 ALR actually affirms that "the rights
of both sexes are the same," but the proclamation of this principle of
equal rights was subject to so many exceptions, especially in marriage
law, that the inequalities outweighed it. Wolff, like Johann Gottlieb
Fichte after him in his *Science of Rights* (especially the chapter "Deductions about Marriage"), had already set the record straight on both
spouses' freedom of contract, interpreting it in the husband's favor.[57]
To rescue the principle of equality, it was assumed that women, through
the "freedom" of the marriage contract, had "tacitly consented to whatever custom brings"; since custom meant nothing less than the "dominance or authority of the husband," however, "the woman was thus
subordinate to the man."[58] Despite the General Code's principles of equality, and with the help of such subtle "deductions," the man was explicitly
considered even there to be "the head of the conjugal union" and "his
decisions [were] final in matters of mutual concern." (§ 184 I.1 ALR). His
wife shared his residence, his name, and his social standing, was obligated
to keep his house, could neither run her own business nor enter into an
employment contract without his consent, and so on. It goes without saying that the husband was also the administrator and beneficiary of any
common property. Yet at the same time, the woman was at least partially competent to transact business and own property; in order to fulfill her housewifely duties, she possessed the *Schlüsselgewalt*, and she was
recognized as an independent legal person if her husband was incapaci-
tated or in regard to property that was expressly "reserved" to her by
contract [*Vorbehaltsgut*].

By contrast, common law was surprisingly liberal in its marital property stipulations, especially in the specific sense that it conferred upon women the status of legal subject, determined by the capacity to own property, on the understanding that "the individual is human only in so far as free, and free only in so far as a proprietor of himself."[59] Common law recognized the principle, adapted from the late-Roman "free union," that marriage did not influence the legal status or property relations of the spouses. As a result, it had no adverse impact on women's capacity to undertake legal and business transactions.[60] A peculiarity of Roman marriage law was the dowry system; the woman contributed to shouldering "marital burdens" with a dowry that became part of her husband's property but was to be returned if the marriage ended. Otherwise, separation of property was the prevailing norm; wives, like unmarried women, could enter into binding obligations, administer their property independently, and be employed outside the home. In a statement that seems surprisingly liberal, Georg Puchta points to his colleagues' vain attempt "to derive compulsory household service" from Latin sources.[61]

Yet it goes almost without saying that this law, while favorable to women, was modified in many ways by legal custom, through local and state regulations, into a privilege for men.[62] For example, in the Hanseatic states (early Lübeck law is typical), the prevailing system of community property allowed businessmen rapid disposition over their wives' property. The connection between law and social reality is indicated by the different common-law marital property regimes in Hesse. There the Roman dowry system applied to "the nobility, the educated, and government officials," while the petty bourgeoisie and peasantry normally followed the Germanic-law regime of joint ownership of subsequently acquired property—a so-called community of acquisitions referred to today as the surplus.[63]

The liberal logic arising from the link between freedom and property was ultimately spun out ad absurdum under French law. Married women were competent to own property but were entirely prohibited from transacting business.[64] At common law or under the Prussian General Code, married women could, at least legally, conduct advantageous business transactions; but under the *Code civil* wives were subject to the absolute domestic authority of their husbands and could undertake no legal transactions without their husbands' authorization, which had to be reissued in each case. Nor could they appear in court, even as women engaged in business, and even where separation of property had been agreed upon. They could neither give away nor dispose of their property without their husbands' consent, nor could they acquire anything, according to Arts. 215 to 217 of the *Code civil* (Cc). The Code purported to be liberal on marital property law, leaving it to the spouses to choose among various forms of marital property and thus respecting the principle of freedom of contract; yet it nevertheless expressly prohibited evasion of the husband's authority through contract or any agreement to relinquish the *puissance maritale*. (Art. 1388 Cc). Thus, despite her capacity to own property, the wife's assets, as well as her earnings, were subject to her husband's exclusive administration and use. As Ernst Holthöfer summarized women's unequal rights under the Code, "Freedom and equality extended only as far as the *père de famille*"; in fact, it turned out that "within the family, the monarchical principle was resurrected as *royauté domestique*."[65]

From the point of view of comparative law, the *Code civil* actually takes the prize for inconsistency. Differences of detail did arise, along with greater or lesser leeway, in the family laws of various jurisdictions. Nevertheless, it can be concluded that, aside from such achievements in civic rights as the ability to own property, the relationship between the sexes in bourgeois matrimonial law was based on relations of power and dominance that were ensured on two levels: through the duty of obedience and the subjugation of the woman under the man's "authority to command," and through her economic dependence, guaranteed by the husband's rights to her property and labor. This is exactly how Emma Oekinghaus defined the structural principle of patriarchal dominance in her study of the status of women in legal history and sociology; on the pretext of protecting not only the woman, but also the family, it ensures the "authority of the head of the household" and "takes control of the woman's property and labor."[66]

Paternal Authority and Children's Rights

This survey has so far dealt with only one dimension of the legal relationships within the bourgeois family; we will now touch upon another aspect from a comparative legal perspective. Woman's status as mother and her legal relationship with her children were of crucial importance for women. Of particular interest here, aside from the regulations regarding parental authority, are the rights of women who bore children outside a legitimate relationship, a civil marriage. These unwed mothers represent the flip side of the bourgeois family and its "order." In a polemical broadside against the introduction of the Napoleonic Code in Baden, August Wilhelm Rehberg, an opponent of the French Revolution and of what he termed "equality dreamers,"[67] attempted to appeal to a righteous sense of civic duty: "The natural incapacity of illegitimate children, the exclusion of those not worthy of inclusion in society . . . are the only means to defend the sacred bond upon whose universality the civic order rests."[68] It is no accident that legal sources on this theme were so extensive and that the legislative materials, in particular, contained a wealth of arguments and rationalizations and attracted so much attention from makers and ideologues of family policy.[69] The treatment of unwed mothers and their children was apparently a litmus test of the entire order of bourgeois values.

In all the family laws considered here, "parental authority," from the point of view of practical law, meant the authority of the father. Even where the mother's right to take part was expressly mentioned, the father's decision was final in all questions of personal care and child rearing. In the Roman legal tradition, however—and this meant under French and common law—the father's authority was almost unlimited, even despotic. Article 376 of the *Code civil* even allowed the father to imprison children up to sixteen years of age for up to a month, with no judicial supervision. Older children could be imprisoned for even longer periods, albeit with the cooperation of the courts (Art. 377 Cc). As far as the mother was concerned, the father had the right to place the children elsewhere at any time—for example, in a foundling home or orphanage; that is, he had the right to take the children away from her. This was a (paternal) practice that Jean-Jacques Rousseau, theoretician of the French Revolution and educator of girls, remorsefully praised in his *Confessions*, even representing it as a republican virtue, in the belief that he was behaving like a "citizen and a father, and . . . a member of Plato's Republic."[70]

In Prussian and Saxon law, too, the father's decision was final in all questions of raising children; however, the mother had an express right to be involved, and before the child "had passed its fourth year," the father was not allowed to remove it from the mother's care and supervision against her will (§ 70 ALR II.2).[71] Even this small concession to mothers' rights demonstrates the extent to which the law's generally patriarchal nature was taken for granted. In the history of the German women's movement, this failure to acknowledge mothers' rights played a significant role in creating an awareness of injustice.[72]

The differences between French and Germanic law—including the Baden General Law, based on the *Code civil*—are even more extreme regarding the legal status of children born out of wedlock. Here, too, differing legal traditions played a major role. In addition, however, the law of illegitimacy provides insight into the disparate history of the family and the process of development of civil society, which was studied in detail, especially in France, where scholars discovered a "history of childhood"[73] and a late "mother love" that corresponded to the lengthy dominance of paternal authority.[74]

The Prussian states had become a "paradise for women," in the opinion of critics of the General Code (ALR), because it granted unmarried women and their out-of-wedlock children claims against the father that far outstripped the relatively solicitous, centuries-old practices of common and Germanic law. Under the provisions of the General Code, the father of a child born out of wedlock—or, if he was unable to pay, even his parents—was expected to pay more than just alimony; he owed the "respectable, single woman or widow" a settlement, in addition to the costs of lying in and other expenses, that could amount to as much as a quarter of his total assets. If there had been an engagement, the woman could even demand "satisfaction," which included all the rights of a woman divorced through no fault of her own. The only people denied such preferential treatment were prostitutes—women who spent time in "public whorehouses" or had sexual relations with "men for payment" (§§ 1027–1131 II.1 ALR and §§ 592–665 II.2 ALR).

Since the Middle Ages it had been customary under common law, influenced by canon and Christian natural law,[75] to grant all "natural" children, as well as those resulting from adulterous relationships, a claim to support and the mother a claim to marriage or a settlement.[76] At the same time, however, common law permitted the *exceptio plurium concumbentium*, that is, the defense that the woman had had several lovers, in which case she could no longer assert a claim. Other particularist laws, however, including Saxon law, made the various potential fathers jointly liable (§ 1872 Saxon BGB).[77]

In the Germanic legal traditions, the legal basis for this was the principle of the blood relationship, which was being replaced more and more by considerations of care and fairness, under the influence of the Church and hand-in-hand with the battle against concubinage. However, French law's intolerance toward out-of-wedlock children can be only partially explained by the strictness of traditional Roman law, which fundamentally denied any relationship between the father and children born out of wedlock. The exceptionally rigid regulations in the *Code civil* regarding out-of-wedlock children were even harsher than those of the customary law (*coutumes*) common under the ancien régime, in contrast to written law (*droit écrit*). The rigidity of the *Code civil* can be better explained as a "backlash against opposing excesses of revolutionary legislation,"[78] or the "result of a special development" in which "the conservative currents of bourgeois, patriarchal morality were completely dominant."[79]

Under the *Code civil*, a child born out of wedlock legally had neither a father nor a mother. French law further distinguished between so-called natural children and those born of adulterous relations. Only the former could be acknowledged by a father and mother and thereby achieve a similar legal status to those born in wedlock, especially with regard to rights of inheritance. But while it was possible to establish maternity in court, investigating paternity was absolutely prohibited. An exception was made only for kidnapping of the woman (Art. 340 Cc). Neither the mother nor the child had any claim against a man as long as he refused to voluntarily acknowledge the child as his. "No other civilized country," wrote Marianne Weber indignantly, "has, supposedly in the interests of female morality, given such carte blanche to male promiscuity."[80]

Even the Baden General Code, which otherwise tracked the French Code, failed to go along with this; an amendment permitted paternity investigations in cases other than kidnapping (Art. 340a).[81] And even Rehberg, the commentator on the Napoleonic Code, was irate about

it, though hardly out of compassion for the female sex: "If one gets involved with a mistress, he should at least pay for his foolishness by con-
tributing some money toward raising a child that he actually has nothing
to do with."[82]

Baden's legal reformers also introduced a small amount of modera-
tion into the French divorce law, because it seemed too harsh to place
"such narrow restrictions on the rights of women, who have been ac-
customed until now to equality here."[83] At issue were the inequitable
prerequisites for divorce, according to which adultery by the man was
only grounds for divorce under Art. 230 Cc if he brought the "sexual
partner" into the marital residence.

It is typical of the irrationality of this legal history that the limited
options for divorce in the 1804 Code, at first almost rejected for the
sake of Baden's Catholics, were maintained in the parts of Germany
governed by French law. In France, on the other hand, in the plainest
sign of the Restoration, divorce was banned between 1816 and 1884.
This was so despite the fact that Baden, "having learned from the great
errors committed by philosophers in the revolution of law in France,"
was not prepared to reap all the fruits of that revolution, under which
men, supposedly, "changed women as easily as they did their shirts."[84]

Divorce law, the flip side of bourgeois family morality, will not be
pursued further in this context, even though it often played a prominent role in the legal debates of the transitional periods.[85] The fact that
in all periods the majority of divorces had been sought by women is
evidence that divorce law was primarily women's law; given the authoritarian structure of marriage, it offered some legal freedom, as a kind
of "deficiency guarantee."[86] It will suffice to note here that Prussian
divorce law, condemned by legal scholars as overly generous, "lax
and frivolous," became clearly more restrictive beginning in the mid-
nineteenth century at the latest. With the adoption of the German Civil
Code around 1900, German law then came to resemble the *Code civil*
in many respects. This resemblance can be seen in almost all the legal
issues discussed here, with respect to the women as a legal person, her
capacity to own property, and especially the laws concerning parent-
child relations and out-of-wedlock children. The process of standardizing the laws was concluded in France by 1804 with the enactment of
the *Code civil*, but not completed in Germany until passage of the Civil

Code around 1900. It remains to be determined whether this can be described as part of the process of development of bourgeois society, and how it dealt with the legal status of women.

Bourgeois Patriarchy as Reaction

Particularly noteworthy are the lack of simultaneity, the varied rhythms of legal change, as well as the fact that legal standardization and the development of bourgeois society as a rule worsened conditions, at least for married women. Because it was introduced in the course of law reform, the "typical downward spiral" in the law of out-of-wedlock children is the most obvious example of this.[87] A bill initiated by the upper chamber of the Prussian parliament made explicit reference to the rigid provisions of the *Code civil*. Enacted into law on 24 April 1854, it considerably diminished the legal rights of single mothers, permitted the defense of multiple sexual partners, and eliminated grandparents' liability. It was justified on the grounds that, as a result of the state regulations, "Licentiousness had become a profitable business for the female sex . . . and in this way morality had been subverted."[88] Even contemporary critics argued that "we liberate from all bonds and increase the male sex's aggressiveness, and say in justification that the female half will become all the more cautious and moral."[89] These provisions were incorporated unchanged into the Civil Code (BGB) and signified a worsening of the status of women, even, for example, in comparison with the Saxon Civil Code.

In regard to their right to own property, married women ultimately found themselves in a worse position under the German Civil Code than previously under common law or the Prussian General Code (ALR). In disputed cases, courts increasingly based their decisions on a legal presumption in favor of male property; that is, the burden of proving ownership of property was, as a general rule, placed upon the woman.[90] In their decisions after 1870, neither the higher courts nor the Reich Supreme Court ever made any attempt, amidst the confusion of marital property law, to standardize the law or reconcile its various sources to the advantage of women; if anything, they did so to women's disadvantage.[91] Those who codified the Civil Code in 1900 also blatantly took the "protection of the man's interests"[92] as the standard for their decisions, against the express wishes of the now-organized women's movement.[93]

Throughout the nineteenth century, as far as we can determine, courts never dealt with women as legal persons or with their competence to conduct business, outside of disputes over property. Thus in this area, too, legal scholars were free to lay the groundwork for the double standard of men's and women's rights in the Civil Code.

The capacity to possess independent rights and duties is the legal dimension through which the freedom and equality of the individual are guaranteed by the private law of civil society. Under the estates system, legal capacity was graduated and only partial, and the individual, as a "person," "enjoys only certain rights in civic society" (according to § 1 I.1 ALR). Now, however, the "idea that every person is, by virtue of his inherent dignity, capable of being a person in the legal sense and thus legally competent" was lauded by legal scholars as an achievement of law and a necessary "legal abstraction" from all "individual circumstances" and peculiarities.[94] Nevertheless, jurisprudence, which set out in the nineteenth century "to gain mastery of the chaotic mass of legal material by revealing the legal concept," had difficulty abstracting from one particular human characteristic: that of "sex."[95] Conspicuously, the difference between the sexes, viewed "as a natural state," led only to special rules, inconsistencies, and breaches of the system in regard to the female sex. This was initially true for all women in Germany as well as France.

Unmarried women, too, if they had freed themselves from paternal authority, were excluded throughout the nineteenth century from all the privileges deemed public or "semi-public," as offices.[96] That is, they could not take on sureties or similar transactions or guardianships, and as a remnant of gender tutelage, they could neither appear in court nor serve as witnesses.[97] All these restrictions were called "legal favors" and justified, for as long as possible, with reference to the aforementioned "weakness and foolishness" of the female sex, on the basis of a Roman decree dating from the first century C.E. Only tradeswomen were excepted from these limitations on capacity to transact business, always and almost everywhere.[98] In both France and Germany legal scholars never considered the inclusion of women within the ambit of rights of political participation, such as suffrage; women were, however, explicitly excluded from political organizations and professional societies,[99] as well as from representation in local government.[100]

One might very well interpret this legal inequality of all women as a vestige of a pre-modern, patriarchal system, and at the same time a postponement, by no means accidental, of the granting of civic rights also overdue in other areas of law. However, the particular legal status of married women in nineteenth-century family law in fact had a different quality, a significance whose basis was quite new. The nature of the underlying system is apparent in the fact that family law became specifically women's law; as Bernhard Windscheid states, "The duty is primary and the rights are only there for the sake of duty; while for all other rights, the duty is only the other side of the right."[101]

It would be taking the wrong track to follow German legal scholars, who based the necessity of the "authority of the man in the house" on the deeper concept of family, especially the German family, "and [on] the special moral force which the German spirit attaches to this natural union."[102] Equally unconvincing are purely psychological explanations, according to which Napoleon's misogyny was the decisive reason for his Code's "massive backlash" with regard to women's rights.[103] Instead, one should understand the Napoleonic system of laws as a reaction not only to the new possibility of freedom and equality for women as well as men but also to the beginnings of implementation of rights. Early stirrings of this implementation can be found in the *droit intermédiaire*, the laws of the brief phase of revolutionary legislation between 1789 and 1804, actually only until 1795; these have heretofore been wrongly viewed as interesting only for their role in paving the way for the Code, as in A. H. Huussen's study of marriage laws in the course of the Revolution.[104] The Code, as the first French civil code, is hardly a direct continuation of feudal law in every respect, nor necessarily a sign of legal progress from it. Instead, in essential legal questions, typically enough in marriage and family law, it failed to reach the level achieved by the *droit intermédiaire*.

The most widely discussed example is divorce law. Whereas in the eighteenth century philosophers and legal reformers felt it proper to demand the right to divorce as one of the basic freedoms, after 1789 there began, in the name of human rights, a "true war of the pamphlets between defenders and opponents of divorce."[105] For the former, the indissolubility of marriage constituted "slavery" and denied the individual right to freedom and even "the pursuit of happiness," which was the necessary reverse side of the newly won political freedoms. For the latter, more was at stake in questions of marriage and family. In their eyes, legitimate marriage was always a "cornerstone" of the social order; the supposedly high divorce rates[106] were proof of a "crisis of marriage," a prevailing immorality in which, in an *"excès funeste,"*[107] the desire for divorce was given free rein among women in particular. At first, only the elimination of church authority went unchallenged; separation of church and state power—that is, the secularization of marriage—was seen as a fundamental achievement of this bourgeois revolution. Recognition of marriage as a civil contract was thus already a result of the Constitution of 1791, and the enactment of the marriage and divorce law of 20 September 1792 was one of the clearest breaks in Year One of the Republic. Many legal problems that affected the status of women were discussed in connection with these reforms and further proposals, none of which were carried out. Examples include questions of the education of women, child rearing, social aspects and improvement of rights to alimony following divorce, and the necessary division of marital property. One noteworthy suggestion was that of Deputy Sédillez of the legislative assembly, who proposed that divorce courts be staffed with women if a man petitioned for a divorce that was contested, and vice versa.[108]

Early on, however, Jean E. M. Portalis, the main architect of Napoleonic family law, used social arguments to demand restrictions on grounds for divorce, in consideration of the inadequate support afforded women.[109] The first three drafts of a new family law presented by Cambacérès to the legislative commission between 1793 and 1796 still breathed the "individualist spirit of the great intellectual and social movement" and attempted to let equality reign even in the relationship between spouses.[110] The consolidation of a new bourgeois order asserted itself in the fourth proposal, presented by Jacqueminot in 1799, in which a clear distinction was made between "good" morals, worthy of retention, and "bad" morals.[111] Accordingly, it retained divorce only as a necessary evil, prohibited married women from participating in trials, and limited their capacity to do business, thus ensuring their subordination to their husbands in all marital matters. In particular, the abolition of common administration of marital property, a system that supposedly diminished the husband's rights, was interpreted by Philippe Sagnac as a victory of legal and traditional ideas over the demands of philosophers.[112] Essentially, however, the tide had already turned by 1795, when the Directorate issued a decree on divorce law admonishing that morals and customs—which according to them provided that "the respectable woman belongs in her household, like the farmer at his plow"—be taken into account in applying the laws.[113]

No less dramatic was the legislation and surrounding debate on the rights of children and their emancipation from paternal authority. An important act in itself was the law of 28 August 1792, uniformly fixing majority at twenty-one years of age for both sexes. Without doubt an even more revolutionary step was the introduction of equal rights of inheritance on 4 June 1793, not only for children of both sexes but also for "natural" children, that is, children born out of wedlock; the only children excluded were those born of adultery. This generous social policy was immediately restricted by a subsequent decree, on 2 November 1793, providing that only children freely acknowledged by the father as his own possessed rights of inheritance. In other words, the revolutionary legislators were concerned about the "danger of blackmail," disagreements, and the scandals that could be brought upon the "most respectable families" by such equality.[114] Thus they invented a rule that had not been part of either written or customary law under the ancien régime: "Investigation of the paternity of a child is prohibited" (later Art. 340 Cc). The next day, 3 November 1793, Olympe de Gouges was guillotined. De Gouges, author of "The Declaration of the Rights of Woman and Citizen," a declaration of human rights that included women, had insisted in Article 11, regarding freedom of thought and opinion, that "one of the most precious rights of woman" was the freedom to be sure of the paternity of fathers and the legitimacy of their children.[115] "With all the force of reaction," wrote Sagnac, summarizing the law's historical development, and "from inequality to inequality, the Consul's Code succeeded in turning woman, whom the Revolution had made equal to man, into his slave. Her role was now defined by refinement of dignity, by humiliation and silence, while the man was permitted tyrannical power, brutality, even cruelty."[116]

Similarities and Distinctions

Despite different timing, the explanatory patterns for patriarchal privilege in both French and German culture are similar, and the justification for restoring the authority of husbands and fathers is the same in all legislative materials and motivations; it was political. Thus for J. E. M. Portalis, the family was not only the nucleus or "nursery of the state;"[117] he insisted that "husbands' authority, paternal authority . . . [are] republican institutions. . . . In absolute monarchies, in despotic states, the power that wishes to enslave us seeks to weaken all other powers. In republics, on the other hand, one strengthens domestic authority in order to safely moderate political and civic authority."[118] Portalis's commentary on his family law—and Portalis is but one example among many other contemporaries and imitators[119]—follows the philosophical doctrines that Rousseau wrote in his pedagogical novel *Emile, or On Education*, in 1762. Portalis wrote, "People have long argued over the superiority or equality of the two sexes. Nothing is more foolish than this argument. . . . The superiority of the man is based in the predispositions of his nature, which subject him to no necessity and allow him greater freedom to use his time and abilities. This superiority is the source of the protective authority that the arrangement bestows upon the man."[120] In Germany, Fichte enjoyed similar importance as a theorist of family law. In his *Science of Rights* (1796), he justified the subordination of women on the basis of the "morality" of marriage. After the divorce law reform initiated by Friedrich Carl von Savigny, minister of legislation, in the period before the March Revolution in 1848, "the dignity of marriage as an institution" had developed into an explicit, reactionary method of discipline used against women alone;[121] it gave husbands control not only of their wives' property but also of their wives' labor and even, because the faithfulness requirement applied only to wives, of their bodies.

The anchoring of new patriarchal privileges despite basic equality of civic rights in France and Germany—in the *Code civil* of 1804 and in German legal doctrine developed since mid-century and codified in the Civil Code of 1900—can be described, following René König, as "a patriarchal backlash" or "secondary patriarchy."[122] This form of patriarchy not only preserved traditional privileges; in a state of social anomie after the dismantling of the estates system and the fundamental questioning of traditional inequality during the French Revolution, it sought new support and basis, at least in the private sphere, in the family.

In France, this patriarchal reaction unfolded between 1789 and 1804 as a dramatic spectacle, with all its ideological arguments and legal harshness. The reaction of the bourgeois patriarchs, and even of many revolutionaries, and their return "to the orthodoxy of the new bourgeois values" was more acute and despotic in the "transformation of mentalities" because the work of doing away with the old regime was more thorough and radical.[123] The collaboration and political participation of women in the French Revolution, the feminist challenge of the first liberal women's movement, and the demands for human rights for women as well as men had contributed to provoking harsher repression and reactions in France than in Germany, where it was still possible at this time to appease the situation through authoritarian benevolence. It is true that here, too, at a time when "human rights were proclaimed loudly from the rooftops," some scattered democrats like Theodor Gottlieb von Hippel of Königsberg advocated granting women "not only privileges, but equal rights."[124] More representative of public opinion was a foundational essay in *Annals of Legislation* in 1804 by Ernst Ferdinand Klein, coauthor of the Prussian General Code. In it he wrote, "Our sex is still the dominant one. Furtive incursions into our territory cannot be considered an extension of the mutual borders. Civic power is still located in our hands alone, and we probably could not use it for a more noble purpose than to protect the weaker sex."[125]

The patriarchal reaction in legal practice and politics did not take hold in Germany until after mid-century, following the 1848 revolution and the first emergence of a women's movement in Germany. Repression was most apparent in the exclusion of women from politics after 1850 through the association and press laws; these were propped up from within and below by the reactionary backlash in family law. The specific bourgeois form of patriarchy, however, lost its benevolent and caring aspect in the competition for income and jobs; it became shriller in tone, antifeminist and more misogynist, as the women's movement became increasingly confident toward the end of the century and demanded rights for women more publicly.

Nevertheless, in the transition from an estates-based to a bourgeois society, men were able, with the help of a new "order in the family" and a specific bourgeois system of family law, to gain ground, at least in the private sphere.[126] This was the double standard that would characterize bourgeois society from then on, a hidden base developing beneath the "sphere of private people come together as a public" in the process of the polarization of state and society, and representing and maintaining the contradictions of its other, darker side.[127] Because the subordination and labor of women in the family form an obviously indispensable foundation, contradictions would constantly resurface, and the realization of equal rights for women, even with the help of concessions, could no longer be put off. As long as the family is organized on the basis of an unequal, gender-specific division of labor, like a "royauté domestique," feminism will not accept it. Making freedom and equality possible in the family remains the promise of a truly civil society.

Human Rights Are Women's Rights

Chapter 8

Dimensions of Feminist Legal Criticism

"HUMAN RIGHTS HAVE no gender" was the defiant and self-confident conclusion drawn by Hedwig Dohm, writer and women's rights activist, in her 1876 book *Der Frauen Natur und Recht* (Women's Nature and Privilege), in which she demanded suffrage for women as their "natural right," since it was a civil right and a human right on which all other rights were based.[1] Her slogan, "Human rights have no gender," was simultaneously a response to and protest against the opinion—as prevalent now as it was then—that human rights "had one gender"; that is, that they did not apply, or at least did not apply adequately, to women. The claim that human rights—which have served as standards for justice, rule of law, and respect for human dignity since the French Revolution—are universal has been questioned repeatedly throughout the world, even in the Western industrialized nations. The fundamental standard in Article 1 of the Declaration of the Rights of Man of 1789, that "Men are born and remain free and equal in rights," has failed to be realized for two hundred years due to inequalities of social standing, class, property, religion, ethnicity, and especially gender.

"Women's rights are human rights." This equation, expressed in the present tense, was part of the closing declaration of the Fourth World Conference on Women, held in 1995 in Beijing. And "women's rights as human rights" has been, at least since the 1993 World Conference on Human Rights in Vienna, the slogan of an international campaign

of women's movements and organizations combating violence and discrimination against women. Irrespective of, and initially unnoticed by,
scholarly feminist discourse on the meaning of equality and/or difference, an extremely vocal women's movement for human rights has be-
gun to make itself heard, demanding answers to questions that are by
no means new. But how should we assess this new international discourse, which has made a significant difference both at the international
policy level (for example through the appointment of a special United
Nations rapporteur) and in the growing amount of scholarly literature
on the subject? It is interesting to observe how various standpoints have
rearranged themselves, shifting sides as the discourse progresses. The
question is whether feminist criticism of the androcentrism of human
rights will have an impact on the discussion of their universality, encouraging a reinterpretation and/or redefinition of human rights.

Therefore, in the first part of this chapter I would like to discuss
the meaning of human rights for women from a philosophical and theoretical perspective, summarizing the different dimensions of feminist legal criticism. In the second part, I shall ask to what extent human rights
can respond to the specifically female experience of injustice. In an-
swering this question, I will undertake a historical and empirical investigation, using examples of injustice, to determine whether and, if so,
how the generally worded universal concepts of human rights can be
understood and interpreted in a way that responds to these specifically
female experiences of injustice.

Feminist Criticism of the Androcentrism of Human Rights

The limitation of human rights to male rights, and thus the exclusion
of women, has been treated at various levels,[2] not only from a feminist
perspective.[3] Critical feminist research has repeatedly emphasized that
the problem is not merely one of "oversight," forgetfulness, or a mere
delay in achieving women's rights vis-à-vis men's. That is, it is not a
matter of disadvantage in reality versus openness in principle. In fact,
it is a question of systematic exclusion, in which the standards and premises of law are perceived and validated as purely male. This critique
is grounded in, and discussed on, three levels of epistemological and
legal theory.

THE GENDER PHILOSOPHY OF THE ENLIGHTENMENT, OR GENDER AS A POLITICAL CATEGORY

The first level of criticism is based on the epistemological premises of Enlightenment philosophy and its political consequences. While discourse in the early Enlightenment period still allowed for the possibility of an equality that was not gender-specific, definite limits were set on the struggle for liberty and equality for one "half of humankind" (Condorcet) by political theorists of civil society, especially the philosophers who paved the way for the French Revolution. Once the fetters of origin and birth had been done away with, or at least called into question, gender emerged, along with the formation of social classes and other structural inequalities, as a political category that characterized and constituted the developing bourgeois society.

Lieselotte Steinbrügge has analyzed in detail the theoretical changes that took place in the French Enlightenment, from "genderless reason" (Poulain de la Barre, 1673) to the "turn to sensuality" (for example, Pierre Roussel, 1775) and the sexualization of female life in medical discourse, to Rousseau's concept of femininity as "based in nature" and women as the "moral sex."[4] Cartesian Poulain de la Barre's expression "reason has no gender" (l'esprit n'a pas de sexe) assumed the separation of mind and body and posited that reason is a special capacity of human beings, placing them above all other living things. The development of the empirical sciences, however, and medical knowledge of the physiology of women as distinct from that of men, led to the concept of a dualism of body and mind. This served as the model for a "polarization of the nature of gender," apparently legitimizing different lifestyles and a gender-specific division of labor.[5] The sciences of generic "man" "and his woman" were emerging as separate disciplines towards the end of the eighteenth century. These included primarily philosophy, but also the natural sciences, medicine, and education. "In the period of the Enlightenment, [they] enthroned the difference between the sexes, making it the all-elucidating basis of science and civilization."[6] Western concepts of civilization, science, progress, rationality, and, in particular, law are thus marked by a philosophy of gender roles in which the man embodies the norm and normalcy, an equal among equals, while the woman represents the deviation, the "second sex," and the inferior.[7]

The human being (as man), with the help of reason and a modern understanding of science, assumed authority over the world—including nature. Continuing this thought, "woman" was defined by this same science, on the basis of her physical make-up, sexuality, and function for the reproduction of the human species, as belonging on the side of nature. In *Emile*, his novel about education, Jean-Jacques Rousseau described how little the woman in the age of reason corresponded to her "nature"—how much conditioning was in fact necessary in order to guide her to her true calling as "housewife, wife, and mother."[8] Based on his protagonist Sophy, he developed an educational program that many generations of educators of girls would attempt to implement. It contributed to upholding not only the family order but bourgeois society as a whole.

Particularly in response to the call for equality of all humankind, great effort was made, not only in education, but politically as well, to quiet the "querelle des femmes"—the scholarly dispute on the nature of woman that had been in progress since the beginning of the modern age—and to ward off the possibility that women would be liberated along with men.[9] The impact and significance of Rousseau's gender philosophy, a part of his social theory as a whole, obviously resulted from the fact that he successfully identified the gender problem in a modern, functional manner. At the same time, he knew how to make the cultural and moral significance of "femininity" palatable, even to his female readers.[10] Rousseau's anthropology of the difference between the sexes was not innovative; it could be traced back to Aristotle. Commonplace in Western philosophy, it was a typology derived from the position during the sex act.[11] What was new was that from then on it would be used to justify legal inequality based on gender. By way of Kant, and especially Fichte's *The Science of Rights*, this philosophy has guided legal theory and practice to the present day.[12]

In addition to this implicit gender philosophy of the Enlightenment, referred to in feminist scholarship as a gender-specific "dialectic of Enlightenment," the exclusion of women from political and legal discourse is based primarily on the social contract.[13] All theories of the state from the sixteenth to the eighteenth centuries started with the idea that the social contract could be entered into only by men, and more precisely, as a union of landowners. The category of gender, or of women, appears neither in these theoretical explanations nor in the discussion on, and responses to, the theories. According to the political theory of possessive individualism, women should be treated like other persons living "in the peace of the house," because they are not "proprietors of their own capacities" or lack "freedom from dependence on the wills of others."[14] The only individuals who are potential parties to the social contract are property owners, or "proprietors," those in a position to "provide for themselves."[15] The early social contract theorists were at least careful and consistent enough to draw up the marriage contract, a special contract that they referred to explicitly as the counterpart to the social contract. It defined women's place in the political and private spheres, and thus the subjection of women. In contrast to these early theorists, the contract's later bourgeois or liberal proponents simply presupposed women's subordination in the family. This is why the significance of marriage (and family) as a special institution that stabilized social conditions, "as the nursery of humankind" (Samuel von Pufendorf), was treated so extensively in all theories of law and the state. In this private-law marriage contract, the wife "voluntarily" subordinated herself to the conjugal authority of the husband, giving him all rights over her; thus she was obliged to obey him, like a subject his ruler. The unique, specifically bourgeois aspect lay in the idea that the subjection of the woman in marriage was compatible with matrimonial love; as Fichte put it, "As the moral impulse of woman manifests itself as love, so in man that impulse manifests itself as generosity." "[Woman's] continuous necessary wish . . . to be so subjected" excluded her from all individual rights, according to Fichte. "Her husband is, therefore, the administrator of all her rights in consequence of her own necessary will."[16]

In her study of social contract theories, Carole Pateman concludes that the exclusion of women from the contract of the state and their simultaneous inclusion in the private sphere were firmly established as a "sexual contract," which appeared as a "natural" rather than socially negotiated right of men. In contrast to traditional patriarchy, which was attended by certain male privileges in the estates-based order, Pateman characterizes the modern social contract as an agreement, not only among heads of families, but among brothers following patricide, wherein the "law of the father" was replaced by a fraternal agreement.

Following Freud's analysis in *Totem and Taboo*, Pateman interprets the motive of this collective fraternal action to be "not merely to claim the natural liberty and right of self-government, but to gain access to women." She continues:

> The separation of "paternal" from political rule, or the family from the public sphere, is also the separation of women from men through the subjection of women to men. . . . The fraternal social contract creates a new, modern patriarchal order that is presented as divided into two spheres: civil society or the universal sphere of freedom, equality, individualism, reason, contract and impartial law—the realm of men or "individuals"; and the private world of particularity, natural subjection, ties of blood, love and sexual passion—the world of women, in which men also rule.[17]

In Pateman's analysis, the transition to modern civil society was thus accompanied by a very specific, new form of domination over women, "a transition which the contract stories encapsulate theoretically involved a change from a traditional (paternal) form of patriarchy to a new *specifically modern* (or fraternal) form: patriarchal civil society."[18] Pateman thereby identified the duality of bourgeois or civil society. She put her finger on a point supported by the findings of numerous feminist social analyses: that the separation of the private sphere from the political, public sphere—a gender-specific assignment—is central and constitutive to this civil society and to the specifically modern structure of gender relations.[19] Nevertheless, I fear that her psychological and psychoanalytical explanation for the motives of these "brothers" could all too easily be misunderstood as a feminist conspiracy theory, thereby obscuring her decisive argument. Moreover, whereas Pateman exposed or unmasked the social (fraternal) contract, in my argumentation the division between public and private spheres leads to a duality of civil society, which I discern as the "hidden base" beneath the bourgeois or civil society it maintains. As for the system of law, it is significant that the social and marriage contracts represent two different levels, and that the marriage contract plays a major role in political theories dealing with the organization of civil society. This is the only way to explain why matrimonial and family law has for so long remained a domain of patriarchal special interests[20] and why, despite all formal steps toward equal rights, this area of law continues to this day to be defended against the right to equality in specific cases.[21]

In his interpretation of social contract theories as models for a theory of justice, John Rawls did not explicitly consider gender relations; aside from a reference to "heads of families," Rawls evidently assumed as a matter of course that "family institutions are just" and play an important socializing role in developing "the corresponding sense of justice."[22] Feminist theorists have good reason to view such casual assumptions with skepticism, especially the presupposition that the family, as a private, unlegislated sphere, is a place that is just. Joining the moral theory debate surrounding Carol Gilligan's ideas on a "female" morality,[23] Seyla Benhabib has criticized the form of abstraction in Rawls's theory, which involves an image of the human being, the concept of an autonomous self, that is evidently "disembedded and disembodied." Characteristic of modern theories of justice is Hobbes's image of human beings in their natural state, viewed "as if but even now sprung out of the earth, and suddenly, like mushrooms, come to full maturity, without all kind of engagement to each other."[24] Benhabib continues, "Yet this is a strange world: it is one in which individuals are grown up before they have been born; . . . a world where neither mother, nor sister, nor wife exist. . . . The point is that in this universe, the experience of the early modern female has no place."[25] She questions the image of a "'veil of ignorance'" from a feminist perspective, because "'the other as different from the self, disappears'" and "'[d]ifferences . . . become irrelevant.'" "The Rawlsian self does not know 'his place in society, his class position or status; nor does he know his fortune in the distribution of natural assets and abilities, his intelligence and strength, and the like.'" The question must then be posed, "'Are these individuals human selves at all'" . . . who "'can know anything at all that is relevant to the human condition?'"[26]

Susan Moller Okin also found it problematic to leave an ethic of care out of a theory of justice. She, however, attempted to correct Rawls's concept of justice by adding to his theory a "notion of equal concern for others" in place of the "mutual disinterest" he postulated. In Okin's view, "the only coherent way in which a party in the original position can think about justice is through empathy with persons of all kinds in all the different positions in society, but especially with the least well-off in various respects. . . . It is to think from the point of view of everybody, of every 'concrete other' whom one might turn out to be."[27] However, Okin also stresses, "But such an emphasis at the same time draws attention to the fact that the theory as it stands contains an internal paradox. Because of Rawls's assumptions about the gendered family, he has not applied the principles of justice to the realm of human nurturance, which is so crucial for the achievement and the maintenance of justice."[28]

Whatever their reasons for criticizing the different contract theories, feminist critics of the exclusionary process in social contract theories reach essentially the same conclusions. Although bourgeois or civil society obligated itself, in its proclamations and principles, to ensure liberty and equality for all human beings, the unequal and subordinate status of women that is anchored in law remains a part of its structure. Beneath the "sphere of private people come together as a public"—the male citizens—society has maintained and safeguarded a private sphere, the family, as a hidden base, as it were—a contradiction. The systematic exclusion of women is grounded in the separation of state and society, a basic feature of liberalism. This separation of public and private spheres goes hand in hand with a corresponding gender-specific and hierarchical division of labor. In response to feminist criticism, even Jürgen Habermas has since conceded, in his preface to the revised German edition of *The Structural Transformation of the Public Sphere:* "It has been shown that the exclusion of women was constitutive for the political public sphere, in the sense not only that a portion of this sphere was dominated by men, but that its very structure and its relationship to the private sphere was gender-specific. Unlike the exclusion of underprivileged men, the exclusion of women had a structuring power."[29] However, Habermas refrained from drawing any further conclusions for his analysis of society.[30]

ON THE CONTROVERSY OVER A FEMALE MORALITY AND THE RELATIONSHIP BETWEEN LAW AND MORALITY

The difficulty in dealing with the theory and practice of law for both women and men lies in the complexity and ambiguity of the concept of law. This concept has a dual or dialectic nature, to the extent that it encompasses "legal norms as both enforceable laws and laws of free-dom."[31] After all, law means, on the one hand, positive, valid law, which can be extremely unjust in its substance or impact. On the other hand, the concept of law encompasses not only the entire body of regulations and norms, which, in contrast to other social norms such as custom, practice, and convention, can be enforced through a legal staff and state coercion.[32] It also includes individual legal claims and expectations grounded in the ideas of "correct" law, justice, and a legitimate order anchored by the medium of law.

In her 1982 book *In a Different Voice*, Carol Gilligan presented her thesis of a separate female morality with different moral orientations and practices—a female "ethic of care" and "empathy," in contrast to a fundamental and universal male ethic of justice. The ensuing debate surrounding the book triggered a far-reaching feminist legal discussion. Although the methodological and empirical bases of her findings on the "two ethics" have since been subjected to diverse criticisms and modified by more recent studies,[33] the question remains why these theo-ries sparked such a broad, ongoing controversy throughout the world.[34] This debate, like the extensive discussion of John Rawls's theory of jus-tice (1971), is evidently more than a discourse on theories of morality. It deals with the consequences of a shift in values; increasing individu-alization and the questioning of standards in both the private and po-litical spheres; and social change as a result of the impact of new social movements, among them the women's movement.

The ethics debate is interesting in this context because of its sig-nificance for feminist discourse on law, whereby it is important not to blur the distinction between ethics and law.[35] Law is less than ethics, to the extent that it covers only some of the requirements of morality; and at the same time it is stronger, in that it uses external coercion to validate its rules. The extent of the overlap between law and ethics at any one time is one of the recurring, fundamental questions of legal theory.[36]

In numerous studies, Ingeborg Maus has continued a critique be-gun by Franz L. Neumann. Thinking specifically of German history and the Nazi perversion of the legal order and destruction of the rule of law, she stresses the formal structure of law, which can only be guaranteed by a democratic legislative process, the "universality of the law," and the determinacy of its content.[37] Maus shows that it was not so-called legal positivism but "the substantive uncertainty" of Nazi legislation that made "a farce of all legal obligation"—aside from the fact that law, in a democratic, constitutional sense, did not exist at this time in any case.[38] At the same time, Maus criticizes the restoration of natural law after 1945 and the "actual remoralization of law" through German Federal Constitutional Court rulings, since these could not be limited or controlled by any sovereign power.[39] Because law, in the form of individual laws and as a result of democratic legislative processes, has coercive authority at its disposal, there is good reason why its prerequisites are more demanding than those of ethics.[40] Thus it is only possible to explain law on moral grounds if ethics and law are kept distinct. "As an independent perspective, it [ethics] forms . . . a potential for resistance in society that must be employed all the more urgently to confront the state's lawmaking process because legal procedures never automatically guarantee just results. . . . To this extent, the ability to criticize democratically established law at a moral level presupposes the separation of law and ethics."[41] This also demonstrates the possible significance of a feminist debate on ethics for a critique of valid law. At the same time, it suggests the ways in which theories of morality and the discourse on justice initiated by social movements can influence and change the legal standards of equality. However, these new ideas of justice can only become valid law if they are negotiated in a democratic legislative process and granted legitimacy in the form of laws.

EQUALITY AND/OR DIFFERENCE: AN ENDLESS DEBATE

Another dimension of feminist legal critique deals with the international discussion on the relationship between equality and/or difference. To be sure, the dissension has toned down in recent years, and some degree of pragmatic agreement has been reached. The choice between either a right to equality or a right to difference is now seen as a false and misleading alternative, since equality can only emerge as an issue or a demand in the face of differences between individuals.[42] Nevertheless, the debate has contributed to a much more nuanced understanding of equality and equal rights. The objections, as well as the references, to equality and/or difference play a significant role in international discourse on human rights as women's rights, and can serve to clarify the conditions for asserting rights, including human rights for women. The global discourse on gender difference thus on the one hand indicates cultural and social change, in the course of which issues of justice in gender relations have called into question ways of thinking and acting long taken for granted. On the other hand, other cultural, social, and ethnic differences, and even differences among different groups of women, must be considered as part of a critical perspective on difference; they challenge any understanding of equality that is too formal, mechanical, or andro- or ethnocentric.

Contrasting equality and difference as mutually exclusive or reciprocal points of reference in feminist theory and politics is not a new argument. It has accompanied the modern history of the struggle for women's rights since the French Revolution. This antinomy is therefore also referred to as "Wollstonecraft's dilemma."[43] It characterizes the difficulties connected with rejecting the presumptions of traditional bourgeois femininity and working to change or eliminate the hierarchical model of gender relations, while at the same time basing emancipatory politics on "womanness," or female experience and orientation. Expressed in legal terms, it is an apparent paradox to demand the right to equality while at the same time insisting that differences be taken into consideration and acknowledged.

Both positions were represented in the various currents of the first historical women's movements in almost all the countries in which they existed. Though bourgeois women's rights advocates focused more on the notion of difference, of the "culture of women's uniqueness," proletarian women demanded equality with men. And middle-class radicals attempted to justify their demands for strict equality on the grounds of different, female, pacifist goals.[44] The second-wave women's movement, too, cannot be identified strictly with a position of difference, despite its opposition to formal equal rights. In her analysis of second-wave feminism, Judith Evans spoke of at least five different phases and forms of feminist politics along the axis of equality and difference, which were also superimposed and intersected by the terms "sameness" or "identity" and "inequality."[45]

Using the principle of legal equality as an instrument or goal of feminist politics has been fundamentally questioned and "deconstructed" by two more recent currents of feminist theory. According to the first, "equality" as a basic legal principle of modern times, and thus law it-self, is a "male standard"[46] that excludes women per se, maintains the gender hierarchy, and only guarantees equality for women on condi-tion that they adapt to male values and lifestyles. Equality as a promise and as the prevailing legal practice is thus revealed to be "adaptation to the male model"[47] or "sameness."

The epistemological objection registered by poststructuralist and postmodern criticism is even more serious. Since this critique questions the concept of the subject, the holder of rights, it challenges feminist legal theory as a whole; that is, it considers a theory that makes "the woman" or the category "sex" a basis for individual rights to be mis-guided, theoretically and politically. Doubt was first raised politically when black women confronted white, Western feminism; epistemologi-cally, the questioning began with a basic philosophical critique of the subjectivity of Western philosophy, the Enlightenment concept of rea-son and rationality, and modern social contract theories. The harshest criticism comes from the fundamental opposition to a legal discourse expressed by DIOTIMA, a group of Italian women in philosophy, fol-lowing the ideas of Luce Irigaray. This critique is based on the idea of an "original" difference predating history and the "undeniable reality" of two genders, since "the human being is two."[48] This presupposition implies, however, that everything supported and constituted by the do-minion of *one* patriarchal world order must be discredited: "the con-cept of equality, . . . freedom, democracy, etc. The traditional political vocabulary *in toto* is suspect."[49] Luce Irigaray formulated a radical cri-tique of the neglect and absence of women in present-day civilization and in its symbolic, social, and political order, especially in the language of law and the subconscious. Consequently, she developed proposals for a female legal order based in women's special experience of injustice. Most important in this context is her demand for special protection of women's dignity—in concrete terms, "legally safeguarding virginity as part of the female identity" and "the right of motherhood."[50] This way of revaluing female forms of experience as a normative orientation has repeatedly been criticized as problematic, as has the ease with which her essentialism might be misunderstood.[51] Nevertheless, Irigaray's fun-damental criticism of existing law within the overall context of culture, language, and symbolic order intensified and accentuated the feminist critique, thus providing an essential contribution to a feminist analysis of law.

In contrast to these ontological positions on the theory of difference, Judith Butler aims to "deconstruct" the binary framework of gender philosophy with an epistemological critique of the category "gender" and even the subject of identity and especially that of "women." This deconstruction is necessary, according to Butler, because the binary of masculine/feminine tends to maintain and reproduce the hierarchical "system of the duality of gender."[52] Starting with the differentiation between biological "sex" and culturally constructed "gender," a distinction commonly made in feminist theory, Butler sees not only the gendered body, but also the sexed body as a "site of cultural interpretation"; that is, it is a social construction maintained through binary oppositions such as man/woman, mind/body, and reason/desire, ruling out all ambiguities, incoherences, and nonheterosexual practices. Butler understands person, sex, sexuality, the "being" of gender, and the idea of the subject as the outcome of hegemonial discourse and prevailing heterosexual practice.[53] However, she also stresses that "the death of that subject is not the end of agency, of speech, or of political debate."[54]

Various pragmatic answers have been offered to resolve the theoretical and political dilemma of a feminist theory that calls into question its own point of reference, "woman" as subject. Christine di Stefano, for example, responded to the question with another question—how helpful or politically sensible is it to abandon the modern concept of justice, self-determination, and changing gender roles, "at the moment when women have just begun to remember their selves and claim an agentic subjectivity," and demand self-determination not only as individuals, but as a group.[55] Nancy Fraser, too, proposed eliminating "false antitheses" and assuming a pragmatic stance. She stressed that an analysis of language, meaning, and discourse should be supplemented with sociological studies of societal structures and institutions, and of law and the economy.[56] From a legal perspective, and based on a highly nuanced analysis of the history of women and law in the United States, Deborah Rhode has called for moderately extensive strategies, "for a less dualistic, more contextual approach. . . . Rather than thinking in terms of either/or—sameness vs. difference, difference vs. gender, difference vs. disadvantage—we should focus on issues of when and why."[57]

In my opinion, in the feminist discussion of equality and difference, legal questions have to some degree been concealed and dominated by a philosophical analysis of discourse that is primarily poststructuralist. As a result, the institutions and structural conditions, as well as the historical, empirical, and doctrinal contexts, of the respective legal cultures have been neglected. American theorists have continually dealt with the "sameness versus difference dilemma," which is distinct from the "equality versus difference" contrast. Their analyses have caused some confusion among European theorists, in view of the different legal traditions and legal situations; they have failed to take the different European context into account and have inappropriately generalized from the U.S. legal system. For example, German law after 1949 and U.S. law differ significantly in that the introduction of the equal rights article—Art. 3, Sec. 2 of the German Basic Law—ruled out the possibility of an Aristotelian interpretation of the equality clause.[58] But an Aristotelian line of reasoning—according to which only likes are to be treated alike, and unlikes according to their respective natures—forms the prerequisite for American authors' arguments preferring "sameness" to "equality." An example here is the work of Catherine A. MacKinnon. She interprets the issue of equal rights according to the U.S. legal system, and thus on the basis of an Aristotelian interpretation; she argues that the equality principle works only with the precondition of being treated alike. Yet this reasoning is not applicable to most European constitutions, with their special provisions establishing the legal equality of men and women and thus explicitly excluding consideration of gender difference.[59] In MacKinnon's view, the legal inequality of women is clearly a result of male power, and gender difference is identical with gender dominance, since, following Aristotle, the man is "the measure of all things."[60] Consequently, the claimed gender neutrality of law can mean nothing but "be the same as men." "Gender neutrality is simply male standard."[61] MacKinnon thus concludes that the legal concept of equality fundamentally presupposes "sameness"—that is, equality in the sense of identity.[62]

As demonstrated by West German legal history since 1949 and the anchoring of equal rights in Art. 3, Sec. 2 of the Basic Law, legal practitioners and the administrators of justice were very reluctant to implement a constitutional standard that revolutionized gender relations. Even the promulgation of an equal rights law, required by the year 1953 under article 117 of the Basic Law, was delayed by legislators until 1957. Equal rights were not laid down in private law until the 1976 reform of matrimonial and family law, and further amendments remained necessary—for example, with respect to laws regarding the wife's taking of the husband's last name.[63]

Elisabeth Selbert, one of four women in the Parliamentary Council, spoke out effectively in 1949 in favor of equal rights laws. She condemned the patriarchal resistance to legal equality and criticized polemic misinterpretations of the law that claimed it would "make everything the same" or create "mechanical" equality. Selbert argued, "It is a basic misconception to assume that equal rights means sameness. Equality is based on equal worth, which acknowledges difference."[64] Erna Scheffler, the first woman to serve as a German federal constitutional judge, foresaw the hidden loopholes for renewed discrimination in this argumentation. She attempted to clarify the dangers to legal doctrine and court rulings created by referring only to "equal worth":

> The doctrine generally prevailing today says equal rights means that legislation, administration, and judicial decisions are required to treat equal conditions in the same way. If in addition to the general principle of equal rights, the legislators further declare that men and women have equal rights, this can only mean that the *natural* difference between the genders cannot be valued *legally* as different conditions. . . . Precisely because men and women are psychologically and physically different, the legislators have created explicit norms for their legal equality. The principle "equal rights despite gender difference" cannot then be restricted using the argument of gender difference. That would contradict the inherent logic of the principle of equal rights.[65]

German constitutional court decisions over the past decades were at first quite contradictory, and only some of the court's rulings were positive for women. The negative impact was sustained by a landmark 1953 decision in which a legal loophole allowed the Aristotelian legal interpretation to be applied in court rulings. Contrary to the explicit prohibition of gender distinctions under Art. 3, Sec. 3 of the Basic Law, the court allowed not only "objective biological differences between men and women"[66] to be used as the basis for legal distinctions, "but also functional ones" related to the division of labor. This decision lent legitimacy to the detrimental consequences of the traditional gender-specific division of labor.[67] Not until the 1970s did the rulings of the Federal Constitutional Court start to reflect an understanding of equality that was no longer determined by traditional gender roles. In the 1980s, however, it was more likely to "consider social differences," pursuing the goal of "allowing a compensatory balance favoring women."[68]

All in all, after many detours and much resistance regarding the interpretation of the equal rights article, a "prevailing opinion" has developed, with the help of important advocates, briefs, and court rulings. According to the compromise formulated by a joint constitutional commission, Art. 3, Sec. 2 refers to "the actual implementation of equal rights of women and men," and the state has been assigned the task of working towards the "elimination of existing disadvantages" and *creating* equality.[69] The legislature has obligated itself not only to combat discrimination based on certain characteristics, including gender, but also expressly to support women as a group, even if occasional instances of discrimination against the dominant group (men) could arise.[70] The gradual development of European law has also played an important role in this process; still, given that this law aims primarily to create a common European market and thus deals with women mainly in terms of their participation in the workforce, joint efforts by feminist lawyers in Europe continue to be necessary to prevent the adoption of market-oriented "male standards."[71]

Against the background of these new legal conditions, the reasons for becoming involved in the legal discourse on equality and difference are not only pragmatic; empirical facts and historical achievements also encourage participation. And it makes no sense for a feminist theory that is skeptical of law, and justified in criticizing the fact that equal rights have not yet been achieved, to allow its interpretations of the equality clause to fall behind the present state of valid law and interpretation, and instead employ the arguments of the opponents of equal rights.

In summary, it should be emphasized once more that equality, a legal concept as controversial as it is meaningful in historical struggles, is neither an absolute principle nor a firm standard; it is a dynamic, discursive concept.[72] It must first be determined in what respect two persons or things are viewed as equal, with reference to a third party, the so-called *tertium comparationis*. This third party can never simply be "man" or the status of men; it must be a standard that is fair to both genders. The meaning of equality in past and present legal practice thus cannot be determined at the level of doctrinal formulas or "argumentative logic";[73] it can only be determined by taking into account the conditions under which the question of equality is posed. "The function of the equality clause will only become recognizable to the extent that the historical conflict over it enters our field of vision."[74]

Thus my empirical and theoretical point of reference for participation in the equality discourse, particularly where the rights of women are concerned, is the women's movements and the experiences of injustice expressed within these movements. They have stood for a sense of justice, legal subjectivity, and the political agency of the participants. These movements have given a voice to the suffering of the disadvantaged and oppressed and the outrage and injustice these women experience; and they have struggled and fought in the legal arena for recognition of their differences and of the views of equality they consider relevant.

The autonomy that has been demanded and practiced in second-wave women's movements on the basis of formal equal rights typifies their demand for recognition and acceptance of difference; that is, it is a self-determined manifestation of the principle of equality that is not oriented toward male standards and lifestyles. An audacious new aspect was the claim to self-determination in the private as well as public spheres, thus encompassing the domain to which women were explicitly assigned in bourgeois society. Turning this into a general, political demand was a provocative act, succinctly expressed in the slogan "the personal is political." As a political demand, this did not mean "simply" personal self-determination; it also meant political self-determination. This form of autonomous politics—that is, insisting on self-determination, including political self-determination—and involvement in current policymaking on legal and equality issues are therefore not contradictory; they belong together. Thus modified, the two sides of feminist discourse on equality and difference unite to create a dynamic understanding of "equality in difference" that varies depending on time and place.[75]

Basic Rights and Human Rights as a Response to Fundamental Experiences of Injustice

Rather than a philosophical, ethical, or normative explanation, we shall now turn our attention to the empirical and concrete historical level of injustice and the emergence of demands for rights. As demonstrated by the history of human and civil rights, human rights as standards for just and humane conditions have been developed in response to concrete historical experiences of injustice and crises in the modern world.[76] The United Nations' 1948 Universal Declaration of Human Rights was the first set of international legal rules and standards recognized worldwide in various pacts and special agreements. According to the preamble, it was a reaction to "barbarous acts" committed by the Nazis during World War II that "outraged the conscience of mankind." Human rights thus do not represent an unbroken faith in the progress of Western societies; on the contrary, they reflect the concerns of the international community and perceived threats to it. In view of the injustices committed by the Western world in the twentieth century, in the form of racism, imperialism, and genocide, they also represent an "attempt to find a new way to protect humanity in the face of fundamental threats to human dignity."[77]

Even though they were not part of the positive, valid legal order, human rights have remained an important point of reference for individuals in the struggle for justice since the French Revolution, and even more so for social movements. The main condition is that they must not concern "merely" matters of individual suffering, misfortune, or fate, but a "collective experience of violated integrity" that can be expressed as an injustice.[78] The question remains, when do such experiences of injustice lead to the claiming of rights or to social protest. Several factors must evidently coincide before this step is taken. In his comprehensive and detailed study, *Injustice: The Social Bases of Obedience and Revolt*, Barrington Moore provided concrete historical evidence, citing the German working-class and the labor movement, that "moral anger and a sense of social injustice have to be discovered and that the process of discovery is fundamentally an historical one."[79] The wealth of his material clearly illustrates the extent to which individuals are capable of tolerating and coming to terms with maltreatment, rather than rebelling. Accordingly, it is plainly not the experience of pain and suffering alone that moves a person to resist. The idea that such pain and suffering is not inevitable and that its societal distribution is unjust is the necessary prerequisite to action.

This suggests that the ability to articulate experiences of wrongdoing and injustice is tied to the ability to understand the experiences and intentions of others; it involves having knowledge and opinions on justice and injustice from a particular locus. This experience is socially transmitted and therefore time- and context-dependent. Everyday experience, and thus everyday consciousness, serves an important orienting function in everyday life, influencing routines, communication, and modes of conduct. This explains why people are reluctant to call their own "conscious experience" and familiar patterns into question. As confirmed in empirical studies on everyday consciousness,[80] or sociological examinations of the contentment of workers on the job,[81] or the satisfaction of housewives,[82] admitting to discontent would disrupt the laboriously maintained daily balance between self-image and expectations. An additional factor is required; that is, the everyday routine must be disrupted. The chance to question one's experiences as unjust, or unjust with respect to others, does not emerge until one's life situation and social context become problematic or change, "in crisis situations in which routinely practiced patterns of action fail to yield the familiar success,"[83] or if new standards and comparisons are created—for example, in the process of so-called globalization through international communication and information.

Perceiving human rights as a response to "fundamental" and "exemplary experiences of injustice"[84] can possibly become a basis for understanding, especially in international and intercultural dialogue. By referring to the "fundamental" interests at stake in human rights violations, we are reminded of the fact that in all previous, or classical, lists of rights, certain objects of legal concern have been viewed as deserving protection above all else, since they deal with a "core" of rights, "without which it is not possible to become aware of one's self as a person."[85] However, which rights to include in this "core" is a matter of debate: the right to live under the protection of law at all or to even have rights,[86] the "right to security of the person," or the classical catalogue of liberties, characterized, depending on context, as "basic liberties," "basic needs," or "natural and social primary goods."[87]

Winfried Brugger's phrase "exemplary experiences of injustice" refers to events and situations, the experience of which "by the persons involved or the awareness of which by a third party would result in an elementary and like-minded judgment as 'unjust,' even when the persons involved and the third party belong to different groups and cultures." This means that the experience of suffering must also exist for others; it must be generalizable. The exemplary or representative character involves a "universal element," beyond its expression in a specific culture, that—it is further assumed—transcends presuppositions of "just" or "unjust" that apply in a specific group, class, race, gender, or culture.[88]

Despite the expansion of this approach to include a gender-specification of the problem, an explicit "core" of women's rights has so far been so lacking in all legal theories that additional information is needed to clarify what it encompasses. This may require a modification of theoretical assumptions and a different history of law, one that fills the existing gaps in current legal history. In the following section, some systematic or paradigmatic examples from the history of the women's movement that describe the steps in the development and explication of law will be presented.

HISTORICAL INJUSTICES

All modern women's movements entered the public arena first and foremost with demands for more rights, as rights struggles and rights movements. The impetus for a women's social movement appeared only when there was "not only injustice," but "outrage," as Bertolt Brecht phrased it in his poem "An die Nachgeborenen." It was necessary that individual, isolated experiences of suffering and injustice—that is, of lack of freedom and of legal incapacity or exclusion from equal participation—were no longer considered individual misfortunes, but experienced as injustice by and with others and asserted to be an infringement of rights. The immediate causes, the social and political conditions that triggered awareness and political action, differed greatly in the various historical phases. But the form of rights violations, the systematic exclusion of women, and the reactions to women's movements were structurally the same, at least in the period of emerging civil society. I have identified three historical stages of legal development in the modern history of struggles for women's rights, corresponding to typical experiences of injustice:

1. The experience of exclusion from civil rights and political participation in the context of the bourgeois revolution and democracy movements of the eighteenth and nineteenth centuries.
2. Denial of civic liberties, individual autonomy, and rights of property for women, in the form of gender tutelage and conjugal authority of husbands, in matrimonial and family law.
3. Sexual exploitation and violence against women, not only because they violate personal and physical integrity, but also as structural violence and a curtailment of life options and agency for women; this was also the impetus for and focus of the international campaign "Women's Rights Are Human Rights," supported by the 1995 United Nations World Conference on Women.

These examples of basic experiences of injustice and women's demands for rights are not merely concrete manifestations of the above-mentioned levels of feminist legal criticism. They also correspond to the historical reconstruction, which has recently received considerable public attention, of the three dimensions of "social rights of citizenship," according to Thomas H. Marshall.[89] He illustrated his delineation of periods with events in Great Britain. Accordingly, the conflict over civil rights took place primarily in the eighteenth century, the struggle for rights of political participation in the nineteenth century, and basic social rights were an outcome of the welfare-state politics of the twentieth century. Not only the lack of simultaneity, but also the different order in which women's and men's rights were recognized, indicates fundamental, structural differences in both a qualitative and quantitative sense. The forms of rights violations and the types of experiences of injustice show that it is virtually impossible to interpret the issue of women's rights simply as a delay in the process of democratization.

THE EXPERIENCE OF EXCLUSION FROM THE
CATEGORY OF CITIZENS

In connection with the bourgeois revolutions in Europe and the United
States, women began to demand, first and foremost, political rights. The
shared motivating force was the experience of exclusion—exclusion
from the category of active citizens—and thus the "unfulfilled promise" of the bourgeois revolutions. This was true of the collective protest by women in the French Revolution, in which they demanded not
only bread but human rights and political participation. In the most
important women's political document of the period, the Declaration
of the Rights of Woman and Citizen, written in 1791 by Olympe de
Gouges,[90] the specific injustices experienced by women were indicated
in the parallels with, and particularly in the deviations from, the "universal" Declaration of the Rights of Man and Citizen. At the same time,
de Gouges paved the way for the radicalization of the principle of democracy as a social contract between men and women. De Gouges's concept of politics expressly provided for the compatibility of motherhood
and civil rights. In fact, the main reason she directly demanded basic
liberties in this catalogue of rights was to assure that existential gender-
specific differences be taken into consideration and recognized. For instance, the right to free communication of thoughts and opinions could
obviously mean different things to men and to women. The passage that
seems far too detailed and inappropriately worded for such a document
nevertheless characterized a fundamental experience of injustice by
women. This was the demand that paternity—that is, the fathers' responsibility and obligation to support even children born out of wedlock—
be investigated and made public.[91] This direct connection between the
role of citizen and that of mother was a provocation and a protest, and
not only against contemporary legal practice; it also contradicted modern constitutional and legal theory, which excluded mothers and wives
from the category of active citizens through the marriage contract. This
point had systematic significance for Olympe de Gouges, as demonstrated by the fact that, in addition to this women's rights declaration
and numerous other works, she drafted a marriage contract as a social
contract between a man and a woman.[92] The aim of this gender contract was to eliminate the two-tiered structure of bourgeois legal orders
that separated the private and political spheres on the basis of gender.

In this way she put her finger on the contradiction, inherent in gender relations in civil society, between the publicly expressed promise of equality of all human beings and the private despotism and violence in the so-called unlegislated realm of the family.

Further examples of claims for universal basic and human rights could be mentioned that legitimized the efforts of the nineteenth-century women's movements. The Declaration of Sentiments, adopted in 1848 at the first U.S. Women's Right Convention in Seneca Falls, is a paraphrase of the 1776 Declaration of Independence with a few significant modifications. In addition to the demand for equal, inalienable rights for men and women, which are listed as including especially, "life, liberty, and the pursuit of happiness," the Declaration of Sentiments also contained a negative list of "repeated injuries and usurpations on the part of man toward woman, having in direct object the establishment of an absolute tyranny over her."[93] This document is an example of the self-confident and legally pragmatic point of departure of the first U.S. women's movement.

The experience of women's exclusion and their disappointment in their revolutionary comrades-in-arms repeated itself in European history in the revolutions of 1830 and 1848.[94] Again and again, throughout Europe, women who had participated in bringing about democratic movements and had taken a stand for liberty, democracy, and the unity of their country were forced to admit that they had been "forgotten" and that the political sphere had been established as a male domain and as men's business. This is why Louise Otto's comment in 1849 in the women's journal she published, "I am recruiting women citizens for the realm of freedom," struck a chord in many women: "Liberty is indivisible! Thus free men shall tolerate no enslaved men beside them—and no enslaved women. We must doubt the honest will and intellect of all freedom fighters who stand up for the rights of men, but not at the same time for the rights of women."[95]

There was still a long way to go before equal rights of citizenship would be achieved, until 1918, when equal democratic suffrage would be established in most countries of the Western world. The international women's suffrage movement that developed out of diverse initiatives in the late nineteenth century insisted that "human rights have no gender" and demanded the right to political self-determination as the "foundation," the starting point, for the implementation of all other rights demanded by its members. Explaining why women need "the suffrage" always brought together two lines of reasoning, one claiming equality and one defending difference.[96] Whereas the suffragists initially supported the general political discourse that demanded equality "as a human right," it was always emphasized that the goal was never to "be the same as men." Depending on the political context, reference to gender difference, female particularity, and women's contribution to the general good turned out to be a strategic advantage and mobilizing bond at the end of the nineteenth century. Nonetheless, this only confirms the fact that, after the decline of the German empire and the defeat in the war, women were not granted the right to vote as an act of magnanimity. Instead, women's suffrage was achieved due to the efforts of a broad-based women's movement with an international network. Yet suffrage, as the "paradigm for rights in general," did not, as the pioneering women had hoped, bring about fundamental changes in gender relations in state and society after 1918.[97] This had more to do with the other side of this persistent exclusion of women from politics—that is, with their inclusion in the private sphere by means of family law.

LEGAL INCAPACITY AND PERSONAL DOMINANCE IN PRIVATE LAW

Refusing to grant women citizenship status, and thus excluding them from all public and political rights, was, from a legal perspective, closely tied to the "special role" played by women in the family, according to theorists of civil society. "Women are the representatives of love, just as men are representatives of law in a general sense."[98] This condensed gender assignment hit the nail succinctly on the head with respect to civil society.

This is why various attempts at personal liberation and emancipation from private constraints were necessary prior to the mobilization and protests that took place within the context of the 1848 March Revolution. The participating women were concerned with being recognized as persons, individuals, and holders of rights, and with claiming the "right to freely develop one's personality and the right to freedom of opinion and conscience." Contemporary women's literature confirmed this concern:

We now demand from the new age a new system of law. . . .
Whoever encroaches upon this right of personality is commit-
ting a brutal act of violence. . . . This right of mine has been
violated; my only recourse is to use my freedom of speech! My
matter speaks for itself; it is its own advocate. But it is not my
matter alone.[99]

A "new age," with new political and social conditions and public forums, made it possible to speak of the personal experience of suffering
as an experience of injustice. It became clear that this experience could
be generalized and could be understood by many others as such. From
the outset, conditions of marriage had been characterized as especially
problematic and in need of change. Louise Dittmar's harsh criticism of
the "marriage of convenience" or the "essence of marriage" is an example of this. She criticized its significance on the basis of her insight
into the social context:

A lot of relationships are being shaken in recent times; a lot of
injustice eliminated; a lot of nonsense and convention done
away with. . . . [But conditions of marriage carry the] brand of
slavery. . . . In its political relationships, marriage corresponds
to the representative system, . . . since the man embodies
virtually all authority, since he is the representative of political
sovereignty, the absolute monarchy, the unrestricted government. . . . The political status of the man in contrast to the
woman is that of the patrician to the plebeian, of the freeman
to the slave.[100]

Nevertheless, such radical critiques were rare at first. Louise Dittmar
and Louise Aston were pioneers of an emancipation movement, but the
middle- and working-class women's movements were unable to create
public interest in such emancipation until social and political conditions changed once again in the late nineteenth century. In Germany,
while the internal trigger for women was the experience of injustice in
everyday married life, the external impetus for a discourse on rights
among women was the codification of the German Civil Code in 1900,
after a prolonged discussion that began following the founding of the
German Empire in 1871.[101]

> Full legal capacity and civic equality are necessary for wives and
> mothers, not only out of personal interest, for the sake of their
> own human dignity, but also in the interests of the family, in
> the interests of the state, . . . in the interests of all new social
> obligations and all tasks for the common good that today's
> woman must perform, which she can only fulfill as a free
> person, in consciousness of her full human responsibility. . . .
> What a contradiction it is to refer again and again to her so-
> called destiny, her vocation as mother and her purpose for the
> species. . . and then for her to be so shamefully low in society's
> estimation, precisely in this vocation.[102]

The legal struggles and mass protests of the women's movement in much
of the Western world were directed against matrimonial and family laws
that were anachronistic and patriarchal and against the double standard according to which prostitution, for example, was tolerated by the
state and only the women were prosecuted. Indignation over this
"boundless injustice" sparked the international movement of abolition-
ists, led by Josephine Butler.[103] They mobilized against state regulation
of prostitution and, like many other campaigns of the morality movement, made sexual violence in gender relations the focus of their critique of society.[104] The struggle for legal capacity in marriage (unmarried
women essentially had equal rights under the new Civil Code) was
largely unsuccessful—especially as the Civil Code's matrimonial and
family laws remained unchanged even after the attainment of equal citizenship rights, thus undermining women's capacity to act in political
and civil matters. Not until 1977 were full equal rights formally guaranteed in West German matrimonial law.

SOCIAL RIGHTS AND VIOLENCE

In the late nineteenth and early twentieth centuries the women's movement made an important contribution, through all its endeavors and
areas of concern, to the discussion and resolution of social problems,
though this has gone largely unnoticed in the history of the welfare
states. Like the labor movement, the women's movement helped lay
the groundwork for state welfare and social policies. Under the motto
of "a policy of organized motherliness,"[105] it organized a variety of
sociopolitical projects even before social security rights were achieved,

making a decisive contribution to social reform and, in particular, to the professionalization of social work.[106] This served to create the institutions and professions of community and welfare activities, which today make up the "social," caring side of the welfare state, the social services that are an indispensable component of the welfare state, beyond transfer payments and public benefits.

Several important examples of self-help projects and achievements are the establishment of employment agencies, vocational counseling, and legal aid offices, where movement activists provided other women free of charge with advice and support in legal matters and disputes. The movement for moral reforms was led primarily by radical middle-class women; the proletarian women's movement agitated for equal pay for equal work, extended maternity rights, and protective labor legislation for women. Aside from these movements, the bourgeois women's movement enjoyed its greatest success in the area of education and training, especially since its emphasis on gender differences enabled it to explain women's special contribution to culture as "a politics of difference."[107] In fact, access to higher education for girls, to university study, and to special women's professions was a prerequisite for social participation, self-determined action, and the development of female individuality. Thomas H. Marshall, in his broad conception of social rights, described the right to education as "a genuine social right of citizenship," and as a "necessary prerequisite of civil freedom."[108]

The modern women's movement essentially took up the issues left unresolved by the earlier movement. On the basis of formally recognized equal rights, the newer movement was able to articulate, more clearly and confidently than the previous generation could, the deeper experiences of injustice concealed within the private sphere—the persistent sore spot in gender relations. These private injustices—domestic violence in particular—were articulated in so-called consciousness-raising groups. The German term for such "self-experience" groups, *Selbsterfahrungsgruppen*, underlines the significance that sharing experiences may have for the individual and collective learning process. Their central demands were no longer "simply" equal rights; instead they called for private and political autonomy. This included, in particular, bodily autonomy and exposure of the many scandalous forms of violence against women that are protected because they take place in the private

sphere. Violence against women was recognized not only as direct physical violence, but also as structural violence. The exclusion of private
experience from the legal domain, and thus from the protection of the
law, was again called into question. This was more than an effort to
assure protection from violence and secure women's quality of life; it
was and is about the extension of political agency. In a broad sense, it
is about empowering women. In the concept of citizenship rights, this
space for women to act is viewed as an ensemble of political, civil, and
social rights, marking the point of departure for an international feminist legal critique that has found a political platform in the international
"Women's Rights are Human Rights" campaign.

The International "Women's Rights are Human Rights" Campaign: Summary and Prospects

But how, in view of gender as well as cultural differences, can agreement be reached on the validity of universal human rights? And how
can the extent of suffering and human rights violations that has gone
undocumented thus far, especially as experienced by women, become a
subject of public discussion, when at the same time the victims are prevented from speaking, lack information about human rights, and are
unable to express their experiences as injustice? Human rights cannot
be imported or prescribed; they apply only if the people involved are
in a position to claim or defend them as rights.

A summary of the theoretical as well as the historical, empirical
evidence indicates that women's elementary experiences of injustice are
difficult to perceive and discuss as human rights violations largely because the neglect, legal incapacitation, and degradation of women, the
violation of their physical integrity, and the failure to recognize them
as equals or holders of rights in almost all cultures are accepted aspects
of gender arrangements, and thus of women's role. Cultural traditions,
customs, and everyday routines often lend legal legitimacy to the very
violence of these relationships. There is obvious common ground among
the different sufferings and injustices women experience. Women's vul-
nerability generally derives from their gender role, their ability to bear
children, and the "invisible" work they perform in the family. Yet this
private, unlegislated sphere is so firmly rooted in historic traditions and

cultural characteristics that violations, discrimination, and restricted living conditions cannot even be discussed, let alone added to the canon
of fundamental violations of rights, unless conditions change. It is not
merely a characteristic of Western civilization, but a fundamental element of the structure of all patriarchal societies, that subordination, legal
incapacity, obedience, a hierarchical division of labor, and the authoritarian nature of sexual relations are the substance and core of the traditional role assigned to women. Claiming rights in this situation is often
not only next to impossible, it also contradicts the internalization of
these roles and the image of women's identity. Consequently, the women
involved often feel they are imperiling their human relationships, since
the structure of these relations are so firmly entrenched in their everyday lives and thus in routines, religious rules, or cultural traditions.

From an intercultural and international perspective, the unique aspect of human rights violations against women lies in the fact that they
often take place in the nonpublic, intimate, private sphere of the family, where they are tolerated and go unpunished, and thus are not subject to public law or protection by the state. The systematic separation
of public from private law is therefore again one of the main obstacles
to the safeguarding of human rights for women.

The international campaign for the worldwide recognition of
women's rights as human rights has specifically addressed this problem,
with a twofold aim. On the one hand, it has adopted feminist criticism
of the androcentrism of positive law and human rights, and criticizes
the inadequacy of human rights protections for women. On the other
hand, it not only claims the universality of human rights, but aims to
expand them, "redefining" them with respect to women's specific concerns.[109] The dimensions of feminist legal criticism thus become even
more clearly evident: (1) the "maleness" or androcentrism of the definitions of crimes and of human rights; (2) the dialectic of equality as a
universal human right versus consideration and recognition of gender-
specific differences; and finally, (3) the distinction between public and
private law, which is problematic for the protection of women's rights.
The vehement defense of protection of the family and of religiously and
culturally rooted family law as a state task, even a state interest, proves an
additional barrier, especially for international human rights protections
targeted at states and their institutions. Nor has the common hierarchy

of human rights by "generation" offered any helpful points of reference for women's rights discourse. Women in the Southern Hemisphere, in particular, have rejected this way of prioritizing rights—political and civil rights as the first generation, followed by economic, social, and cultural rights, and finally by the third generation of collective or group rights, such as the rights to development, a livable environment, and peace.[110] Linking women's rights to the so-called third generation rights, as group rights, has been shown to be a trap, since international development policies, as well as women's participation in nationalist movements and in the decolonization process, have tended to support male economic dominance at the expense of women's interests.[111]

The United Nations and its committees have not yet proven the best defenders of women's rights. Nor have the achievements of existing human rights agencies created under the United Nations charter been very positive in protecting women.[112] The United Nations has had a Commission on the Status of Women since 1947—an official, political agency that drafts all conventions dealing specifically with women and initiated a procedure for the protection of the human rights of women in 1983. In 1979, the United Nations adopted the Convention on the Elimination of All Forms of Discrimination against Women (CEDAW).[113] CEDAW went into force in 1981 and has since been ratified by sixteen countries, though over eighty of them registered serious reservations, especially regarding marriage and family rights. Feminist critics have pointed out that the approach to discrimination taken in this convention is also based on male standards; that is, equal rights are defined as equal status in the public sphere ("The States Parties to the present Convention . . . Have agreed on the following" "To establish legal protection of the rights of women on an equal basis with men . . . " Pt. I, Art. 2c.) On the other hand, there is danger that separating out rights specific to women from the general human rights committees and issues could again lead to the marginalization of women's claims. Finally, far too few women who could exercise influence have been represented up to now on the various committees. Not until 1993 was "gender-specific violence [defined] as discrimination against women" in a supplemental protocol, referring to the special significance of oppression in the private sphere.[114]

Nevertheless, owing not least to international public discussion by women, a movement for the human rights of women has emerged amidst human rights theories and political practice. It is not led by women from the Northern Hemisphere; quite the contrary. The development of publicity and discussion by women at the international level was decisive and was furthered by the United Nations Decade of the Woman, from 1975 to 1985, which led to change, or at least to increased attention to women, in development policies. Several World Conferences on Women have taken place since 1975 under the auspices of the United Nations, at which unofficial forums organized by nongovernmental organizations (NGOs) have helped create a new global public concerned with women's issues.[115] In addition to the resources that the United Nations has made available in preparation for the Conferences, a mobilization network of local and national organizations and projects has formed to discuss and prepare the topics and issues of dispute. These projects and activists have freed the human rights campaign from suspicions that it is a manifestation of elitist or Western feminism. Like the 1985 World Conference on Women in Nairobi, they have demonstrated the strength and self-confidence of women from other parts of the world.[116] A decisive step for women from non-Western cultures in demanding human rights was, however, that they themselves began to define the substance and meaning of their cultures, using their own experience and legal systems to confront patriarchal practices and interpretations.[117]

In addition, the subject of women's human rights has been deliberately placed on the agenda of United Nations conferences by various organizations since 1991. This effort has been assisted by systematic documentation of human rights violations against women throughout the world, and through the organization of a women's tribunal in conjunction with the 1993 human rights conference in Vienna, supported by hundreds of thousands of signatures from more than 120 countries. The main subject, and the point on the agenda that brought together all experiences of injustice at the Vienna conference, was "violence against women." Thus the Fourth World Conference on Women in 1995 in Beijing included the following statement in its Declaration and Platform for Action:

> Violence against women both violates and impairs or nullifies
> the enjoyment by women of human rights and fundamental
> freedoms. Taking into account the Declaration on the Elimina-
> tion of Violence against Women and the work of Special
> Rapporteurs, gender-based violence, such as battering and other
> domestic violence, sexual abuse, sexual slavery and exploita-
> tion, and international trafficking in women and children, . . .
> [etc.] are incompatible with the dignity and the worth of the
> human person and must be combated and eliminated.[118]

The driving force of the human rights campaign, "putting these issues squarely on the world's doorstep," is therefore a dynamic and participatory concept of human rights that must still prove itself workable, especially in view of cultural differences.[119] The goal remains the elimination of androcentric assumptions, a redefinition of human rights, and the introduction of the specific experiences of women to the practical discourse on human rights, without once again separating out and isolating questions of women's rights. Those concerned are well aware of the many questions that remain unanswered and of how little human rights have so far changed in practice. Yet the history and range of this feminist discourse on human rights are unique in international law. They are political issues that demand attention in their own right.

Notes

Foreword

1. Joan Scott, *Only Paradoxes to Offer: French Feminists and the Rights of Man* (Cambridge: Harvard University Press, 1996), 3.

Introduction

1. Iris Young, *Justice and the Politics of Difference.* (Princeton, N.J.: Princeton University Press, 1990), 25.

Chapter 1   *The Meaning of Equality with Regard to Difference*

On the following, see also Otto Dann, *Gleichheit und Gleichberechtigung* (Berlin: Duncker & Humblot, 1980), 16ff., and Konrad Hesse, "Der Gleichheitsgrundsatz im Staatsrecht," in *Archive des öffentlichen Rechts* 77 (1951–1952): 172.

1. See Wilhelm Windelband, *Über Gleichheit und Identität* (Heidelberg: Winter, 1910).
2. Aristotle, "Ethica Nicomachea," trans. W. Ross (London: Oxford University Press, 1972), book 13, 1131a–b; cited in Catherine MacKinnon, *Towards a Feminist Theory of the State* (Cambridge: Harvard University Press, 1989), 225. See also Gerhard Leibholz, "Die Gleichheit vor dem Gesetz und das Bonner Grundgesetz," in *Deutsches Verwaltungsblatt* (1951): 195; and Günter Beitzke, "Gleichheit von Mann und Frau," in *Die Grundrechte*, ed. Franz L. Neumann, Hans C. Nipperdey, and Ulrich Scheuner (Berlin: Duncker & Humblot, 1954), 2:208.
3. Windelband, *Gleichheit und Identität*, 9.
4. Gustav Radbruch, *Rechtsphilosophie*, 4th ed. (Stuttgart: Koehler, 1950), 126, 129.
5. *Verhandlungen des Deutschen Juristentages in Frankfurt/Main 1950* (Tübingen: Mohr 1951), 38:5.
6. *BverfGE* (Bundesverrtassungsgericht-Entscheidenung, Decision of the Federal Constitutional Court), 10: 59f.; see also, in greater depth, Ines Reich-Hilweg, *Männer und Frauen sind gleichberechtigt* (Frankfurt/Main: Europäische Verlags-Anstalt, 1979); for a critical view, see Hans D. Jarass and Bodo Pieroth, *Grundgesetz-Kommentar* (Munich: Beck, 1989), on Art. 3, marginal no. 46.
7. See Günter Beitzke, *Familienrecht*, 19th ed. (Munich: Beck, 1977), 5. Though

many had abandoned such ideas by this time, Beitzke still supported them, even as late as 1977.

8. Theodor Maunz, Günter Dürig, and Roman Herzog, *Grundgesetz Kommentar*, (Munich: Beck, 1996), note on Art. 3 II, marginal no. 11, emphasis in original; on this point, see especially Günter Dürig, Art. 3 II GG, from a constitutional law standpoint, in *Fam RZ* (1954), 2–5, according to which the "succinct sentence 'men and women have equal rights' can be read, based on its substantive content, as 'women have equal rights with men.'"

9. See Hildegard Krüger, in Hildegard Krüger, Ernst Breetzke, and Kuno Nowak, *Gleichberechtigungsgesetz. Kommentar* (Munich: Beck, 1958), E. marginal no. 21.

10. Maunz, Dürig, and Herzog, *Grundgesetz Kommentar*, Art. 3 I, marginal no. 3.

11. See also Ernst Benda, *Rechtsgutachten zur Gleichstellung der Frau im öffentlichen Dienst* (Freiburg: Institut für öffentliches Recht, 1986), 153.

12. Hesse, "Gleichheitsgrundsatz," 177, emphasis in original.

13. Karl Marx, *Capital*, trans. Samuel Moore and Edward Aveling, ed. Friedrich Engels, vol. 1, part 6: Wages, ch. 19: "The transformation of the value (and respective price) of labour-power into wages" (para. 13) (1867; Moscow: Progress Publishers, 1887); accessed via the Internet.

14. Karl Marx, "Critique of the Gotha Program" (Karl Marx's Marginal Notes to the Program of the German Workers Party, part one), in *The Marx-Engels Reader*, ed. Robert C. Tucker, 2nd ed. (London: W. W. Norton, 1978), 525–541; here, 530; emphasis in original.

15. On this, in detail, see Ute Gerhard, *Verhältnisse und Verhinderungen. Frauenarbeit, Familie und Rechte der Frauen im 19. Jahrhundert* (Frankfurt/Main: Suhrkamp, 1978), 13f., 180f. On Marxist legal theory, I refer specifically to Oskar Negt, "Thesen zur marxistischen Rechtstheorie," in *Kritische Justiz* (1973), 1–19; Lelio Basso, "Die Rolle des Rechts in der Phase des Übergangs zum Sozialismus," in *Kritische Justiz* (1973), 239–263; and Wolf Rosenbaum, "Zum Rechtsbegriff bei Stucka und Pasukanis," in *Kritische Justiz* (1971), 148–165; see also Hubert Rottleuthner, ed., *Probleme der marxistischen Rechtstheorie* (Frankfurt/Main: Suhrkamp, 1975).

Chapter 2　**In the Footsteps of the Philosophers**

1. Ernst Bloch, *Natural Law and Human Dignity*, trans. Dennis T. Schmidt (Cambridge: MIT Press, 1987), 184.

2. Karl Larenz, *Methodenlehre der Rechtswissenschaft*, 5th ed. (Berlin: Springer, 1983), 183f., here, 187.

3. These are only a sampling of the large number of studies of history, theory of the state, and political science written from a feminist perspective. Despite different foci and hypotheses, all of them reinterpret, fundamentally question, and reveal the androcentrism in the great philosophies, democratic theories, and heritage of the Enlightenment. See, for example, Seyla Benhabib and Linda J. Nicholson, "Politische Philosophie und die Frauenfrage," chapter 12, in Iring Fetscher and Herfried Münkler, eds., *Pipers Handbuch der politischen Ideen* (Munich: Piper, 1987); Heidemarie Bennent, *Galanterie und Verachtung* (Frankfurt: Campus, 1985); Evelyn Fox Keller, *Reflections on Gender and -Science* (New Haven, Conn.: Yale University Press, 1985); Ursula Pia Jauch, *Immanuel Kant zur Geschlechterdifferenz* (Vienna: Passagen, 1988); Genevieve Lloyd, *The Man of Reason: "Male" and "Female" in Western Philosophy* (London: Methuen, 1984); Lieselotte Steinbrügge, *Das moralische Geschlecht* (Weinheim:

Beltz, 1987); see also Elisabeth List and Herlinde Studer, eds., *Denkverhältnisse. Feminismus und Kritik* (Frankfurt/Main: Suhrkamp, 1989). The fact that these fundamental works of feminist critique of scholarship and ideology were published almost simultaneously is astounding. They were evidently long overdue.

4. On the following, see in particular, Ernst Bloch, *Antike Philosophie. Leipziger Vorlesungen zur Geschichte der Philosophie*, vol. 1 (Frankfurt/Main: Suhrkamp, 1985); and Otto Dann, *Gleichheit und Gleichberechtigung. Das Gleichheitspostulat in der alteuropäischen Tradition und in Deutschland bis zum ausgehenden 19. Jahrhundert* (Berlin: Duncker and Humblot, 1980).

5. Bloch, *Antike Philosophie*, 108.

6. See Benhabib and Nicholson, "Politische Philosophie," 522; for an extensive discussion of Plato and Aristotle, see Susan Moller Okin, *Women in Western Political Thought* (Princeton, N.J.: Princeton University Press, 1979), 15ff., and Jean Bethke Elshtain, *Public Man, Private Woman* (Princeton, N.J.: Princeton University Press, 1981), 19ff.

7. See Johann Jakob Bachofen, *Das Mutterrecht* (1861; Frankfurt/Main: Suhrkamp, 1975); on this, see Uwe Wesel, *Der Mythos vom Matriarchat* (Frankfurt/Main: Suhrkamp, 1981).

8. All quotes taken from Sophocles, *The Theban Plays*, trans. E. F. Watling, reprint (Harmondsworth, Middlesex, U.K.: Penguin Books, 1987): *Antigone*, 126–162, here, 128 and 138.

9. Erik Wolf, "Profanes Naturrecht," in *RGG* (*Reichsgrundgesetz*, Reich Basic Law), (Tübingen: Mohr, 1960), 4:1351.

10. Georg Wilhelm Friedrich Hegel, *Hegel's Philosophy of Right*, trans. with notes by T. M. Knox (London: Oxford University Press, 1978), § 166:114–115.

11. Bachofen, *Mutterrecht*.

12. Bloch, *Natural Law*, 113–114.

13. *Hegel's Philosophy of Right*, § 166: 115.

14. Sophocles, *The Theban Plays*, *Antigone*, 140, 144.

15. Cited from the German translation: Rossana Rossanda, *Einmischung* (Frankfurt/Main: Suhrkamp, 1980), 173; original: Rossana Rossanda, *La altre. Conversazioni a Radiotre sui rapporti tra donne e politica, libertà fraternità, uguaglianza, democrazia, fasicismo, resistenza, stato, partito, rivouzione, femminismo* (Milano: Casa editrice Valentino Bompaini, 1979).

16. See Seneca, "On Consolation," in *Moral Essays*, vol. 2, trans. John W. Basore (Cambridge: Harvard University Press, 1935): "But who has asserted that Nature has dealt grudgingly with women's natures and has narrowly restricted their virtues? Believe me, they have just as much force, just as much capacity, if they like, for virtuous action."

17. Galatians 3:28.

18. See, especially, Gerda Weiler, *Ich verwerfe im Lande die Kriege* (Munich: Frauenoffensive, 1984); see also Heide Göttner-Abendroth, *Die Göttin und ihr Heros* (Munich: Frauenoffensive, 1980) and Hanna Wolff, *Jesus der Mann*, 4th ed. (Stuttgart: Radius, 1979).

19. Leonore Siegele-Wenschkewitz, "Feministische Theologie ohne Judaismus," in Leonore Siegele-Wenschkewitz, ed., *Verdrängte Vergangenheit, die uns bedrängt* (Munich: Kaiser, 1988), 12–53, here, 25f. There are a number of other essays in the same volume that are worthwhile reading, by Marie-Theres Wacker, "Matriarchale Bibelkritik—ein antijudaistisches Konzept?," 181–242, and Luise Schottroff, "Die große Liebende und der Pharisäer Simon," 147–163. See also Bernadette J. Brooten, *Women Leaders in the Ancient Synagogue:*

Inscriptional Evidence and Background Issues (Chico, Calif.: Scholars Press, 1982); Elisabeth Schüssler Fiorenza, *Bread Not Stone: The Challenge of Feminist Bible Interpretation* (Boston: Beacon Press, 1984).

20. See also Josephine Butler, "Christus der gefährliche Gleichmacher" (1869), in *Frau und Religion*, ed. Elisabeth Moltmann-Wendel (Frankfurt/Main: Fischer, 1983), 52–55.

21. 1 Corinthians 14:34.

22. Elisabeth Moltmann-Wendel, *Das Land, wo Milch und Honig fließt* (Gütersloh: Gütersloher Verlags-haus, 1985), 90.

23. St. Ambrose (Super I Cor. 2) and St. Augustine (Quest. Vet. et Nov. Test. Qu. 106), quoted in Robert Bartsch, *Die Rechtsstellung der Frau als Gattin und Mutter* (Leipzig: Veit, 1903), 50.

24. St. Thomas Aquinas, *Summa Theologica*, ed. and trans. Fathers of the English Dominican Province (Hampshire, U.K.: Eyre and Spottiswoode, 1947), part 1, qu. 92, objection 1.

25. Bartsch, *Die Rechtsstellung der Frau*, 50, 55; see also Marianne Weber, *Ehefrau und Mutter in der Rechtsentwicklung* (Aalen: Scientia, 1971; reprint of Tübingen: Mohr, 1907), 207.

26. Claudia Honegger, ed., *Die Hexen der Neuzeit. Studien zur Sozialgeschichte eines kulturellen Deutungsmusters* (Frankfurt/Main: Suhrkamp, 1978), 56.

27. Bloch, *Antike Philosophie*, 474.

28. Elisabeth Moltmann-Wendel, *Ein eigener Mensch werden. Frauen um Jesus* (Gütersloh: Gütersloher Verlagshaus, 1980), 15; and Elisabeth Moltmann-Wendel, *Das Land, wo Milch und Honig fließt*, 89f. See also Rosemary Radford Ruether, ed. *Religion and Sexism. Images of Women in the Jewish and Christian Tradition* (New York: Simon and Schuster, 1974); and Luise Schottroff and Marie-Theres Wacker, eds., *Kompendium, Feministische Bibelauslegung* (Gütersloh: Kaiser, 1998).

29. Moltmann-Wendel, *Ein eigener Mensch werden. Frauen um Jesus.*

30. See Edith Ennen, *Frauen im Mittelalter* (Munich: Beck, 1984), 110f.; Honegger, *Die Hexen der Neuzeit*, 45f.; Moltmann-Wendel, *Ein eigener Mensch werden*, 36f.; the entry "Frau" in *Religion in Geschichte und Gegenwart* 2: IIIa and IIIb.

31. See also Malwida von Meysenburg, *Memoiren einer Idealistin*, 3 vols. (Leipzig: Schuster & Loeffler, 1875); Weber, *Ehefrau und Mutter*, 211; Emma Oekinghaus, *Die gesellschaftliche und rechtliche Stellung der deutschen Frau* (Jena: G. Fischer, 1925), 10f.; see also Dann, *Gleichheit und Gleichberechtigung*, 121f.

32. On the United States and the influence of the Quakers on the organization of the women's movement, see Eleanor Flexner, *Century of Struggle*, rev. ed. (Cambridge: Harvard University Press, 1975). This corresponds in Germany to the exceptional involvement of women in the so-called Freie Gemeinde (free congregations) in the 1848 revolution; see Catherine M. Prelinger, "Religious Dissent: Women's Rights and the Hamburger Hochschule für das weirbliche Geschlecht in Mid-Nineteenth-Century Germany," *Church History* 45 (March 1976): 42–45; and Sylvia Paletschek, *Frauen und Dissens. Frauen im Deutschkatholizismus und in den freien Gemeinden 1841–1852* (Göttingen: Vandenhoeck & Ruprecht, 1990).

33. Louise Otto, in Ute Gerhard, Elisabeth Hannover-Drück, and Romina Schmitter, eds., *"Dem Reich der Freiheit werb' ich Bürgerinnen." Die Frauenzeitung von Louise Otto* (Frankfurt/Main: Syndikat, 1979), 106; hereafter cited as *Die Frauen-Zeitung.*

34. Hedwig Dohm, *Was die Pastoren denken* (Berlin: Schlingmann, 1872).

35. Elisabeth Malo, "Eine Anfrage an die Herren Theologen Deutschlands aus den Kreisen christlich gebildeter Frauen" (1891), in *Frau und Religion*, Moltmann-Wendel, 87–98, here, 87f.

36. Erik Wolf, *Große Rechtsdenker der deutschen Geistesgeschichte* (Tübingen: Mohr, 1963), 396; see also the homage to the "German scholar without misery" in Bloch, *Natural Law*, appendix, 281–316.

37. Friedrich von Spee, *Cautio Criminalis oder rechtliches Bedenken wegen der Hexenprozesse* (1631; Munich: Deutscher Taschenbuch Verlag, 1982).

38. [Christian Thomasius], *Über die Hexenprozesse*, ed. Rolf Lieberwirth (Weimar: Böhlau, 1967), 109; see also Bloch, *Natural Law*, 306ff.

39. See, for example, Franz Wieacker, *Privatrechtsgeschichte der Neuzeit* (Göttingen: Vandenhoeck & Ruprecht, 1967), 314, arguing that: "Thomasius's empiricism" enriched the law of reason "with practical ethical experience and postulates while dangerously weakening its philosophical substance."

40. See Keller, *Reflections on Gender and Science*, 37–39, citing Francis Bacon, *The Masculine Birth of Time* (*Temporis Partus Masculus*), trans. Benjamin Farrington, *Centaurus* (1951): 1.

41. See Honegger, *Hexen der Neuzeit*, 136.

42. See especially Keller, *Reflections on Gender and Science*, part one, chapters 1–2: 21–42; here, 7, 36, 38–39. Words in brackets are from Keller.

43. Max Horkheimer and Theodor W. Adorno, *Dialectic of Enlightenment*, trans. John Cumming (published in German, 1944; New York: Continuum, 1972), 4.

44. In this context, I shall not even attempt to outline them, since research on legal history displays gaps on the issue of women's rights. See also chapter 7 in this book; and Ute Gerhard, ed., *Frauen in der Geschichte des Rechts von der Frühen Neuzeit bis zur Gegenwart*, (Munich: Beck, 1997). For the best overviews available to date, see Bartsch, *Rechtsstellung der Frau* (1903); Manfred Erle, *Die Ehe im Naturrecht des 17. Jahrhunderts*, university dissertation (Göttingen, 1952); and, once again, Weber, *Ehefrau und Mutter*.

45. See Hermann Conrad, *Deutsche Rechtsgeschichte 2*: "Neuzeit bis 1806" (Karlsruhe: Müller, 1966), 377.

46. Also on the following, see Wieacker, *Privatrechtsgeschichte*, 249ff., and Erik Wolf, "Naturrecht," in *RGG* (1960), 4:1353.

47. Wieacker, *Privatrechtsgeschichte*, 268.

48. Hugo Grotius, "On the Law of War and Peace," in Edward Dumbauld, *Life and Legal Writings of Hugo Grotius* (Norman: University of Oklahoma Press, 1969), 57–82, here, 62; originally published as *De jure belli ac pacis* (Paris: Buon, 1625).

49. Thomas Hobbes, *Leviathan*, ed. C. B. Macpherson (Harmondsworth, Middlesex, U.K.: Penguin Books, 1968), 185.

50. John Locke, *Two Treatises of Government*, II § 123–124 (1690; London: Cambridge University Press, 1970), 368–369.

51. Ibid., chapters 4–6 (§ 22–76): 301–336.

52. Christian Wolff, *Grundsätze des Natur-und Völckerrechts* (Halle, 1754; Hildesheim: Olms, 1980), part 1, § 70 (emphasis added); on this general subject, in detail, see Dann, *Gleichheit und Gleichberechtigung*, 93ff.

53. See Steinbrügge, *Das moralische Geschlecht*, 38, 121.

54. See Carole Pateman, *The Sexual Contract* (Stanford, Calif.: Stanford University Press, 1988).

55. See Erle, *Die Ehe im Naturrecht*, 28f. (esp. 31, 48); and Wieacker, *Privatrechtsgeschichte*, 297.

56. Locke, *Two Treatises*, I § 49: 194.
57. Ibid., II § 82: 339.
58. See Erle, *Die Ehe im Naturrecht*, 141f., 270.
59. Ibid., 244f.
60. Christian Thomasius, *Von der Kunst Vernünfftig und Tugenhafft zu lieben. Als einzigem Mittel zu einem glückseligen, galanten und vergnügten Leben zu gelangen, Oder Einleitung zur Sitten Lehre* (1692; reprint, Hildesheim: Olms, 1968), 357; see also Werner Schneiders, *Naturrecht und Liebesethik* (Hildesheim: Olms, 1971), 143ff.
61. See Thomas Hobbes, *De Cive* (The Citizen) [1651], dedication and preface, "Man to Man is an arrant Wolfe" (homo homini lupus).
62. See Bloch, *Natural Law*, 300–302. I have not yet been able to confirm Erle's claim that Thomasius took a decisive step backward in a later work, *Fundamenta*. There he supposedly justified the subordination of the wife to her husband's authority on the basis not of law but of ethics and what is considered proper. On this point, Wieacker's (*Privatrechtsgeschichte*, 316) complaint of Thomasius's "empiricism" and his "radical separation of law and morality" might have been cause for confusion. Erle at least conceded that Thomasius did not change his views regarding the rights of women.
63. On the history leading up to Prussia's General Code (Allgemeines Landrecht, ALR), see Reinhart Koselleck, *Preußen zwischen Reform und Revolution* (Stuttgart: Klett-Cotta, 1975); on the legal status of women in the General Code, see Ute Gerhard, *Verhältnisse und Verhinderungen. Frauenarbeit, Familie und Rechte der Frauen im 19. Jahrhundert* (Frankfurt/Main: Suhrkamp, 1978), 154ff.
64. Christian Wolff, *Grundsätze des Natur- und Völckerrechts* (1754), part 3, § 870.
65. Ibid., § 856.
66. Weber, *Ehefrau und Mutter*, 297.
67. Poulain de LaBarre, *De l'égalité des deux sexes: discours physique et moral; où l'on voit l'importance de se défaire des préjugez* (Paris: du Puis, 1690); see also Poulain de LaBarre, *The Equality of the Two Sexes*, trans. with an introduction by A. Daniel Frankforter, *Studies in the History of Philosophy* 11 (Lewiston, N.Y.: Mellen, 1989).
68. Steinbrügge, *Das moralische Geschlecht*, 105; see also Heidemarie Bennent, *Galanterie und Verachtung. Eine philosophiegeschichtliche Untersuchung zur Stellung der Frau in der Gesellschaft und Kultur* (Frankfurt/Main; Campus, 1985), 46ff.; and Inge Baxmann, "Von der Egalité im Salon zur Citoyenne—einige Aspekte der Genese des Bürgerlichen Frauenbildes," in *Frauen in der Geschichte*, ed. Annette Kuhn and Jörn Rüsen (Düsseldorf: Schwann, 1983), 3:109–137; on Rousseau and against the feminist repression hypothesis, see esp. Christine Garbe, "Sophie oder die heimliche Macht der Frauen. Zur Konzeption des Weiblichen bei Jean-Jacques Rousseau," in *Frauen in der Geschichte*, ed. Ilse Brehmer, J. Jacobi-Dittrich, and E. Kleinau et al., (Düsseldorf: Schwann, 1983), 4:65–87.
69. Claudia Honegger, "Weibliche Selbstreflexion um 1800," *Feministische Studien* 2 (1989): 3–22; and Claudia Honegger, *Die Ordnung der Geschlechter. Die Wissenschaften vom Menschen und das Weib, 1550–1859* (Frankfurt/Main: Campus, 1991).
70. See, for example, Karin Hausen, "Die Polarisierung der 'Geschlechtscharaktere'—Eine Spiegelung der Dissoziation von Erwerbs- und Familienleben," in *Sozialgeschichte der Familie in der Neuzeit Europas*, ed. Werner Conze (Stuttgart: Klett-Cotta, 1976), 363–393; see also Ute Frevert, *Frauen-*

Geschichte: zwischen bürgerlicher Verbesserung und neuer Weiblichkeit (Frankfurt/Main: Suhrkamp, 1986); and on studies on the social history of the family, see for example: Heidi Rosenbaum, ed., *Familie und Gesellschaftsstruktur* (Frankfurt/Main: Suhrkamp, 1978).

71. Crawford B. Macpherson, *The Political Theory of Possessive Individualism: Hobbes to Locke* (Oxford: Clarendon Press, 1962). In any case Macpherson indicated (125–126, and 296, n. 1) that the right to vote demanded by the Levellers in the English Civil War in the seventeenth century clearly referred only to male suffrage and that even the "Petition of Women" of 5 May 1649 merely demanded civil rights protection in the sense of relief from arbitrary legal proceedings, as guaranteed in the Habeas Corpus Act of 1679; equal political rights were not demanded. On this, see also Dann, *Gleichheit und Gleichberechtigung*, 107f.

72. At least with respect to a marriage contract, according to the natural law theory women were explicitly viewed as equals and thus as eligible to enter into a contract. But the conclusion of that contract marked the end of their legal competence.

73. This is evidently treated so much as a matter of course that even John Rawls, referring to these theories as an example of individuals in their natural state, spoke of "heads of families"; see John Rawls, *A Theory of Justice* (London: Oxford University Press, 1971), 128.

74. Macpherson, *The Political Theory of Possessive Individualism*, 3, 264.

75. Locke, *Two Treatises*, II § 79: 337–338, and § 87: 341–342.

76. Macpherson, *The Political Theory of Possessive Individualism*, 3, 263.

77. Locke, *Two Treatises*, II § 85: 340–341.

78. On this context in general, see Otto Brunner, "Das 'Ganze Haus' und die alteuropäische Ökonomik," in *Familie und Gesellschaft*, ed. Ferdinand Oeter (Tübingen: Mohr, 1966).

79. Locke, *Two Treatises*, II § 86: 341.

80. Cited in Koselleck, *Preußen zwischen Reform und Revolution*, 54, on the context in general, see 52f.; see also Gerhard, *Verhältnisse und Verhinderungen*, 81f.

81. Locke, *Two Treatises*, II § 86: 341.

82. Jürgen Habermas, *Structural Transformation of the Public Sphere: An Inquiry into a Category of Bourgeois Society*, Studies in Contemporary German Social Thought (Cambridge: MIT Press, 1991), 27.

83. Adolf von Knigge, *Über den Umgang mit Menschen*, 1st ed. (Hannover: Schmidt, 1788), 1:196.

84. Cf. Jean-Jacques Rousseau, *Emile*, trans. Barbara Foxley (London: J. M. Dent & Sons, 1911; reprint, 1963), 322.

85. See Ursula Floßmann, "Die Gleichberechtigung der Geschlechter in der Privatrechtsgeschichte," in *Rechtsgeschichte und Rechtsdogmatik*, ed. U. Floßmann (Vienna: Springer, 1977), 119–144, here, 131; and Christina Damm, "Die Stellung der Ehefrau und Mutter nach Urteilen des Reichsgerichts von 1879 – 1914" (Ph.D. dissertation, Marburg, 1983), 32; on gender tutelage and its significance, see also chapter 7 of this book.

86. Dorothea Christina Leporin, *Gründliche Untersuchung der Ursachen, die das weibliche Geschlecht vom Studieren abhalten* (1742; reprint, Hildesheim: Olms, 1975), 22.

87. Adalbert von Hanstein, *Die Frauen in der Geschichte des deutschen Geisteslebens des 18. und 19. Jahrhunderts* (Leipzig: Freund & Wittig, 1899), 1:173f, here, 174.

88. Johann Gottlieb Fichte, *The Science of Rights*, trans. A. E. Kroeger (New York: Harper and Row, 1970), 133.
89. Ibid., 441.
90. Ibid., 133.
91. Ibid., 393–401.
92. Ibid., 10.
93. Ibid., 402.
94. Ibid., 76–78.
95. Ibid., 441.
96. Ibid., 392.
97. Kurt Nowak, *Schleiermacher und die Frühromantik* (Weimar: Böhlau, 1986), 284.
98. Fichte, *The Science of Rights*, 435.
99. Ibid., 403.
100. Ibid., 393, 397, 398.
101. Especially in Aristotle, see Okin, *Women in Western Political Thought*, 82.
102. Iring Fetscher, *Rousseaus politische Philosophie* (Frankfurt/Main: Suhrkamp, 1988), 15.
103. Steinbrügge, *Das moralische Gechlecht*.
104. Rousseau, *Emile*, 322.
105. Ibid., 321.
106. Elisabeth Blochmann, *Das "Frauenzimmer" und die "Gelehrsamkeit"* (Heidelberg: Quelle & Meyer, 1966), 26f.
107. Mary Wollstonecraft, *A Vindication of the Rights of Women*, ed. Mary Brody (1792; reprint, London: Penguin Classics, 1985), 125.
108. Rousseau, *Emile*, 322. Advocates of the first German women's movements often cited the last sentence with indignation, but it is interesting that the "moderate" women active in the area of educational policy ignored the sexual context. See Helene Lange, *Die Frauenbewegung in ihren modernen Problemen* (Leipzig: Quelle & Meyer, 1908), 27.
109. Rousseau, *Emile*, 323.
110. Ibid.
111. On Fichte see Gertrud Bäumer, *Fichte und sein Werk* (Berlin: Herbig, 1921); Weber, *Ehefrau und Mutter*, 306f; Gerhard, *Verhältnisse und Verhinderungen*, 14 ff; Hannelore Schröder, *Die Rechtlosigkeit der Frau im Rechtsstaat* (Frankfurt/Main and New York: Campus, 1979); see also Bennent, *Galanterie und Verachtung*, 113f. On Rousseau see, for example, Silvia Bovenschen, *Die imaginierte Weiblichkeit* (Frankfurt/Main: Suhrkamp, 1979); Christine Garbe, "Sophie oder die heimliche Macht der Frauen"; and Steinbrügge, *Das moralische Geschlecht*.
112. Friedrich C. von Savigny, "Darstellung der in den preußischen Gesetzen über Ehescheidung unternommenen Reform" in *Vermischte Schriften* (Berlin: Veit, 1850), 5: 238. On this context in general, see Dirk Blasius, *Ehescheidung in Deutschland 1794–1945* (Göttingen: Vandenhoeck & Ruprecht, 1987); and Gerhard, *Verhältnisse und Verhinderungen*, 167f.
113. Karl Larenz, *Allgemeiner Teil des deutschen bürgerlichen Rechts* (Munich: Beck, 1967), §9: 1; see also Joachim Gernhuber, *Lehrbuch des Familienrechts* (Munich: Beck, 1971), §3: 3.
114. Compare the often cited decision—exemplary in terms of legal opinion—by the German Federal Supreme Court in a 1966 divorce trial. It is definitely on a par with Fichte's crassitudes: "The woman does not satisfy her matrimonial obligation simply by apathetically tolerating sexual intimacy. If she is pre-

vented, by predisposition or some other reason, from finding satisfaction in marital intercourse, marriage nevertheless demands of her the affordance of marital affections and a willingness to make sacrifices, and it prohibits the display of indifference or unwillingness." Cited in *Neue Juristische Wochenschrift* (1967): 1078–79.

115. Gertrud Bäumer, *Fichte und sein Werk* (Berlin: Herbig, 1921).

116. According to Garbe, "Sophie oder die heimliche Macht der Frauen," 68, who counters "feminist animosity" by suggesting that the "repression hypothesis" be reviewed, following Michel Foucault's analysis of power.

117. Steinbrügge, *Das moralische Geschlecht*, 123.

118. Fetscher, *Rousseaus politische Philosophie*, 17.

119. Cited in Hermann Conrad, "Die Rechtsstellung der Ehefrau in der Privatrechtsgesetzgebung der Aufklärungszeit," in *Aus Mittelalter und Neuzeit Festschrift für Gerhard Kallen zum 70 Geburtstag*, ed. Josef Engel and Hans M. Klinkenberg (Bonn: Hanstein, 1957), 268.

120. Immanuel Kant, "The Metaphysics of Morals" (1797), in Kant, *Practical Philosophy*, trans. and ed. Mary J. Gregor, introd. Allan Wood (Cambridge, U.K.: Cambridge University Press, 1996), 353–604, here, 427; emphasis in original.

121. See Erle, *Die Ehe im Naturrecht*, 27.

122. Immanuel Kant, *Groundwork of the Metaphysics of Morals* (1785), in Kant, *Practical Philosophy*, ed. Gregor, 37–108, here, 84; emphasis in original.

123. Immanuel Kant, "Conjectures on the Beginning of Human History," in *Political Writings*, edited with an introduction by Hans Reiss, trans. H. B. Nisbet, 2nd enl. ed. (Cambridge, U.K.: Cambridge University Press, 1991), 221–234, here, 225; emphasis in original. See also a corresponding definition in: Immanuel Kant, "The Metaphysics of Morals" (1797) in Kant, *Practical Philosophy*, ed. Gregor, 353–604, here, 557.

124. Immanuel Kant, "The Metaphysics of Morals" (1797), book 1, in Kant, *Practical Philosophy*, ed. Gregor, 353–604, here, 430; emphasis in original.

125. Though this was claimed by Ursula Pia Jauch, *Immanuel Kant zur Geschlechterdifferenz*, 178; see also Elisabeth Conradi, "Die Kehrseite der Medaille," *Feministische Studien* 2 (1989): 85–93, here, 90f.

126. See, for example, Immanuel Kant, "An Answer to the Question: What is Enlightenment?" (1784), in Kant, *Practical Philosophy*, ed. Gregor, 11–22.

127. Immanuel Kant, "The Metaphysics of Morals" (1797), book 1, in Kant, *Practical Philosophy*, ed. Gregor, 353–604, here, 458.

128. Carol Hagemann-White, "Sexismus," in *Frauenhandlexikon*, ed. Johanna Beyer, Franziska Lamott, and Birgit Meyer (Munich: Beck, 1983), 260.

129. Bloch, *Natural Law and Human Dignity*, 75.

130. Theodor Gottlieb von Hippel, "On Improving the Status of Women," excerpt in *Women, the Family, and Freedom: The Debate in Documents*, ed. Susan Groag Bell and Karen M. Offen, 2 vols. (Stanford, Calif.: Stanford University Press, 1983), 1: 116–119; here, 117.

131. Nowak, *Schleiermacher*, 277.

132. Lange, *Die Frauenbewegung*, 23.

133. An interesting exception is Wilhelm J. Behr, *System der allgemeinen Staatslehre* (Bamberg and Würzburg: Goebhardt, 1804), 1:§796. Behr did not want to exclude women or servants and wage workers from citizenship contracts and thus from civil rights. Only married women were "as regards their own dignity . . . totally lost to their husbands" and thus could not claim civil or civic rights.

134. Nowak, *Schleiermacher,* 279.
135. Schleiermachers "Katechismus der Vernunft für edle Frauen," cited in Lange, *Die Frauenbewegung,* 118.

Chapter 3   Human Rights for Women as Well as Men

1. Baron Charles-Louis de Montesquieu, *The Spirit of the Laws,* trans. Thomas Nugent (New York: Hafner, 1949).
2. Jean-Jacques Rousseau, *The Social Contract,* trans. Charles Frankel (New York: Hafner, 1947), 33–34.
3. Lorenz von Stein, *Geschichte der sozialen Bewegung in Frankreich von 1789 bis auf unsere Tage* (1850; Munich: Drei Masken, 1921), 1:213–214.
4. See Title III of the Constitution of 1791. Cited in Walter Grab, ed., *Die Französische Revolution. Eine Dokumentation* (Munich: Nymphenburger, 1973), 65.
5. Karl Marx in "'On the Jewish Question,' ch. 1: Bruno Bauer, Die Judenfrage (The Jewish Question: Braunschweig 1843)," in *The Marx-Engels Reader,* ed. Robert C. Tucker, 2nd ed. (New York: W. W. Norton, 1978), 26–52; here, 33.
6. Stein, *Geschichte der sozialen Bewegung,* 242–243.
7. Lorenz von Stein, *Schriften zum Sozialismus* (Darmstadt: Wissenschaftliche Buchgesellschaft, 1974), 3, unchanged reprint of the anonymous articles that appeared in *Die Gegenwart,* vols. 1, 7, and 9 (Leipzig, 1848–1854).
8. See Emmanuel Sieyès, *Qu'est-ce que le tiers état?;* in English, see Sieyès, *What is the Third Estate?,* ed. and with historical notes by S. E. Finer, trans. M. Blondel, introduction by Peter Campbell (New York: Praeger, 1963).
9. See Gerhard, *Verhältnisse und Verhinderungen,* 74ff.
10. See Jean Antoine de Condorcet, "Sur l'admission des femmes au droit de cité," in *Oeuvres de Condorcet,* ed. A. Condorcet-O'Connor and M. F. Aragoa, vol. 10 (Paris: Didot, 1847); originally appeared in *Journal de la société,* no. 5 (Paris, 1789).
11. Cited in Lily Braun, *Die Frauenfrage* (Leipzig: Hirzel, 1901; Berlin and Bonn: Dietz, 1979), 83; see also Anna Pappritz, "Die Geschichte der Frauenbewegung in Frankreich," in *Handbuch der Frauenbewegung,* ed. Helene Lange and Gertrud Bäumer, part 1 (Berlin: Moeser, 1901), 363f.; more recently, see the comprehensive survey of relevant literature in Claudia Opitz, "'Die vergessenen Töchter der Revolution'–Frauen und Frauenrechte im revolutionären Frankreich von 1789–1795," in *Grenzgängerinnen,* ed. Helga Grubitzsch et al. (Düsseldorf: Schwann, 1985), 287–312; Susanne Petersen, *Marktweiber und Amazonen. Frauen in der Französischen Revolution* (Cologne: Pahl-Rugenstein, 1987); and Viktoria Schmidt-Linsenhoff, ed., *Sklavin oder Bürgerin? Französische Revolution und neue Weiblichkeit 1760–1830* (Marburg: Jonas, 1989).
12. Cf. Friedrich Schiller's "The Song of the Bell," trans. Henry Wadsworth Longfellow, in *An Anthology for Our Time* (New York: Frederick Ungar Publ., 1959), 237–248. Jules Michelet's *Les Femmes de la Revolution* (Paris: Delahays, 1854) had a significant impact on these myths and falsifications of history. On criticism of the work, see Helga Grubitsch, "Michelets 'Frauen der Revolution'" in *Grenzgängerinnen,* 153–179. Paule-Marie Duhet, *Les femmes et la révolution 1789–1794* (Paris: Julliard, 1971), is the most comprehensive presentation up to now of women in the French Revolution. Though it is not free of clichés influenced by Michelet and of a male, pejorative view, it also contains many interesting sources and references that unfortunately have yet

to be evaluated, let alone translated. For excerpts, see Romina Schmitter, *Die Frauenbewegung im 19. Jahrhundert in den USA und in Europa. Quellen- und Arbeitshefte zur Geschichte und Politik* (Stuttgart: Klett, 1981).

13. See Dann, *Gleichheit und Gleichberechtigung*, 104f.
14. The most comprehensive mention appears in Lily Braun, where she refers to E. Lairtullier, *Les femmes célèbres de 1789 à 1795 et leur influence dans la révolution, pour servir de suite et de complément à toutes les histoires de la révolution française* (Paris, 1840); see also Léopold Lacour, *Trois femmes de la révolution. Olympe de Gouges, Théroigne de Méricourt, Rose Lacombe* (Paris: Plon-Nourrit, 1900). Both authors, who were definitely closer to the sources, cited only excerpts of the declaration.
15. See Hannelore Schröder and Theresa Sauter, "Zur politischen Theorie des Feminismus," *Aus Politik und Zeitgeschichte* 47 (1977): 29–54, here, 31f. For an English translation see: "Olympe de Gouges (1791)," in *Women, the Family, and Freedom: The Debate in Documents*, ed. Susan Groag Bell and Karen M. Offen, 2 vols. (Stanford, Calif. Stanford University Press, 1983), 1:104–109; see also "Olympe de Gouges, 'Declaration of the Rights of Woman and Female Citizen,'" in *Women in Revolutionary Paris, 1789–1795*, ed. Darlene Gay Levy, Harriet Applewhite, and Mary Durham Johnson (Urbana: University of Illinois Press, 1979), 87–96; and Micheline R. Ishay, *The Human Rights Reader: Major Political Essays, Speeches and Documents from the Bible to the Present* (New York: Routledge, 1999), 140–147.
16. See Olivier Blanc, *Olympe de Gouges* (Paris: Syros, 1981); and Ruth Jung, "'Meine Stimme wird sich noch aus des Grabes Tiefe Gehör zu verschaffen wissen.' Olympe de Gouges—Streiterin für Frauenrechte," in *Sklavin oder Bürgerin*, ed. Schmidt-Linsenhoff, 73–87.
17. Jules Michelet, *Les femmes de la révolution*; cited passage translated from the German: *Die Frauen der Revolution*, ed. and trans. Gisela Etzel (Munich: Langen, 1913), 69. Other sources give the year of de Gouges's birth as 1748.
18. Olivier Blanc, *Olympe de Gouges*. See also Benoît Groult, *Olympe de Gouges. Oeuvres* (Paris: Mercure de France, 1986).
19. See Blanc, *Olympe de Gouges*, 162f.
20. Ibid., 189.
21. See the text of both declarations in the appendix of this book.
22. Ernst Bloch, *Politische Messungen. Pestzeit, Vormärz* (Frankfurt/Main: Suhrkamp, 1970), 379.
23. See Franz L. Neumann, *Die Herrschaft des Gesetzes* (Frankfurt/Main: Suhrkamp, 1980), 238f.
24. See Dann, *Gleichheit und Gleichberechtigung*, 64. "Natural law dictates order."
25. See Bloch, *Natural Law and Human Dignity*, 70.
26. Olympe de Gouges, "Declaration of the Rights of Woman and Citizen," prologue, in *Women, the Family, and Freedom*, ed. Bell and Offen, 104.
27. See preamble and postamble by Olympe de Gouges, in ibid., 105, 106–109; see appendix of this book.
28. See Dann, *Gleichheit und Gleichberechtigung*, 39.
29. See Otto Palandt, ed., *Bürgerliches Gesetzbuch* (Munich: Beck, 1978), outline to § 903.
30. Florentinus, D. I. 5.4. (from the "Corpus Juris Justinanum") cited in Helmut Coing, *Grundzüge der Philosophie des Rechts* (Berlin: de Grwyter, 1976), 189.
31. Immanuel Kant, "The Metaphysics of Morals" (1797), book 1, in Kant, *Prac-

  tical Philosophy, trans. and ed. Mary J. Gregor, introduction by Allan Wood (Cambridge: Cambridge University Press, 1996), 353–604, here, 393.

32. Coing wrote, in the explanatory note, "that is, freedom to act"; Coing, *Grundzüge der Philosophie des Rechts*, 35.

33. All of these quotations were taken from Kant, *The Metaphysics of Morals* (1797), book 1, in Kant, *Practical Philosophy*, ed. Gregor, 353–604, here, § 2, § 7, § 8, § 22.

34. Ibid., 394.

35. Ibid., § 26: 428.

36. Immanuel Kant, "Conjectures on the Beginning of Human History," in Kant, *Political Writings*, ed. and with introduction by Hans Reiss, trans. H. B. Nisbet, 2nd ed. (Cambridge: Cambridge University Press, 1991), 221–234, here, 226.

37. Ernst Bloch, *Neuzeitliche Philosophie II* (Frankfurt/Main: Suhrkamp, 1985), 121.

38. Kant referred explicitly to Rousseau in his "Conjectures on the Beginning of Human History," 227–228.

39. Rousseau, *The Social Contract*, 46. But Rousseau later placed restrictions on his principle of equality: "with respect to equality, the word must not be understood to mean that power and riches should be equally divided between all; but that power should never be so strong as to be capable of acts of violence" (46).

40. Coing, *Grundzüge der Philosophie des Rechts*, 135. See also Harold J. Bernan, *Recht und Revolution. Die Bildung der westlichen Rechtstradition* (Franfurt/Main: Suhrkamp, 1991), 192. I would like to thank Helen Schüngel-Straumann and Ilona Riedel-Spangenberger for the precise references to canonical law.

41. This is a similar critique, though coming up against a different "limit" to the one developed by Karl Marx in his response to Bruno Bauer in "On the Jewish Question." Marx referred to the right to own property only as the "practical application of the right of liberty"; see Marx, "On the Jewish Question," 41.

42. Fichte, *The Science of Rights*, 78.

43. Entry: "Frauen" in *Conversations-Lexicon, oder encyclopädisches Handwörterbuch für gebildete Stände*, 7 vols. (Stuttgart: Macklot, 1818–1819), 2: 789.

44. See Hans Welzel, *Naturrecht und materielle Gerechtigkeit* (Göttingen: Vandenhoeck & Ruprecht, 1962), 162f.

45. See Georg Jellinek, *Die Erklärung der Menschen- und Bürgerrechte*, 4th ed. (1895; Munich and Leipzig: Duncker & Humblot, 1927), XI, 42f.

46. Cf. "Marriage is the tomb of confidence and love" in the Postamble to de Gouges's Declaration in *Women, the Family and Freedom*. Bell and Offen, eds., 108.

47. Bloch, *Natural Law*, 65, feminist modification added.

48. The translation of Article 10 was taken from *Women in Revolutionary Paris, 1789–1795*, ed. Levy, Applewhite, and Johnson, 91.

49. "Introduction," in *Observations on "The Spiritual Situation of the Age": Contemporary German Perspectives*, ed. Jürgen Habermas, 2 vols. (Cambridge, Mass.: MIT Press, 1983), 1:1–28, here, 27.

50. Jürgen Habermas, *The Theory of Communicative Action*, trans. Thomas McCarthy (Boston: Beacon Press, 1987), 393.

51. See Olympe de Gouges, "Model for a Social Contract Between Man and Woman," in *Women, the Family, and Freedom*, ed. Bell and Offen, 108–109.

52. See Beate Harms-Ziegler, "Außereheliche Mutterschaft in Preußen im 18. und 19. Jahrhundert," in *Frauen in der Geschichte des Rechts*, ed. Ute Gerhard (Munich: Beck, 1997), 325–344.

53. Ute Gerhard, "Die Rechtsstellung der Frau in der bürgerlichen Gesellschaft

des 19. Jahrhunderts. Frankreich und Deutschland im Vergleich" in *Bürgertum im 19. Jahrhundert*, ed. Jürgen Kocka (Munich: Deutscher Taschenbuch-Verlag, 1988), 1:455.

54. See Ruth Graham, "Loaves and Liberty: Women in the French Revolution," in *Becoming Visible*, ed. Renate Bridenthal and Claudia Koonz (Boston: Houghton Miflin, 1977), 238ff.

55. Olympe de Gouges, in *Marie Olympe de Gouges. Politische Schriften*, ed. Margarete Wolters and Clara Sutor (Hamburg: Buske, 1979), 178: "The French people has become republican, but it shall not become a people of assassins."

56. Marx, "On the Jewish Question," 41, 42.

57. Locke, *Two Treatises of Government*, II, § 27 (ch. V: "Of Property"), 305–306.

58. Marx, "On the Jewish Question," 42.

59. Olympe de Gouges (1791), "Declaration of the Rights of Woman and Citizen," in *Women, the Family, and Freedom*, ed. Bell and Offen, 109.

60. Marx, "On the Jewish Question," 42.

61. Ibid., 46.

62. Ludwig Feuerbach, *The Essence of Christianity*, trans. George Eliot (New York: Harper and Row, Harper Torchbooks, 1957), 3.

63. Fichte, *The Science of Rights*, 402.

64. See Hausen, "Die Polarisierung der 'Geschlechtscharaktere': Eine Spiegelung der Dissoziation von Erwerbs- und Familienleben," in *Sozialgeschichte der Familie in der Neuzeit Europas*, ed. Werner Conze (Stuttgart: Klett-Cotta, 1976), 363–393.

65. Marx, "On the Jewish Question," 46, 34.

66. Rousseau, *Emile*, 321.

67. Bloch, *Politische Messungen*, 346.

68. Bloch, *Natural Law*, 70.

69. Jürgen Habermas, *The Philosophical Discourse of Modernity: Twelve Lectures*, trans. Frederick Lawrence (Cambridge: MIT Press, 1987), 17.

70. See Marx, "On the Jewish Question," 42; and Bloch, *Politische Messungen*, 342f.; and Bloch, *Natural Law*, 177.

71. Bloch, *Natural Law*, 174.

72. Doris Janshen expressed a different opinion, in "Naturrecht versus Naturzerstörung. Zur Verdrängung des Weiblichen aus den Menschenrechten," *Freiheit und Gleichheit* 4 (1983): 30f.

73. See Bloch, *Natural Law*, 167–168. See also Norbert Sommer, ed., *Nennt uns nicht Brüder. Frauen in der Kirche durchbrechen das Schweigen* (Stuttgart: Kreuz, 1985).

74. See Dann, *Gleichheit und Gleichberechtigung*, 138.

75. See Theodor Gottlieb von Hippel, *Über die bürgerliche Verbesserung der Weiber* (Berlin: Voß, 1792; Frankfurt/Main: Syndikat, 1977); for an excerpt in English, see *Women, the Family, and Freedom*, ed. Bell and Offen, 116–119. See also de Condorcet, in *Die Frau ist frei geboren*, Schröder, 55–65.

76. See Rossanda, *Einmischung*, 99f.

77. Bloch, *Natural Law*, 165.

Chapter 4   *Equal Rights or Women's Distinctiveness*

1. See chapter 6, "Getting at the Root of the Evil," in this book, and Ute Gerhard, *"Unerhört." Die Geschichte der deutschen Frauenbewegung* (Reinbek: Rowohlt, 1990).

2. Some examples were Privy Legal Councillor Carl Bulling, Anton Menger, and

very early "friends of women" such as Theodor G. von Hippel and Wilhelm J. Behr.

3. Weber, *Ehefrau und Mutter* (1907).

4. Emma Oekinghaus, *Die gesellschaftliche und rechtliche Stellung der deutschen Frau* (Jena: G. Fischer, 1925).

5. Georg Simmel, "Über das Abenteuer, die Geschlechter und die Krise der Moderne" (1923), in *Philosophische Kultur. Gesammelte Essays* (Berlin: Wagenbach, 1983); see also Georg Simmel, *On Women, Sexuality, and Love*, trans. and with an introduction by Guy Oakes (New Haven, Conn.: Yale University Press, 1984); cf. Marianne Weber's response, "Die Frau und die objektive Kultur," in *Frauenfragen und Frauengedanken* (Tübingen: Mohr, 1919), 95–133; on this, see Theresa Wobbe, *Wahlverwandtschaften. Die Soziologie und die Frauen auf dem Weg zur Wissenschaft* (Frankfurt/Main: Campus, 1995), and Ute Gerhard, "Illegitime Töchter. Das komplizierte Verhältnis zwischen Feminismus und Soziologie," *Kölner Zeitschrift für Soziologie und Sozialpsychologie, Sonderheft* 38 (1998): 343–382.

6. See Jürgen Habermas, *Between Facts and Norms: Contributions to a Discourse Theory of Law and Democracy*, trans. William Rehg (Cambridge, Mass.: MIT Press, 1996), 409–427.

7. Quoted in Franz L. Neumann, "The Change in the Function of Law in Modern Society," trans. and ed. Klaus Knorr and Edward A. Shils, in Neumann, *The Democratic and The Authoritarian State. Essays in Political and Legal Theory*, ed. and with a preface by Herbert Marcuse (Glencoe, Ill.: The Free Press, 1957), 22–68, here, 46. This article is an abbreviated translation of Neumann, "Der Funktionswandel des Gesetzes im Recht der bürgerlichen Gesellschaft," *Zeitschrift für Sozialforschung* (1937), 542–596; also published in Neumann, *Demokratischer und autoritärer Staat* (Frankfurt/Main: Europäische Verlags-Anstalt, 1967), 31–81.

8. On the topic of natural law, see, for example, Werner Maihofer, ed., *Naturrecht oder Rechtspositivismus?* (Darmstadt: Wissenschaftliche Buchgesellschaft, 1966), and Wolf Rosenbaum, *Naturrecht und positives Recht* (Neuwied and Darmstadt: Luchterhand, 1972).

9. *Die Frauen-Zeitung*, 68; reprint of no. 5 (1849).

10. See, in contrast, her reference to other women of the French Revolution in *Die Frauen-Zeitung*, 116; reprint of no. 14 (1849).

11. See Ute Gerhard, "Über die Anfänge der deutschen Frauenbewegung um 1848. Frauenpresse, Frauenpolitik und Frauenvereine," in *Frauen suchen ihre Geschichte. Historische Studien zum 19. und 20. Jahrhundert*, ed. Karin Hausen (Munich: Beck, 1983), 196ff. See also Gerlinde Hummel-Haasis, ed., *"Schwestern zerreißt eure Ketten," Zeugnisse zur Geschichte der Frauen in der Revolution von 1848/49* (Munich: Deutscher Taschenbuch-Verlag, 1982).

12. *Die Frauen-Zeitung*, 86; reprint of no. 7 (1849).

13. This was triggered by an open letter sent by Louise Otto to the "Worker's Alliance" on 27 October 1848. See *Die Frauen-Zeitung*, 57, and numerous articles on "women workers" in *Die Frauen-Zeitung*; reprint of no. 3 (1849).

14. Louise Otto in *Die Frauen-Zeitung*, 41; reprint of no. 1 (1849).

15. *Die Frauen-Zeitung*, 193–194; reprint of no. 37 (1849), emphasis in original.

16. Bloch, *Natural Law and Human Dignity*, trans. Dennis T. Schmidt (Cambridge: MIT Press, 1986), 174.

17. See Renate Möhrmann, ed., *Frauenemanzipation im deutschen Vormärz. Texte und Dokumente* (Stuttgart: Reclam, 1978); and Renate Möhrmann, *Die andere*

Frau. Emanzipationsansätze deutscher Schriftstellerinnen im Vorfeld der Achtundvierziger-Revolution (Stuttgart: Metzler, 1977).

18. Dann, *Gleichheit und Gleichberechtigung*, 203.

19. *Die Frauen-Zeitung*: 39, reprint of no. 1 (1849); 57, reprint of no. 3 (1849); 131, reprint of no. 17 (1849).

20. See Dann, *Gleichheit und Gleichberechtigung*, 204.

21. Ibid., 159; see also Welzel, *Naturrecht und materiale Gerechtigkeit*, 162ff.

22. Louise Otto in *Die Frauen-Zeitung*: 39, reprint of no. 1 (1849); 180, reprint of no. 34 (1849); 262, reprint of no. 21 (1850); emphasis in original.

23. The German Confederation was a loose grouping of German states created in 1815 by the Congress of Vienna to replace the Holy Roman Empire. It was rendered largely ineffective by the rivalry between Austria and Prussia and was dissolved in 1866 after the Prussian defeat of Austria in the Seven Weeks' War. (Cited from the 1996 Grolier Multimedia Encyclopedia.)

24. On the restriction of the rights of coalition of workers, see Volker Hentschel, *Geschichte der deutschen Sozialpolitik 1880–1980* (Frankfurt/Main: Suhrkamp, 1983), 31f. On the history of the suppression of associations of female workers, see Hilde Lion, *Zur Soziologie der Frauenbewegung* (Berlin: Herbig, 1926), and Ottilie Baader, *Ein steiniger Weg*, 2nd ed. (Berlin: Vorwärts, 1931). See especially *Die Staatsbürgerin*, a newspaper published by Gertrud Guillaume-Schack in 1886 and later banned, now reprinted in a volume edited by Hartwig Gebhardt and Ulla Wischermann (Munich: Saur, 1988). Adeline Berger, *Die zwanzigjährige Arbeiterinnenbewegung Berlins und ihr Ergebnis* (Berlin: published by the author, 1889). On the special difficulties male-dominated unions experienced with women workers in general, and with equal pay in particular, see Gisela Losseff-Tillmanns, *Frauenemanzipation und Gewerkschaften* (Wuppertal: Hammer, 1978), and, for details, Gerhard, "Unerhört."

25. For details, see Ute Gerhard, "Grenzziehungen und überschreitungen. Die Rechte der Frauen auf dem Weg in die politische Öffentlichkeit," in *Frauen in der Geschichte des Rechts. Von der Frühen Neuzeit bis zur Gegenwart*, ed. Ute Gerhard (Munich: Beck, 1997), 509–546, here, 524ff.

26. "Gesetz, die Angelegenheiten in der Presse betreffend," 14 March 1851, no. 23, *Gesetz- und Verordnungsblatt für das Königreich Sachsen vom Jahre 1851* (Dresden: Meinhold, 1851), § 12; on this, see also Louise Otto's commentary in *Die Frauen-Zeitung* 51 (1850): 328.

27. Louise Otto, "§12 des Entwurfs eines Preßgesetzes für das Königreich Sachsen," *Die Frauen-Zeitung*, 328; reprint of no. 51 (1850).

28. Quoted in Albert Friedrich Berner, *Lehrbuch des Deutschen Preßrechts* (Leipzig: Tauchnitz, 1876), 61f.; see also Ernst R. Huber, *Deutsche Verfassungsgeschichte seit 1789* (Stuttgart: Kohlhammer, 1978), 2:782f., and Huber, *Verfassungsgeschichte* (1978), 3:136f.

29. See references in Moisej Jakovlevic Ostrogorskij, *Die Frau im öffentlichen Recht. Eine vergleichende Untersuchung der Geschichte und Gesetzgebung der civilisierten Länder* (Leipzig: Wigand, 1897).

30. Thomas Nipperdey, "Verein als soziale Struktur in Deutschland im späten 18. und frühen 19. Jahrhundert," in *Geschichtswissenschaft und Vereinswesen im 19. Jahrhundert. Beiträge zur Geschichte historischer Forschung* (Göttingen: Vandenhoeck & Ruprecht, 1972), 1–44; see also Otto Dann, "Die Anfänge politischer Vereinsbildung in Deutschland," in *Soziale Bewegung und politische Verfassung. Beiträge zur Geschichte der modernen Welt*, ed. Ulrich Engelhardt et al. (Stuttgart: Klett, 1976), 197–232.

31. Jürgen Habermas, *The Structural Transformation of the Public Sphere: An Inquiry into a Category of Bourgeois Society*, trans. Thomas Burger, with the assistance of Frederick Lawrence (Cambridge, Mass.: MIT Press, 1989), the English translation of Jürgen Habermas's *Strukturwandel der Öffentlichkeit*, included a translator's note by Thomas Burger that we would like to include here, as it applies to this translation as well and will hopefully serve to convey some of the difficulty we experienced deciding in each individual case how to properly translate "bürgerlich."—Trans.

> [One] troublesome term is *bürgerlich*, an adjective related to the noun *Bürger*, which may be translated as "bourgeois" or "citizen." *Bürgerlich* possesses both connotations. In expressions such as "civil code," "civil society," "civic duty," "bourgeois strata," and "bourgeois family" the German term for "civil," "civic," and "bourgeois" is *bürgerlich*. *Bürgerlich* also means "middle class" in contrast to "noble" or "peasant." [We may also add in contrast to "working class."] *Bürgerliche Öffentlichkeit* thus is difficult to translate adequately. For better or worse, it is rendered here as "bourgeois public sphere." (Habermas, *The Structural Transformation of the Public Sphere*, xv).

32. Habermas, *The Structural Transformation of the Public Sphere*, 27; see also the foreword to the new 1990 German edition, *Strukturwandel der Öffentlichkeit* (Frankfurt/Main: Suhrkamp), 15.

33. Reinhard Rürup, "Deutschland im 19. Jahrhundert. 1815–1871," in *Deutsche Geschichte*, vol. 3: *19. und 20. Jahrhundert (1815–1945)*, ed. Reinhard Rürup, Hans-Ulrich Wehler, and Gerhard Schulz (Göttingen: Vandenhoeck & Ruprecht, 1985), 3–90, here, 84; see also Habermas, *The Structural Transformation*.

34. See Renate Baader, *Dames de lettres. Autorinnen des preziösen, hocharistokratischen und "modernen" Salons* (Stuttgart: Metzler, 1986); Deborah Sadie Hertz, *Jewish High Society in Old Regime Berlin* (New Haven, Conn.: Yale University Press, 1988).

35. Quoted in Hannah Arendt, *Rahel Varnhagen: The Life of a Jewess*, ed. Liliane Weissberg, trans. Richard and Clara Winston (London: Leo Baeck Institute, 1957), 173.

36. Thomas Vormbaum, *Die Rechtsfähigkeit der Vereine im 19. Jahrhundert. Ein Beitrag zur Entstehungsgeschichte des BGB* (Berlin and New York: Walter de Gruyter, 1976), 27.

37. Ibid., 90f.

38. Cited in Schering, ed., *Allgemeines Landrecht für die Preußischen Staaten mit Anmerkungen und einem ergänzenden Nachtrage*, 4 vols. (Berlin: Nauck, 1863–1869), 2: II, no. 637.

39. Werner Schultze, *Öffentliches Vereinigungsrecht im Kaiserreich—1871 bis 1908*, dissertation (Frankfurt/Main, 1973), 491; on this, see Generalkommission der Gewerkschaften Deutschlands, ed., *Anleitung zur Benutzung des Vereins- und Versammlungsrechts in Deutschland*, 3rd ed. (Hamburg: Legien, 1900), 25f., 41.

40. Judgment of 10 November 1887, *Reichsgerichtsentscheidung in Strafsachen* (RGSt) (1888), 16: 383–386.

41. See, for example, Herrad-Ulrike Bussemer, *Frauenemanzipation und Bildungsbürgertum. Sozialgeschichte der Frauenbewegung in der Reichsgründungszeit* (Weinheim and Basel: Beltz, 1985); Ute Gerhard, *Unerhört. Die Geschichte der Frauenbewegung*, 7ff.

42. Louise Otto, *Das Recht der Frauen auf Erwerb* (Hamburg: Hoffmann & Campe, 1866), 93.

43. See Adolph Lette's famous memorandum as chairman of the Association to Promote the Female Sex's Fitness to Work, quoted in Margrit Twellmann, *Die deutsche Frauenbewegung. Ihre Anfänge und erste Entwicklung. Quellen 1843–1889* (Meisenheim: Hain, 1972), 137ff.; see also the foreword by Joseph Heinrichs to Louise Otto's *Recht der Frauen auf Erwerb*.

44. On this, see Louise Otto-Peters, *Das erste Vierteljahrhundert des Allgemeinen deutschen Frauenvereins* (Leipzig: Schäfer, 1890).

45. Gertrud Bäumer, "Die Geschichte der Frauenbewegung in Deutschland, in *Handbuch der Frauenbewegung*," part 1, ed. Helene Lange and Gertrud Bäumer (Berlin: Moeser, 1901), 1–158, here, 76.

46. Louise Otto-Peters, *Frauenleben im deutschen Reich. Erinnerungen aus der Vergangenheit* (Leipzig: Schäfer, 1876), 259.

47. The German expression *Geschlechtsvormundschaft* has been translated here as "gender tutelage"; it could also be rendered literally as "sex- or gender-based guardianship." As discussed in the following, it refers to the legally sanctioned treatment of women, historically, as, in effect, the property of their husbands (or other male family members)—subject to legal control over most aspects of their lives, in which the husband's control was even greater than traditional paternal authority over minor children.

48. See the sources and cites in Margrit Twellmann, *Quellen*, 2: 167f., 190f., 197f., and Gertrud Bäumer, in *Handbuch der Frauenbewegung*, 68f.

49. Heinrich von Sybel, *Über die Emancipation der Frauen* (Bonn: Cohen, 1870), 11.

50. Marie Louise Janssen-Jurreit, *Sexismus. Über die Abtreibung der Frauenfrage* (Munich and Vienna: Hanser, 1976), 11.

51. Hedwig Dohm, *Women's Nature and Privilege*, trans. Constance Campbell (Westport, Conn.: Hyperion Press, 1976); originally published as *Der Frauen Natur und Recht* (Berlin: Wedekind & Schwieger, 1876). Cited passage has been translated from the German edition.

52. Ibid., 119, 120.

53. See Gertrud Bäumer, in *Handbuch der Frauenbewegung*, 74f., and Gisela Brinker-Gabler, "Die Frau ohne Eigenschaften," *Feministische Studien* 1 (1984): 117.

54. This is the approach in Gertrud Bäumer; cf., in contrast, Theresa Wobbe, "Die Frauenbewegung ist keine Parteiensache," *Feministische Studien* 2 (1986): 58–59, and Bärbel Clemens, *"Menschenrechte habe kein Geschlecht!" Zum Politikverständnis der bürgerlichen Frauenbewegung* (Pfaffenweiler: Centaurus, 1988), 36f.

55. Jellinek, *Erklärung der Menschen- und Bürgerrechte*, 4.

56. Hermann Baumgarten, *Der deutsche Liberalismus. Eine Selbstkritik* (1866; Frankfurt/Main, Berlin, and Vienna: Reimer, 1974), 15.

57. Neumann, "The Change in the Function of Law in Modern Society."

58. Ibid., 53.

59. Friedrich Julius Stahl, *Die Philosophie des Rechts* (1837; reprint, Darmstadt: Wissenschaftliche Buchgesellschaft, 1963), 2:221, quoted in Ingeborg Maus, "Entwicklung und Funktionswandel der Theorie des bürgerlichen Rechtsstaats," in *Der bürgerliche Rechtsstaat*, ed. M. Tohidipur (Frankfurt/Main: Suhrkamp, 1978), 1:33.

60. Gerhard Oestreich, *Geschichte der Menschenrechte und Grundfreiheiten im Umriß* (Berlin: Duncker & Humblot, 1978), 102f.

61. Franz Wieacker, *Privatrechtsgeschichte der Neuzeit*, 430ff.,. here, 443.

62. On the following, see the overview in the prizewinning work by Moisej

Jakovlevic Ostrogorskij of the Paris Legal Faculty, _Die Frau im öffentlichen Recht_; for specifics, see Lida Gustava Heymann, _Das Wahlrecht der Frauen zu den Handelskammern in den deutschen Bundesstaaten_ (Leipzig: Dietrich, 1910), and the reports and speeches on the legal status of women in Marie Stritt, ed., _Der Internationale Frauenkongress in Berlin 1904_ (Berlin: Habel, 1904). See also Gertrud Bäumer, _Die Frau in Volkswirtschaft und Staatsleben der Gegenwart_ (Stuttgart and Berlin: Deutsche Verlagsanstalt, 1914), 223ff.

63. See Emma Oekinghaus, _Die gesellschaftliche und rechtliche Stellung der deutschen Frau_, 124, and Lida Gustava Heymann, _Das kommunale Wahlrecht der Frauen im Deutschen Reich_ (Munich: Kastner & Callwey, 1910).

64. Ostrogorskij, _Die Frau im öffentlichen Recht_, 173. See also chapter 7, "Gender Tutelage, or Women in Nineteenth-Century Legal Doctrine," in this book.

65. The only exception was Ostrogorskij, _Die Frau im öffentlichen Recht_, with its survey of the "history and legislation of civilized countries," whose subject, interestingly, can be credited to a contest sponsored by the Paris university.

66. On the suffrage movement, see chapter 6 of this book.

67. For details on the significance of this theme for the system and the complex legal situation, see chapter 7 of this book.

68. Judgment of the Reich Court for Civil Matters, _Reichsgerichtsentscheidung in Zivilsachen_ (RGZ) (Leipzig, 1887), 16:149.

69. René König, "Familie und Autorität. Der deutsche Vater im Jahr 1955," in René König, _Materialien zur Soziologie der Familie_ (Cologne: Kiepenheuer & Witsch, 1974), 219; see also Ingeborg Weber-Kellermann, _Die deutsche Familie_ (Frankfurt/Main: Suhrkamp, 1975), 117ff.

70. For details, see chapter 7 of this book.

71. Bernhard Mugdan, _Die gesamten Materialien zum Bürgerlichen Gesetzbuch für das deutsche Reich_, vol. 5, _Motive_ (Berlin: Decker, 1899), 124.

72. Rudolph von Jhering, _Der Kampf ums Recht_, 21st ed. (Vienna: Manzsche Verlags- und Universitäts-Buchhandlung, 1926), 7, 98.

73. Hans Hattenhauer, _Zwischen Hierarchie und Demokratie_ (Karlsruhe: Müller, 1971), 179.

74. Emil Preetorius, _Die eheherrliche Vormundschaft und das Bürgerliche Gesetzbuch_ (Berlin: Struppe & Winckler, 1907), 68.

75. See chapter 6 of this book.

76. See the "appeal" by the Federation of German Women's Organizations in _Die Frauenbewegung_ (1896), 114–115.

77. Clara Zetkin, _Zur Geschichte der proletarischen Frauenbewegung Deutschlands_ (Frankfurt/Main: Roter Stern, 1971), 209.

78. August Bebel's 1879 book _Die Frau und der Sozialismus_, which had already gone to fifty editions by 1910, laid the groundwork to this extent. It was published in English as: _Woman under Socialism_, trans. Daniel De Leon (New York: Schocken Books, 1971).

79. Johanna Loewenherz, "Können Sozialdemokratinnen und bürgerliche Frauenrechtlerinnen für gemeinsame Ziele auch gemeinsam kämpfen?" _Sozialistische Monatshefte_ 3 (1897): 356–360, here, 359.

80. Karl Joël, _Die Frauen in der Philosophie_ (Hamburg: Verlagsanstalt und Druckerei, 1896), 47, 66.

81. Immanuel Kant, "An Answer to the Question: What is Enlightenment?" (1784), in _Practical Philosophy_, trans. and ed. Mary J. Gregor, introduction by Allen Wood (Cambridge, U.K.: Cambridge University Press, 1996), 17. See also Immanuel Kant, "What is Enlightenment?" in Kant, _Selections_, ed. and trans. Lewis White Beck (New York: Macmillan, 1988), 462; this translation

refers specifically to "tutelage": "Enlightenment is man's release from his self-incurred tutelage. Tutelage is man's inability to make use of his understanding without direction from another. Self-incurred is this tutelage when its cause lies not in lack of reason but in lack of resolution and courage to use it without direction from another."

82. Immanuel Kant, "Groundwork of the Metaphysics of Morals" (1785), in Kant, *Practical Philosophy*, 37–108, here, 79

83. See Minna Cauer, "Vortrag vor der deutsch-akademischen Vereinigung," *Allgemeine Deutsche Universitäts-Zeitung* 24 (1888): 289.

84. Jürgen Habermas, *The Philosophical Discourse of Modernity: Twelve Lectures*, trans. Frederick Lawrence (Cambridge: MIT Press, 1987), 17.

85. Helene Lange, "Was wir wollen," *Die Frau* (1893): 1f., here, 4.

86. See Georg Simmel, "Zur Philosophie der Geschlechter und Zur Philosophie der Kultur," in *Philosophische Kultur. Gesammelte Essays* (Berlin: Wagenbach, 1983); see also Simmel, *On Women, Sexuality, and Love*, trans. and with an introduction by Guy Oakes (New Haven, Conn.: Yale University Press, 1984); and the response and moderate criticism of Simmel in Marianne Weber, "Die Frau und die objektive Kultur," in *Frauenfragen und Frauengedanken* (Tübingen: Mohr, 1913); see also Oekinghaus, *Die gesellschaftliche und rechtliche Stellung*, 22, 25; Ute Gerhard, "Anderes Recht für Frauen? Feminismus als Gegenkultur," in *Gegenkultur und Recht*, ed. Volkmar Gessner and Winfried Hassemer (Baden-Baden: Nomos, 1985).

87. Gertrud Bäumer, *Die Frau in der Kulturbewegung der Gegenwart* (Wiesbaden: Bergmann, 1904), 36. Analyzing the barriers and disruptions that women for example "encountered in the workshop of male science," Gertrud Bäumer continued, "Women who have worked in science learned from men; they received their standards of value and lack of value from men. In the ever more complicated arrangement of the scientific cosmos, they first had, as students, to chart a long course through male intellectual work before reaching the point at which the independent further development of science began—until then, any feeling of confidence could, nay, had to be dulled. . . . And where could the woman, who was in any case only tolerated, find the confidence to seek out her own paths? It was the man who offered all response to scholarly achievements; this response only reinforced what was in the spirit of his own scientific interests . . . ; what seemed insignificant to him was ignored and fell, unused, into oblivion."

88. Malwida von Meysenbug, *Memoiren einer Idealistin*, 1:296.

89. See Helene Lange, "Frauenwahlrecht," *Kampfzeiten* 1 (Berlin: Herbig, 1928): 186. This was also true of radicals such as Anita Augspurg, Minna Cauer, and Helene Stöcker.

90. "Das Recht der Frau," in *Die Frauenbewegung* (1896), 48–50. There is also a great deal of evidence in the movement's newspapers, especially in *Die Frauenbewegung*, published by Minna Cauer beginning in 1895, and in the newspapers of the suffrage movement: *Die Zeitschrift für Frauenstimmrecht*, first published in 1907, and *Frauen-Stimmrecht*, which began in 1912, both published by Anita Augspurg. Some examples of programmatic writing include Lily Braun, *Die Bürgerpflicht der Frau* (Berlin: Dümmler, 1895): "We demand application of the principles of the modern state—universal human rights—to the other half of humankind as well, the women." (23); and Margarete Treuge, "Die Frau im Staat," in *Jahrbuch der Frauenbewegung* (Leipzig and Berlin: Teubner, 1912),11 ff.

91. Frances Magnus-Hansen, "Ziel und Weg in der deutschen Frauenbewegung des XIX. Jahrhunderts," in *Deutscher Staat und deutsche Parteien* (Munich and Berlin: Oldenbourg, 1922), 219.
92. Oekinghaus, *Die gesellschaftliche und rechtliche Stellung*, 31.
93. Lange, "Frauenwahlrecht," *Kampfzeiten* 2: 189.
94. Alice Salomon, quoted in Monika Simmel, in *Jahrbuch der Sozialarbeit* 3 (Reinbek: Rowohlt, 1979), 44.
95. *Ziel und Aufgaben der Frauenbewegung. Programm des Allgemeinen Deutschen Frauenvereins*, 1905, quoted in Lange, *Die Frauenbewegung*, 122. See Irene Stöhr, "'Organisierte Mütterlichkeit.' Zur Politik der deutschen Frauenbewegung um 1900," in *Frauen suchen ihre Geschichte*, 221–249.
96. Lange, "Was wir wollen," *Die Frau* (1893): 4.
97. Agnes von Zahn-Harnack, *Die Frauenbewegung. Geschichte, Probleme, Ziele* (Berlin: Deutsche Buch-Gemeinschaft, 1928), 78.
98. Gertrud Bäumer, *Die Frau im neuen Lebensraum* (Berlin: Herbig, 1931), 16–17.
99. Stöhr, "Organisierte Mütterlichkeit," 226.
100. Lange, *Kampfzeiten* 1:205.
101. Zahn-Harnack, *Die Frauenbewegung*, 77.
102. Lange, *Kampfzeiten* 1:204.
103. Lange, "Was wir wollen," 4.
104. See Lange, *Die Frauenbewegung*, 17f.
105. Helene Lange, *Lebenserinnerungen* (Berlin: Herbig, 1925), 146.
106. Weber, *Ehefrau und Mutter*, 436–437.
107. Quoted in Lange and Bäumer, *Handbuch der Frauenbewegung*, 1:64–65.
108. Lange, *Die Frauenbewegung*, 19.
109. Li Fischer-Eckart, "Die Stimmrechtsbewegung," in *Der Deutsche Frauenkongreß 1912*, ed. Bund Deutscher Frauenvereine (Leipzig and Berlin: Teubner, 1912), 187.
110. Helene Lange, "Intellektuelle Grenzlinien," *Kampfzeiten* 1:211.
111. Cornelia Klinger, "Abschied von der Emanzipationslogik?" *Kommune* 1 (1988): 39–53. More recently, see, for example, Diotima (Verona women philosophers' group), *Der Mensch ist zwei. Das Denken der Geschlechterdifferenz* (Vienna: Wiener Frauenverlag, 1989).
112. Alice Salomon, "Literatur zur Frauenfrage. Die Entwicklung der Theorie der Frauenbewegung," *Archiv für Sozialwissenschaft und Sozialpolitik* 26 (1908): 460–462.
113. Bäumer, *Die Frau im neuen Lebensraum*, 16.
114. Ibid., 16–17.
115. Salomon, *Literatur zur Frauenfrage*, 461.
116. See Lange, *Die Frauenbewegung*, 58f.
117. Helene Lange, "Feministische Gedankenanarchie," in *Frauenbewegung und Sexualethik. Beiträge zur modernen Ehekritik*, ed. Gertrud Bäumer et al. (Heilbronn: Salzer, 1909).
118. On the following, see also Heide Schlüpmann, "Radikalisierung der Philosophie. Die Nietzsche-Rezeption und die sexualpolitische Publizistik Helene Stöckers," *Feministische Studien* 1 (1984): 10–34, here, 16.
119. Helene Stöcker, "Die Ziele der Mutterschutzbewegung," in *Die Liebe und die Frauen* (Minden: Bruns, 1906), 173.
120. Schlüpmann, *Radikalisierung der Philosophie*, 19.
121. Helene Stöcker, "Die Liebe der Persönlichkeit," in *Die Liebe und die Frauen*, 159.

122. Helene Stöcker, "Unsere Umwertung der Werte," in *Die Liebe und die Frauen*, 14.

123. See Rosa Mayreder, *Zur Kritik der Weiblichkeit. Essays* (Jena and Leipzig: Diederichs, 1905 and 1923), reprint (Munich: Frauenoffensive, 1982). In her treatise on love, Rosa Mayreder had also dealt critically with Fichte's theory of right. See "Der Weg der weiblichen Erotik," in *Zur Kritik der Weiblichkeit*, 216ff.

124. Stöcker, *Umwertung der Werte*, 7, 14.

125. On this, see Minna Cauer, "Staatsbürgerin und Frauenrechtlerin," in *Die Frauenbewegung* (1909), 148.

126. Margarete L. Selenka, quoted in Gisela Brinker-Gabler, *Frauen gegen den Krieg* (Frankfurt/Main: Fischer, 1980), 16.

127. See ibid., 14 et passim.

128. See *Die Frau im Staat* 7–8 (1920): 2.

129. See Lange, *Die Frauenbewegung*, 31: "The truth, that the state is not in fact a free union among completely equal quantities, but an organic structure with a varied division of labor, whose parts in many ways interlock and enter into relations of mutual dependency, which makes illusory any freedom in regard to the whole." With this view of the state, however, she found herself very much a part of the prevailing trend in legal scholarship. The organicist view of the state, developed by Otto von Gierke, for example, from the "organism of human associations," was the basis of the constitutional system of imperial Germany. The ideology of biological, organic community was one of the intellectual roots of the Nazi conception of law and the state. See Wieacker, *Privatrechtsgeschichte*, 454, and Hattenhauer, *Zwischen Hierarchie und Demokratie*, 217.

130. Gertrud Bäumer, "Lage und Aufgabe der Frauenbewegung in der Umwälzung," *Die Frau* (1933): 385.

131. This is meant here in the sense that it was used by Ernst Bloch; see, for example, chapter 3, note 70, of this book.

132. Barbara Brick and Christine Woesler, "Maschinerie und Mütterlichkeit," *Beiträge zur feministischen Theorie und Praxis* 5 (1981): 61–68.

133. Gertrud Bäumer, *Die Frau und das geistige Leben* (Leipzig: Amelang, 1911), 97.

134. But see Irene Stöhr, "Uferlos gemäßigt, aber begrenzt radikal," in *Die Tageszeitung*, 8 March 1986.

135. Cited from the German translation: Rossanda, *Einmischung*, 83; originally published in Italian as *La altre. Conversazioni a Radiotre sui rapporti tra donne e politica, libertà fraternità, uguaglianza, democrazia, fascismo, resistenza, stato, partito, rivouzione, femminismo* (Milan: Casa editrice Valentino Bompaini, 1979).

Chapter 5   *Interim Remarks*

1. Otto Kirchheimer, "Weimar—und was dann? Analyse einer Verfassung," in Kirchheimer, *Politik und Verfassung* (Frankfurt/Main: Suhrkamp, 1964), 21.

2. Lida Gustava Heymann and Anita Augspurg, *Erlebtes—Erschautes. Deutsche Frauen kämpfen für Freiheit, Recht und Frieden*, ed. Margit Twellmann, 2nd ed. (Meisenheim: Hain, 1977), 187.

3. Joachim Perels, "Der Gleichheitssatz zwischen Hierarchie und Demokratie," in *Grundrechte als Fundament der Demokratie*, ed. Joachim Perels (Frankfurt/

Main: Suhrkamp, 1979), 69–75, here, 72; see also Ingeborg Maus, *Entwicklung und Funktionswandel der Theorie*, 38f.

4. Ulrich Scheuner, "Der Gleichheitsgedanke in der völkischen Verfassungsordnung," *Zeitschrift für die gesamte Staatswissenschaft* 99 (1939): 247, quoted in Perels, "Der Gleichheitssatz," 74, 79; see also Werner Hill, *Gleichheit und Artgleichheit* (Berlin: Duncker & Humblot, 1966), 205ff.

5. See Beitzke, *Gleichheit von Mann und Frau*, 208.

6. *BVerfGE* , 3: 225 ff., and many others.

7. See Ines Reich-Hilweg, *Männer und Frauen sind gleichberechtigt*, (Frankfurt/Main: Europäische Verlagsanstalt, 1979), and Vera Slupik, *Die Entscheidung des Grundgesetzes für Parität im Geschlechterverhältnis* (Berlin: Duncker & Humblot, 1988).

8. Gabriele Strecker, *Frausein heute* (Weilheim: Barth, 1965), 67.

9. See Maunz, Dürig, and Herzog, *Grundgesetz-Kommentar*, note on Art.3 II, marginal no. 11.

10. See Carol Smart, *Feminism and the Power of Law* (London and New York: Routledge, 1989), 5.

11. Rüdiger Voigt, "Positionsbestimmungen," in *Verrechtlichung*, ed. Rüdiger Voigt (Königstein/Ts.: Athenaeum, 1980), 13–17, here, 15.

12. Bloch, *Natural Law*, 12.

13. Rape within marriage has been a criminal offense in Germany since July 1997 according to the amended version of § 177 of the penal code.

14. Carol Gilligan, *In a Different Voice: Psychological Theory and Women's Development* (Cambridge: Harvard University Press, 1993), 149.

15. See Carole Pateman, ed., *The Disorder of Women: Democracy, Feminism and Political Theory* (Cambridge, Mass.: Polity Press, 1989), 196–197; Pateman refers to this as "Wollstonecraft's dilemma."

Chapter 6   *"Getting at the Root of the Evil"*

1. Anita Augspurg, "'Gebt acht, solange noch Zeit ist!'" *Die Frauenbewegung* (1895): 4.

2. Ibid.

3. Of the wealth of informational and agitation pamphlets, the following discussion relies on Auguste Kirchhoff, *Zur Entwicklung der Frauenstimmrechtsbewegung* (Bremen: Boesking, 1916); Frieda Ledermann, *Zur Geschichte der Frauenstimmrechtsbewegung* (Berlin: Scholem, 1918); Maria Lischnewska, *Die deutsche Frauenstimmrechtsbewegung zwischen Krieg und Frieden* (Berlin: published by the author, 1915); Anna Lindemann, "Die Frauenstimmrechtsbewegung in Deutschland," *Jahrbuch der Frauenbewegung* (1913): 159–172; Frieda Radel, *Warum fordern wir das Stimmrecht?* (Leipzig: Dietrich, 1910); Marie Walter, *Das Frauenstimmrecht* (Zurich: Grütliverein, 1913); Clara Zetkin, *Zur Frage des Frauenwahlrechts* (Berlin: Buchhandlung Vorwärts, 1907).

4. See "Olympe de Gouges (1791)," in *Women, the Family, and Freedom: The Debate in Documents*, ed. Susan Groag Bell and Karen M. Offen, 2 vols (Stanford, Calif.: Stanford University Press, 1983), 1:104–109; and "Olympe de Gouges, 'Declaration of the Rights of Woman and Female Citizen,'" in *Women in Revolutionary Paris, 1789–1795*, ed. Darlene Gay Levy, Harriet Applewhite, and Mary Durham Johnson (Urbana: University of Illinois Press, 1979), 92–96; see also Micheline R. Ishay, *The Human Rights Reader: Major Political Essays, Speeches and Documents from the Bible to the Present* (New York: Routledge, 1999), 140–147.

5. *Über die bürgerliche Verbesserung der Weiber* (Berlin: Voß, 1792; reprint, Frankfurt/Main: Syndikat, 1977). For an excerpt in English, see *Women, the Family, and Freedom*, ed. Bell and Offen, 116–119.

6. Mary Wollstonecraft, *A Vindication of the Rights of Women* (London, 1792); reprint ed. Mary Brody (London: Penguin Classics, 1985), 125.

7. Robert Blum, ed., *Sächsische Vaterlandsblätter* 3 (1843), 633; see also *Frauen-Zeitung*, 99, reprint of no. 11 (1849).

8. *Memoiren einer Idealistin*, 1st anonymous ed. (Leipzig: Schuster & Loeffler, 1875); see also Helene Lange and Gertrud Bäumer, eds., *Handbuch der Frauenbewegung*, I (Berlin: Moeser, 1901), 30–32.

9. John Stuart Mill, *The Subjection of Women* (London: Longmans, Greed, Reader & Dyer, 1869).

10. Hedwig Dohm, *Women's Nature and Privilege*, trans. Constance Campbell (Westport, Conn.: Hyperion Press, 1976), 150; first published as *Der Frauen Natur und Recht* (Berlin: Wedekind & Schwieger, 1876).

11. August Bebel, *Women Under Socialism*, trans. Daniel De Leon (New York: Schocken Books, 1971); first published as *Die Frau und der Sozialismus* (Zurich: Volksbuchhandlung, 1879).

12. Marie Stritt, "Die Frauenfrage auf dem evangelisch-sozialen Kongreß," *Die Frauenbewegung* (1879): 130–131; and Louise Otto, *Frauenleben im Deutschen Reich* (Leipzig: Schäfer, 1876), 259.

13. Thomas Vormbaum, *Die Rechtsfähigkeit der Vereine im 19. Jahrhundert. Ein Beitrag zur Entstehungsgeschichte des BGB* (Berlin and New York: Walter de Gruyter, 1976), 90f.

14. Quoted in Lily von Gisycki, "Nach links und rechts I," *Die Frauenbewegung* (1895): 33–35, here, 34.

15. Minna Cauer, *25 Jahre Verein Frauenwohl* (Berlin: Loewenthal, 1913), 13.

16. Lischnewska, *Die deutsche Frauenstimmrechtsbewegung*, 4.

17. Lindemann, "Die Frauenstimmrechtsbewegung," 159.

18. Cauer, *25 Jahre Verein Frauenwohl*, 13.

19. Immanuel Kant, *Religion within the Limits of Reason Alone* (1793), trans. T. M. Greene and H. H. Hudson (New York: Harper and Row, 1960), 176.

20. Lily von Gisycki, *Die Bürgerpflicht der Frau* (Berlin: Dümmler, 1895), 19, 23.

21. Lily von Gisycki, "Aus der Frauen bewegung" und "Nach links und recht II" *Die Frauenbewegung* (1895): 28–30 and 49–51, respectively.

22. Else Lüders, *Der "linke Flügel"* (Berlin: Loewenthal, 1904), 50–51; see also Alice Dullo, "Nochmals zur Frage des Frauenstimmrechts," *Die Frauenbewegung* (1906): 83, as well as a debate there ranging over several articles concerning "crown" or "roots."

23. Marie Stritt, "Wiener Eindrücke," *Die Frauenbewegung* (1897): 81.

24. Louise Otto, ed., *Einige Deutsche Gesetz-Paragraphen* (Leipzig: Schäfer, 1876), 2–3.

25. Emilie Kempin, *Die Stellung der Frau nach den z. Zt. gültigen Gesetzes-Bestimmungen sowie nach dem Entwurf eines bürgerlichen Gesetzbuches für das Deutsche Reich* (Leipzig: Schaefer, 1892); see also Sera Proelß and Marie Raschke, *Die Frau im neuen bürgerlichen Gesetzbuch* (Berlin: Dümmler, 1895), and Lüders, Der "linke Flügel," 24.

26. Emil Preetorius, *Die eheherrliche Vormundschaft und das BGB* (Berlin: Struppe & Winckler, 1907).

27. See, for example, Johannes Brenneisen, *Das bürgerliche Gesetzbuch und die Frauen* (Leipzig: Kunze, 1900).

28. Petition to the Social Democratic Party Convention, 1896, quoted in *Die Frauenbewegung* (1896): 126. The periodical *Gleichheit*, published by Clara Zetkin, also regularly reported on the debates and women's initiatives connected with the draft of the BGB; see *Die Gleichheit*, no. 11 (1896): 85 f.; no. 12 (1896): 90f.; and no. 13 (1896): 98f.

29. Weber, *Ehefrau und Mutter*, 434.

30. Proelß and Raschke, *Die Frau im neuen BGB*, 5; see also Marie Stritt, *Das bürgerliche Gesetzbuch und die Frauenfrage* (Frankenberg: Reisel, 1898), and quotes by Stritt in "Das Recht der Frau," *Die Frauenbewegung* (1896): 49.

31. "Aufruf," *Die Frauenbewegung* (1896): 114.

32. Ernst R. Huber, *Deutsche Verfassungsgeschichte seit 1789*, 2nd rev. ed. (Stuttgart, Berlin, Cologne, and Mainz: Kohlhammer, 1982), 4: 275–278. This second, updated edition thoroughly documents all initiatives and petitions in connection with the German Civil Code (BGB), such as that of the conservatives against liability for damage caused by game animals (the embarrassing "hare debate" in the Reichstag). In the entire 1,250–page volume there is not a single word about the women's legal movement against the BGB.

33. "Die Protestversammlung zu Berlin am 29. Juli 1896," *Die Frauenbewegung* (1896): 136–137.

34. Stritt, *Das bürgerliche Gesetzbuch*, 4.

35. Marie Stritt, "Rechtsschutz für Frauen," in *Handbuch der Frauenbewegung*, ed. Lange and Bäumer, part 2 (Berlin: Moeser, 1901), 123f.; Marie Raschke, "Generalbericht der Zentrale deutscher Rechtsschutzstelle für Frauen," *Die Frauenbewegung* (1902): 92f.; Elisabeth Altmann–Gottheinner, ed., *Jahrbuch des Bundes Deutscher Frauenvereine*, address section (Leipzig and Berlin: Teubner, 1918), 61. See also Rosemarie Schade, "Frauen helfen Frauen," *Feministische Studien* 2 (1989): 135–144, which highlights the exemplary legal protection office in Heidelberg, headed by Camilla Jellinek. See also Beatrix Geisel, *Klasse, Geschlecht und Recht: vergleichende sozialhistorische Untersuchung der Rechtsberatungspraxis von Frauen- und Arbeiterbewegung (1894–1933)* (Baden-Baden: Nomos, 1997).

36. Stritt, "Rechtsschutz für Frauen," 127; see also M. Bennewitz, "Rechtsschutzstellen," in *Der Internationale Frauenkongress in Berlin* (Berlin: Habel, 1904), 384f.

37. Raschke, "Generalbericht," 92.

38. Gertrud Bäumer, "25 Jahre Rechtsschutzarbeit," *Die Frau* (1922): 215.

39. Anita Augspurg, "Ein typischer Fall der Gegenwart," *Die Frauenbewegung* (1905): 81.

40. See, for example, Gertrud Bäumer et al., *Frauenbewegung und Sexualethik, Beiträge zur modernen Ehekritik*, 2nd ed. (Heilbronn: Salzer, 1909).

41. Minna Cauer, "Alte Fragen in neuer Beleuchtung," *Die Frauenbewegung* (1905): 49; Cauer, "Einstellung oder Unterstellung," *Die Frauenbewegung* (1905): 105. See also Heide Schlüpmann, "Radikalisierung der Philosophie," *Feministische Studien* 1 (1984): 10–34.

42. "Die Tagung des Verbandes Fortschrittlicher Frauenvereine vom 2.–4. Okt. zu Berlin," *Die Frauenbewegung* (1905): 155.

43. Ross Evans Paulson, *Women's Suffrage and Prohibition: A Comparative Study of Equality and Social Control* (Glenview, Ill.: Scott, 1973), 113. See also Eleanor Flexner, *Century of Struggle*, enl. ed. (Cambridge: Harvard University Press, 1996), chapters 11–16; see also Mary P. Ryan "The Power of

Women's Networks: A Case Study of Female Moral Reform in Antebellum America," *Feminist Studies* 5 (1979): 66–85.

44. Criminal laws against pimping, aggravated procuring, and distributing obscene publications were introduced or tightened with passage of the "Lex Heinze." Under § 184, item 3a of the German penal code (StGB), these prohibitions included publicizing or advertising for contraceptive devices. Paragraph 184a, censoring literature, theater, and the fine arts, was repealed after public protests.

45. Prostitution was decriminalized in a 1927 law; only certain forms of it ("in an obvious manner," etc.) remained subject to punishment. In contrast, § 180 II StGB of this law expressly provided that "keeping a brothel" constituted illegal procuring. Nevertheless, the legal situation remains unclear, as paragraph 3 leaves nonexploitative "provision of accommodation" to prostitutes exempt from punishment. Because this is a question of interpretation, prostitution remains tacitly tolerated.

46. On this, see Ulla Wischermann's essay "Die Presse der radikalen Frauenbewegung," *Feministische Studien* 1 (1984): 39–62.

47. Lida Gustava Heymann and Anita Augspurg, *Erlebtes-Erschautes* (Meisenheim am Glan: Hain, 1977), 50.

48. Lily von Gizycki, "Stimmungsbilder aus der Generalversammlung des Bundes deutscher Frauenvereine in München," *Die Frauenbewegung* (1895): 69.

49. Lüders, *Der "linke Flügel,"* 30 f.

50. Anna Pappritz, "Die Sittlichkeitsfrage auf dem Internationalen Frauenkongress," *Die Frauenbewegung* (1899): 130f.; see also Pappritz, "Die Zwecke und Ziele der Internationalen Abolitionistischen Föderation," *Der Abolitionist* 1 (1902).

51. Pappritz, "Zwecke und Ziele."

52. "Ein Kampf gegen die öffentlichen Häuser in Hamburg," *Beilage der Frauenbewegung, Parlamentarische Angelegenheiten und Gesetzgebung,* nos. 1 and 12 (1902).

53. Heymann and Augspurg, *Erlebtes-Erschautes,* 53.

54. Minna Cauer, "Vogelfrei," *Die Frauenbewegung* (1902): 169.

55. Anita Augspurg, "Schweigen die Frauen?" *Beilage der Frauenbewegung. Parlamentarische Angelegenheiten,* no. 14 (1902).

56. Minna Cauer, "Die Schutzlosigkeit der Frau," *Die Frauenbewegung* (1898): 13; Cauer, "Die Mißgriffe der Polizei," *Die Frauenbewegung* (1902): 187; Augspurg, "Schweigen die Frauen?" 139.

57. "Frl. Doktors Verhaftung" and "Frl. Doktors Plaidoyer," *Die Frauenbewegung* (1902): 172–173.

58. "Beschwerdeschrift von Dr. jur. Anita Augspurg an den Gemeindevorstand der Großherzogl. Sächsischen Haupt- und Residenzstadt Weimar," *Beiträge der Frauenbewegung. Parlamentarische Angelegenheiten,* no. 22 (1902).

59. Cauer, "Die Schutzlosigkeit der Frau." See also Marie Raschke, "Die weibliche Ehre," *Die Frauenbewegung* (1897): 250.

60. "Wieder ein Schlag ins Antlitz der Frau" and "Das Altonaer Schwurgerichtsurteil" in several installments, *Beilage der Frauenbewegung. Parlamentarische Angelegenheiten,* nos. 3, 4, 5, and 6 (1905).

61. Ibid., no. 6.

62. Augspurg, "Schweigen die Frauen?"

63. Helene Stöcker, "Strafrechtsreform und Abtreibung," *Die Neue Generation*

(1908): 399; see also ibid., 211. See also "Sittlichkeitsfrage," *Die Frauen-bewegung* (1908): 190.

64. *Petition des Bundes Deutscher Frauenvereine zur Reform des Strafrechts*, written by Camilla Jellinek (n. p., 1909), 45f. It should be noted that Camilla Jellinek, who supported elimination of § 218, explicitly left this portion of the explanation to Katharina Scheven and documented her different standpoint in *Die Strafrechtsreform und die §§ 218 und 219 StGB* (Heidelberg: Winter, 1909). See also Else Lüders, "Eindrücke von der Generalversammlung des Bundes Deutscher Frauenvereine," *Die Frauenbewegung* (1908): 154.

65. Anna Bergmann, "Frauen, Männer, Sexualität und Geburtenkontrolle. Die Gebärstreikdebatte der SPD im Jahre 1913," in *Frauen suchen ihre Geschichte*, ed. Karin Hausen (Munich: Beck, 1983), 81–108, here, 94. On the German Communist Party and its campaign against § 218 in the 1920s, see Silvia Kontos, "Hausarbeit, Geburtenkontrolle und Frauenautonomie," *Gesellschaft. Beiträge zur Marxschen Theorie* 14 (1981): 12.

66. Helene Stöcker, ed., *Petitionen des Deutschen Bundes für Mutterschutz 1905–1916* (Berlin: Geschäftstelle des Bundes für Mutterschutz, n.d. [1916]), 3.

67. Ibid., 52.

68. Ibid., 17.

69. "Arbeiterinnenschutz," in *Der Internationale Frauenkongreß in Berlin*, ed. Marie Stritt (Berlin, 1905), 445 f.

70. The circumstances of this speech caused a sensation because Helene Simon had to follow the reading of her address from the cordoned-off section reserved for women. See Agnes von Zahn-Harnack, *Die Frauenbewegung, Geschichte, Probleme, Ziele* (Berlin: Deutsche Buch-Gemeinschaft, 1928), 280, 248–249.

71. Helene Simon, "Arbeiterinnenschutz und bürgerliche Frauenbewegung," *Soziale Praxis* (1901): 33.

72. See the literature mentioned in note 3 of this chapter.

73. "Deutscher Verein für Frauenstimmrecht," *Die Frauenbewegung* (1902): 1 f.

74. Lischnewska, *Die deutsche Frauenstimmrechtsbewegung*, 8–9.

75. Ledermann, *Zur Geschichte der Frauenstimmrechtsbewegung*, 22

76. Zetkin, *Zur Frage des Frauenwahlrechts*, 12 f.

77. Kirchhoff, *Zur Entwicklung der Frauenstimmrechtsbewegung*, 9.

78. Lischnewska, *Die deutsche Frauenstimmrechtsbewegung*, 24 f., and Kirchhoff, *Zur Entwicklung der Frauenstimmrechtsbewegung*, 11.

79. See Tony Breitscheid, *Die Notwendigkeit der Forderung des allgemeinen, gleichen und direkten Wahlrechts* (Berlin: Preussischer Landesverein für Frauen-stimmrecht, 1909).

80. Kirchhoff, *Zur Entwicklung der Frauenstimmrechtsbewegung*, 11–12.

81. Rita Bardenhauer, *Woher und Wohin? Geschichtliches und Grundsätzliches aus der Frauenbewegung* (Leipzig: Naturwissenschaften GmbH, 1918), 98.

82. See *Zeitschrift für Frauenstimmrecht*, nos. 23–24 (1917): 48.

83. On this, see "Frauenstimmrechtsbewegung," *Zeitschrift für Frauenstimmrecht*, nos. 19–20 (1917): 41 and nos. 15–16 (1917): 30.

84. Minna Cauer, "Staatsbürgerin und Frauenrechtlerin," *Die Frauenbewegung* (1909): 148.

85. See Rose Rauther, "Rosika Schwimmer. Stationen auf dem Lebensweg einer Pazifistin" *Feministische Studien* 1 (1984): 63–75. See also Marie Louise Degen, *The History of the Women's Peace Party* (Baltimore, Md.: Johns Hopkins University Press, 1939); Gertrude Bussey and Margarete Tims, *Women's International League for Peace and Freedom. 1915–1965. A Record on Fifty Years' Work*

(London: Allen & Unwin, 1965); Catherine Foster, *Women for All Seasons: The Story of the Women's International League for Peace and Freedom* (Athens: University of Georgia Press, 1989); Ute Gerhard, "National oder International. Die internationalen Beziehungen der deutschen bürgerlichen Frauenbewegung," *Feministische Studien* 2 (1994): 34–52; Leila J. Rupp, *Worlds of Women: The Making of an International Women's Movement* (Princeton, N.J.: Princeton University Press, 1997); Leila J. Rupp, "Zur Organisation der internationalen Frauenbewegung vor dem Zweiten Weltkrieg," *Feministische Studien* 2 (1994): 53–65.

86. Aletta Jacobs, Welcome Address," in *International Women's Congress in the Hague, 28 April–1 May 1915, Report,* ed. International Women's Committee of Permanent Peace (Amsterdam, n.d.), 8.

87. See the discussion at the Hague conference, especially Helene Stöcker, "Auch das Stimmrecht wird uns nicht vor dem Ausbruch des Krieges schützen können," in *International Women's Congress in the Hague, 28 April–1 May 1915, Report,* 126, and various pieces in *Die Frau im Staat. Eine Monatsschrift,* ed. Anita Augsburg und Lida Gustava Heymann, vols. 1–15 (1919 bis 1933); see also Ulla Wischermann's essay, "Die Presse der radikalen Frauenbewegung," in *Feministische Studien* 1 (1984), 39–62, wherein she described the monthly journal as strongly pacifist, speaking out for women's issues, international understanding, and peace.

88. Quoted in Gisela Brinker–Gabler, *Frauen gegen den Krieg* (Frankfurt/Main: Fischer, 1980), 16.

89. Oekinghaus, *Die gesellschaftliche und rechtliche Stellung der deutschen Frau,* 118 and 27f.

90. Heymann and Augspurg, *Erlebtes-Erschautes,* 189 f.

91. Internationale Frauenliga für Frieden und Freiheit/Deutscher Zweig (Women's International League for Peace and Freedom, German branch), ed., *Völkerversöhnende Frauenarbeit während des Weltkrieges,* parts 1–4 (Munich: B. Heller, 1920–1933).

92. L. Wäldin-Kobe, "Die Frauen und der Krieg," *Frauenstimmrecht* (1913): 57–58.

93. Maunz, Dürig, and Herzog, *Grundgesetz-Kommentar,* note on Art. 3 II GG, marginal no. 11.

94. Gertrud Bäumer, *Die Frau und das geistige Leben* (Leipzig: Amelang, 1911), 97–98.

95. See Hans Hattenhauer, *Zwischen Hierarchie und Demokratie* (Karlsruhe: Müller, 1971), 159f.

96. Minna Cauer, "'Antwort' auf Leo Rosbacher," *Die Frauenbewegung* (1908): 74–75. See also Cauer, "Staatsbürgerin und Frauenrechtlerin," *Die Frauenbewegung* (1909): 148: "[A] women's rights advocate par excellence can only be consistent by joining the Social Democratic party. . . . All other parties, to the shame of liberalism, it must be said, completely fail in this respect."

97. Barbara Sichtermann, *Weiblichkeit. Zur Politik des Privaten* (Berlin: Wagenbach, 1983), 104.

98. A. L. Elgström, "Gemeinmütterlichkeit," *Die Neue Generation* (1918): 378.

Chapter 7   Gender Tutelage: Women in Nineteenth-Century Legal Doctrine

1. For example, the disagreement between artisans and reformers about whether freedom of trade applied to women as well as men was not decided until the

1869 trade law for the North German Confederation made the decision in favor of women, though here, too, it was restricted for wives. See Ute Gerhard, *Verhältnisse und Verhinderungen. Frauenarbeit, Familie und Recht der Frauen im 19. Jahrhundert* (Frankfurt/Main: Suhrkamp, 1978), 36f.; on suffrage and other civic rights, see chapter 4 of this book.

2. Rudolf Ernst Huber, *Deutsche Verfassungsgeschichte seit 1789*, 2nd ed. (Stuttgart: Kohlhammer, 1975), 2:790.

3. *Die Frauen-Zeitung*, 328; reprint of no. 51 (1850).

4. *Aufruf*, signed by the Legal Commission of the Federation of German Women's Organizations, reprinted in *Die Frauenbewegung* (1986), 114–115.

5. See Dieter Grimm, "Bürgerlichkeit im Recht," in *Bürger und Bürgerlichkeit im 19. Jahrhundert*, ed. Jürgen Kocka (Göttingen: Vandenhoeck & Ruprecht, 1987), 149.

6. Pio Caroni, *"Privatrecht": Eine sozialhistorische Einführung* (Basel and Frankfurt/Main: Helbing & Lichtenhahn, 1988), 102.

7. Otto von Gierke, *Die soziale Aufgabe des Privatrechts* (Berlin: Springer, 1889), 5.

8. Inst. Just. I.1.4, quoted in Caroni, *Privatrecht*, 105.

9. Caroni, *Privatrecht*, 103; see also Heide Wunder, "Herrschaft und öffentliches Handeln von Frauen in der Gesellschaft der Frühen Neuzeit," in *Frauen in der Geschichte des Rechts: Von der Frühen Neuzeit bis zur Gegenwart*, ed. Ute Gerhard (Munich: Beck, 1997), 27–54; and Gerhard Dilcher, "Die Ordnung der Ungleichheit. Haus, Stand und Geschlecht," in *Frauen in der Geschichte des Rechts*, 55–72.

10. Karl Marx, "On the Jewish Question," chapter 1, "Bruno Bauer, Die Judenfrage (The Jewish Question: Braunschweig 1843)," in *The Marx-Engels Reader*, ed. Robert C. Tucker, 2nd ed. (London: W. W. Norton, 1978), 34.

11. On this process, see in particular Reinhart Koselleck, *Preußen zwischen Reform und Revolution. Allgemeines Landrecht, Verwaltung und soziale Bewegung von 1791–1848*, 2nd ed. (Stuttgart: Klett, 1975), 63ff.

12. On the status of women in public law, see Ute Gerhard, "Grenzziehungen und-überschreitungen. Die Rechte der Frauen auf dem Weg in die politische Öffentlichkeit," in *Frauen in der Geschichte des Rechts*, 509–546; Birgitta Bader-Zaar, "Bürgerrechte und Geschlecht. Zur Frage der politischen Gleichberechtigung von Frauen in Österreich, 1848–1918," in *Frauen in der Geschichte des Rechts*, 547–562.

13. See, for example, Hermann Conrad, "Die Rechtsstellung der Ehefrau in der Privatrechtsgesetzgebung der Aufklärungszeit," in *Aus Mittelalter und Neuzeit, Festschrift für Gerhard Kallen zum 70. Geburtstag*, ed. J. Engel and H. M. Klinkenberg (Bonn: Hanstein, 1957), 253–270; Heinrich Dörner, *Industrialisierung und Familienrecht. Die Auswirkungen des sozialen Wandels dargestellt an den Familienmodellen des ALR, BGB und des französischen code civil* (Berlin: Duncker & Humblot, 1974). In contrast, more recently, see the comprehensive *Handbuch der Quellen und Literatur der neueren europäischen Privatrechtsgeschichte*, vol. 2, *Das 19. Jahrhundert*, ed. Helmut Coing (Munich: Beck, 1982), with many sources and references. Unfortunately, Stephan Buchholz's chapter on German law, in contrast to Ernst Holthöfer's on French law, follows the usual legal separation into matrimonial and divorce law, marital property law, and so forth, in which the woman's rights as a person always disappear. An invaluable source for legal history and comparative law remains Marianne Weber, *Ehefrau und Mutter in der Rechtsentwicklung* (Tübingen: Mohr, 1907; reprint, Aalen: Scientia, 1971).

14. This is also true of Ute Gerhard, *Verhältnisse und Verhinderungen*, as well as Christina Damm, "Die Stellung der Ehefrau und Mutter nach Urteilen des Reichsgerichts von 1879 bis 1914. Eine Untersuchung zum Spannungsverhältnis zwischen dem Ideal der Gleichberechtigung und der von Recht und Ideologie legitimierten sozialen Wirklichkeit" (Ph.D. dissertation, Marburg, 1983), and, more recently, the very useful work by Susanne Weber-Will, *Die rechtliche Stellung der Frau im Privatrecht des Preußischen Allgemeinen Landrecht von 1794* (Frankfurt/Main: Lang, 1983); the latter includes a comparative law summary in each chapter.

15. Franz Wieacker, *Privatrechtsgeschichte der Neuzeit unter Berücksichtigung der deutschen Entwicklung*, 2nd ed. (Göttingen: Vandenhoeck & Ruprecht, 1967), 473.

16. See the contemporary quotes in Coing, introduction to Julius von Staudinger, *Kommentar zum Bürgerlichen Gesetzbuch*, 12th ed. (Berlin: Schweitzer, 1980), marginal no. 19–22.

17. Louise Otto, foreword to *Einige deutsche Gesetzparagraphen über die Stellung der Frau*, ed. Allgemeiner deutscher Frauenverein (Leipzig: Schäfer, 1876), 3.

18. Ibid.

19. Von Staudinger, *Kommentar zum Bürgerlichen Gesetzbuch*, marginal no. 25.

20. This was, without doubt, a considerably larger number at the end of the century than at the beginning, when the General Code claimed only subsidiary validity in Prussia, after the individual laws of the various provinces. But I know of no survey for the earlier period.

21. Von Staudinger, *Kommentar zum Bürgerlichen Gesetzbuch*, marginal no. 24.

22. Reinhart Koselleck, *Preußen zwischen Reform und Revolution* (Stuttgart: Klett-Cotta, 1975), 23f.; here, 24.

23. See also Wieacker, *Privatrechtsgeschichte der Neuzeit*, 332f.

24. "Patent wegen Publication des neuen allgemeinen Gesetzbuches für die Preußischen Staaten," in *Allgemeines Landrecht* (Berlin, 1794), 1.

25. Johann Georg Schlosser, *Briefe über die Gesetzgebung überhaupt und den Entwurf des preußischen Gesetzbuchs insbesondere* (Frankfurt/Main: Fleischer, 1789; reprint, Glashütten: Auvermann, 1970), 279.

26. Emilie Kempin, *Die Stellung der Frau nach den zur Zeit in Deutschland gültigen Gesetzesbestimmungen sowie nach dem Entwurf eines bürgerlichen Gesetzbuches für das Deutsche Reich*, ed. Allgemeiner Deutscher Frauenverein (Leipzig: Schäfer, 1892), 10.

27. See Carl Georg Haubold, *Lehrbuch des königlichen-sächsischen Privatrechts* (Leipzig: Hahn, 1847), Part I, § 7.

28. See Wieacker, *Privatrechtsgeschichte der Neuzeit*, 459.

29. On this, see also Franz Wieacker, *Industriegesellschaft und Privatrechtsordnung* (Frankfurt/Main: Athenäum, 1974), 15, which describes the German civil code as the "late-born child of the science of pandects and the national democratic movement . . . led by liberalism since 1848."

30. Stephan Buchholz, "Einzelgesetzgebung Deutschland," in *Handbuch der Quellen und Literatur der Neueren Europäischen Privatrechtsgeschichte*, ed. Helmut Coing, vol. 3, *Das 19. Jahrhundert*, book 2 (Munich: Beck, 1982), 1626–1773; here, 1639.

31. W. Andreas, "Die Einführung des Code Napoléon in Baden," *Zeitschrift der Savigny-Stiftung für Rechtsgeschichte, German. Abt.* (Weimar, 1910): 182–234. See also Elisabeth Fehrenbach, *Traditionale Gesellschaft und revolutionäres Recht. Die Einführung des Code Napoléon in die Rheinbundstaaten*, 2nd ed. (Göttingen:

Vandenhoeck & Ruprecht, 1978), 26, and Elisabeth Fehrenbach, *Der Kampf um die Einführung des Code Napoléon in den Rheinbundstaaten* (Wiesbaden: Steiner, 1973), 9, 15.

32. See Wieacker, *Privatrechtsgeschichte der Neuzeit*, 342–346.
33. In the words of J. N. F. Brauer, who was crucial in preparing the way for the *Code civil* in Baden and also wrote commentaries on it, quoted in Andreas, 223; see J. N. F. Brauer, *Erläuterungen über den Code Napoléon und die Großherzoglich Badische bürgerliche Gesetzgebung* (Karlsruhe, 1811).
34. See Murad Ferid, *Das französische Zivilrecht*, vol. 1 (Frankfurt/Main: Metzner, 1971), marginal note 1 A 59.
35. Quoted in Fehrenbach, *Der Kampf um die Einführung*, 9.
36. Ernst Holthöfer, "Zivilgesetzgebung Frankreich," in *Handbuch der Quellen und Literatur der neueren europäischen Privatrechtsgeschichte*, vol. 3, *Das 19. Jahrhundert*, book 1, ed. Helmut Coing (Munich: Beck, 1982), 863–1068, here, 884.
37. See Ferid, *Das französische Zivilrecht*, marginal no. 1 A 50.
38. Fehrenbach, *Traditionale Gesellschaft*, 23.
39. Marianne Weber, *Ehefrau und Mutter*, 320, 318.
40. Karl Friedrich Eichhorn, *Einleitung in das deutsche Privatrecht mit Einschluß des Lebensrecht*, 5th ed. (Göttingen: Vandenhoeck & Ruprecht, 1845), VII.
41. Wieacker, *Privatrechtsgeschichte der Neuzeit*, 353.
42. Carl Friedrich von Gerber, *System des Deutschen Privatrechts* (Jena, 1863), 81–82.
43. Ibid., 573.
44. Georg Beseler, *System des gemeinen deutschen Privatrechts* (1847; Berlin: Weidmann, 1873), 480–481.
45. Wilhelm Theodor Kraut, *Die Vormundschaft nach den Grundsätzen des deutschen Rechts*, 3 vols. (Göttingen: Dietrich, 1835–1859).
46. For details, see Ernst Holthöfer, "Die Geschlechtsvormundschaft. Ein Überblick von der Antike bis ins 19. Jahrhundert," in *Frauen in der Geschichte des Rechts*, 390–451; Susanne Weber-Will, "Geschlechtsvormundschaft und weibliche Rechtswohltaten im Privatrecht des preußischen Allgemeinen Landrechts von 1794," in *Frauen in der Geschichte des Rechts*, 452–459; David Warren Sabean, "Allianzen und Listen: Die Geschlechtsvormundschaft im 18. und 19. Jahrhundert," in *Frauen in der Geschichte des Rechts*, 460–479.
47. Kraut, *Die Vormundschaft*, 2:299.
48. Ibid., 291f., 322.
49. Ibid., 320.
50. Ibid., 321.
51. Judgment of 13 July 1886, *Entscheidungen des Reichgerichts in Zivilsachen* (Leipzig, 1887), 16:148f.
52. Carl Josef Anton Mittermaier, *Grundsätze des gemeinen deutschen Privatrechts*, 7th ed. (Regensburg: Manz, 1847), 2:347.
53. In "Die Stellung der Ehefrau und Mutter," note 4, p. 37, Christina Damm also points out the absence of any judgments on ability to conduct business apart from the marital property law.
54. Ibid., 46.
55. See Christian G. Haubold, *Lehrbuch des Königlich-Sächsischen Privatrechts* (Leipzig: Hahn, 1820 and 1847), § 153, §154.
56. See Conrad, "Die Rechtsstellung der Ehefrau," 260.
57. Johann Gottlieb Fichte, *The Science of Rights*, trans. A. E. Kroeger (New York:

Harper and Row, 1970), 392; originally published 1796 as *Grundlage des Naturrechts nach Prinzipien der Wissenschaftslehre*.

58. Christian Wolff, *Grundsätze des Natur- und Völkerrechts, worin alle Verbindlichkeiten und alle Rechte aus der Natur des Menschen in einem beständigen Zusammenhang hergeleitet werden können* (Halle: Renger, 1754, reprinted Königstein: Scriptor, 1980), 638.

59. Macpherson, *The Political Theory of Possessive Individualism*, 264.

60. See Johann Friedrich Ludwig Göschen, *Vorlesungen über das Civilrecht* (Göttingen: Vandenhoeck & Ruprecht, 1839), 3, 38–41, and Georg Puchta, *Pandekten*, 8th ed. (Leipzig: Barth, 1856), 586.

61. Puchta, *Pandekten*, 586.

62. This is the reason the organized women's movement in Germany supported the common-law system of marital property at the time the Civil Code was passed. See *Schriften des Bundes deutscher Frauenvereine, Petition und Begleitschrift betreffend das Familienrecht* (Leipzig: Schäfer, n.d. [1895]).

63. Otto, "Foreword," in *Einige deutsche Gesetzparagraphen*, 17.

64. On this, see the chapter by Ursula Vogel, "Patriarchale Herrschaft, bürgerliches Recht, bürgerliche Utopie. Eigentumsrechte der Frauen in Deutschland und England," in *Bürgertum und bürgerliche Gesellschaft*, 406–438.

65. Holthöfer, "Zivilgesetzgebung Frankreich," 906.

66. Emma Oekinghaus, *Die gesellschaftliche und rechtliche Stellung der deutschen Frau* (Jena: Gustav Fischer, 1925), 7f. See also Ernst Manheim, "Beiträge zu einer Geschichte der autoritären Familie," in *Studien über Autorität und Familie*, ed. Erich Fromm et al. (Paris: Alcan, 1936), 2:523ff., and Max Weber, *Economy and Society: An Outline of Interpretive Sociology*, 2 vols., ed. Guenther Roth and Claus Wittich (Berkeley and Los Angeles: University of California Press, 1978), 1:231–235; 2:1006–1013.

67. See Otto Dann, *Gleichheit und Gleichberechtigung. Das Gleichheitspostulat in der alteuropäischen Tradition und in Deutschland bis zum ausgehenden 19. Jahrhundert* (Berlin: Duncker and Humblot, 1980), 144f.

68. August Wilhelm Rehberg, *Ueber den Code Napoléon und dessen Einführung in Deutschland* (Hanover: Hahn, 1814), 151.

69. See, for example, the reports of the Prussian auditor, which are a fertile source for social history: *Gesetz. Revision-Pensum* 15 (Berlin, 1930).

70. Jean Jacques Rousseau, *Confessions*, intro. R. Niklaus (London: J. M. Dent & Sons, 1964), 9.

71. See, in contrast, a later Reich Supreme Court judgment, cited in Damm, "Stellung der Ehefrau und Mutter," 129f.

72. See Otto, "Foreword," in *Einige deutsche Gesetzparagraphen*, 2.

73. See Philippe Ariès, *Centuries of Childhood: A Social History of Family Life* (New York: Knopf, 1962); originally published as *L'Enfant et la vie familiale sous l'Ancien Régime* (Paris: Plon, 1960).

74. See Elisabeth Badinter, *Mother Love: Myth and Reality—Motherhood in Modern History* (New York: Macmillan, 1981); originally published as *L'amour en plus: histoire de l'amour maternel (17th–20th centuries)* (Paris: Flammarion, 1980).

75. Anke Leineweber, *Die rechtliche Beziehung des nichtehelichen Kindes zu seinem Erzeuger in der Geschichte des Privatrechts* (Königstein: Hanstein, 1978), 55f.

76. Damm, *Stellung der Ehefrau und Mutter*, 158.

77. See Hermann Conrad, "Die Stellung der unehelichen Kinder in der neuzeitlichen Privatrechtsentwicklung Deutschlands, Frankreichs, Österreichs und der Schweiz," *Zeitschrift für das gesamte Familienrecht* (1962): 325f.

78. According to Anton Menger, *Das bürgerliche Recht und die besitzlosen Klassen* (Tübingen: Laupp,1908; reprint, Darmstadt: Wissenschaftliche Buchgesellschaft, 1968), 72.
79. Leineweber, *Die rechtliche Beziehung,* 249.
80. Marianne Weber, *Ehefrau und Mutter,* 325.
81. See also Andreas, *Einführung des Code Napoléon in Baden,* 221.
82. Rehberg, *Ueber den Code Napoleon,* 155.
83. Johann N. F. Brauer, *Erläuterungen über den Code Napoleon und die Großherzoglich Badische bürgerliche Gesetzgebung* (Karlsruhe: Müller, 1809), 1:200.
84. Quoted in Andreas, *Einführung des Code Napoléon in Baden,* 190, 221.
85. During the French Revolution, for example, as well as in Germany around 1848; see Gerhard, *Verhältnisse und Verhinderungen,* 167f.
86. Dirk Blasius, "Bürgerliche Rechtsgleichheit und die Ungleichheit der Geschlechter. Das Scheidungsrecht im historischen Vergleich," in *Bürgerinnen und Bürger. Geschlechterverhältnisse im 19. Jahrhundert,* ed. Ute Frevert (Göttingen: Vandenhoeck & Ruprecht, 1988), 67–84.
87. Buchholz, "Einzelgesetzgebung Deutschland," 1678.
88. Quoted in Heinrich Dernburg, *Lehrbuch des preußischen Privatrechts* (Halle: Verlag der Buchhandlung des Waisenhauses, 1881), 3:194.
89. Brüggemann, *Stenographischer Bericht der 1. Kammer von 1853,* 1:44, quoted in Damm, *Stellung der Ehefrau und Mutter,* 148.
90. See Dernburg, *Lehrbuch des Preußischen Privatrechts,* 3: 81.
91. For greater detail, see Damm, *Stellung der Ehefrau und Mutter,* 37f.
92. Bernhard Mugdan, *Die gesamten Materialien zum Bürgerlichen Gesetzbuch für das deutsche Reich,* vol. 4, *Familienrecht: Motive* (Berlin: Decker, 1899), 124.
93. See the two petitions in *Einige deutsche Gesetzparagraphen* and *Schriften des Bundes Deutscher Frauenvereine, Petition und Begleitschrift betr. das Familienrecht im Entwurf des neuen bürgerlichen Gesetzbuches* (Leipzig, 1895).
94. Enneccerus and Nipperdey, *Allgemeiner Teil des Bürgerlichen Rechts,* 15th ed., book 1 (Tübingen: Mohr, 1959), § 83 II.1.
95. Wilhelm Bornemann, *Systematische Darstellung des Preussischen Civilrechts,* (Berlin: Jonas, 1834), 1:77.
96. I will not consider here the unequal, complicated process for the emancipation of unmarried daughters under the Prussian General Code, § 230 II. 2. See Dörner, *Industrialisierung und Familienrecht;* and Weber-Will, *Die rechtliche Stellung der Frau,* 199f.
97. This was finally eliminated by § 102 of the Tutelage Law [*Vormundschaftsordnung*] of 5 July 1875; see also Weber-Will, *Die rechtliche Stellung der Frau,* 220f.
98. For greater detail, see Weber-Will, *Die rechtliche Stellung der Frau.,* 197f., 230f., 274f.
99. Particularly serious cases included the prohibition of political women's organizations in France in 1793 and in the German Confederation after 1850.
100. For details, see Moisej Ostrogoskij, *Die Frau im öffentlichen Recht. Eine vergleichende Untersuchung der Geschichte der Gesetzgebung der civilisierten Länder* (Leipzig: Wigand, 1897).
101. Bernhard Windscheid, *Lehrbuch des Pandektenrechts,* 7th ed. (Frankfurt/Main, 1891), 1:93.
102. Gerber, *System des Deutschen Privatrechts,* § 221.
103. See Hermann Conrad, "Die Rechtsstellung der Ehefrau," 267; and Weber, *Ehefrau und Mutter,* 320.

104. A. H. Huussen, Jr., "Le droit du mariage au cours de la révolution française," *Tydschrift voor Rechtsgeschiedenis* (1979), 10.
105. Huussen, "Le droit du mariage," 45. On the overall context, see especially Philippe Sagnac, *La législation civile de la révolution française (1789–1804)* (Paris: Hachette, 1898).
106. See Huussen, "Le droit du mariage," 15, in which he views the few available data for Paris and a few other cities as hardly representative or capable of interpretation.
107. Sagnac, *La législation civile*, 292.
108. Huussen, "Le droit du mariage," 49.
109. Ibid., 106.
110. Conrad, "Die Rechtsstellung der Ehefrau," 265.
111. See P. Lerebours-Pigeonniére, "La famille et le code civil," in *Le Code civil. 1804–1904. Livre du centenaire* (Paris: Rousseau, 1904), 270.
112. Sagnac, *La législation civile*, 299f.
113. Huussen, "Le droit du mariage," 104 n. 317.
114. See Paul Viollet, *Histoire du droit civil français* (Paris: Larose & Tenin, 1905; reprint, Aalen: Scientia, 1966), 511.
115. See Ute Gerhard, "Menschenrechte auch für Frauen. Der Entwurf der Olympe de Gouges," *Kritische Justiz* 2 (1987): 127–140.
116. Sagnac, *La législation civile*, 376.
117. Jean Etienne Marie Portalis, *Discours. Rapports et travaux inédits sur le code civil* (Paris: Joubert, 1844), 162.
118. Quoted in Conrad, "Die Rechtsstellung der Ehefrau," 269.
119. For example, Mirabeau, in his public education program; see J. Portemer, "Le statut de la femme en France," *Receuils de la société Jean Bodin pour l'histoire comparative des institutions* 12, part 2 (Brussels, 1962): 487.
120. *Exposé de motifs fait par J. E. M. Portalis* (1803), quoted in Conrad, "Die Rechtsstellung der Ehefrau," 268–269.
121. In the words of Friedrich Carl von Savigny, who translated this theory into family law practice. See Gerhard, *Verhältnisse und Verhinderungen*, 167ff.
122. René König, "Familie und Autorität: Der deutsche Vater im Jahre 1955," in *Materialien zur Soziologie der Familie* (Cologne: Kiepenheuer & Witsch, 1974), 218.
123. Michel Vovelle, *Die Französische Revolution. Soziale Bewegung und Umbruch der Mentalitäten* (Munich: Oldenbourg, 1982), 52; originally published in Italian as *Breve storia della rivoluzione francese* (Rome: Gius. Laterza and Figli Spa, 1979).
124. Theodor Gottlieb von Hippel, *Über die bürgerliche Verbesserung der Weiber* (Berlin: Voß, 1792; reprint, Frankfurt/Main: Syndikat, 1977), 45; for an excerpt in English see *Women, the Family, and Freedom*, ed. Bell and Offen, 116–120.
125. E. F. Klein, "Muß das weibliche Geschlecht mit dem männlichen durchgehends gleiche Rechte haben?" *Annalen der Gesetzgebung und Rechtsgelehrsamkeit von den Preußischen Staaten* 17 (Berlin: Nicolai, 1788), 203.
126. See Jacques Donzelot, *The Policing of Families*, trans. Robert Hurley (Baltimore, Md.: Johns Hopkins University Press, 1997).
127. Habermas, *The Structural Transformation of the Public Sphere*, 27.

Chapter 8 *Human Rights Are Women's Rights*

1. Dohm, *Women's Nature and Privilege*, 142.
2. On this discussion, see Ute Gerhard, Mechthhild Jansen, Andrea Maihofer,

Pia Schmid, and Irmgard Schulz, eds. *Differenz und Gleichheit. Menschenrechte haben (k)ein Geschlecht* (Frankfurt/Main: Helmer, 1990).

3. See Konrad Hilpert, "Menschenrechte: Männerrechte—Frauenrechte?," *Jahrbuch für christliche Sozialwissenschaften* 34 (1993): 35–72.

4. Lieselotte Steinbrügge, *Das moralische Geschlecht. Theorien und literarische Entwürfe über die Natur der Frau in der französischen Aufklärung* (Weinheim and Basel: Beltz, 1987).

5. Karin Hausen, "Die Polarisierung der 'Geschlechtscharaktere'—Eine Spiegelung der Dissoziation von Erwerbs- und Familienleben," in *Sozialgeschichte der Familie in der Neuzeit Europas*, ed. Werner Conze (Stuttgart: Klett, 1976), 363–393.

6. Claudia Honegger, "Sensibilität und Differenz," in *Gleichheit und Differenz*, ed. Gerhard et al., 241–247, here, 245; see also Claudia Honegger, *Die Ordnung der Geschlechter. Die Wissenschaften vom Menschen und das Weib* (Frankfurt/Main: Campus, 1991).

7. See Evelyn Fox Keller, *Reflections on Gender and Science* (New Haven: Yale University Press, 1985); Genevieve Lloyd, *The Man of Reason: "Male" and "Female" in Western Philosophy* (London: Methuen, 1984).

8. Rousseau, *Emile*; see also Elisabeth Blochmann, *Das "Frauenzimmer" und die "Gelehrsamkeit"* (Heidelberg: Quelle & Meyer, 1966); see also part 1 of this book.

9. The dispute was launched by the book by Christine de Pizan, *Le livre de la cité des dames* (Paris, 1405). For the English translation, see Christine de Pizan, *The Book of the City of Ladies*, trans. Earl Jeffrey Richards, foreword by Natalie Zemon Davis (New York: Persea Books, 1998). See also Heide Wunder, *"Er ist die Sonn', sie ist der Mond." Frauen in der Frühen Neuzeit* (Munich: Beck, 1992), 63.

10. See Silvia Bovenschen, *Die imaginierte Weiblichkeit* (Frankfurt/Main: Suhrkamp, 1979); Christine Garbe, "Sophie oder die heimliche Macht der Frauen. Zur Konzeption des Weiblichen bei Jean-Jacques Rousseau" in *Frauen in der Geschichte*, ed. Ilse Brehmer (Düsseldorf: Schwann, 1983), 4:65–87.

11. See Rousseau, *Emile*, 322–323.

12. On specific related aspects, see chapter 2 in this book.

13. With reference to Max Horkheimer and Theodor W. Adorno, *Dialectic of Enlightenment*, trans. John Cumming (New York: Continuum, 1972); first published as *Dialektik der Aufklärung*, (Amsterdam: Querido, 1947).

14. Macpherson, *The Political Theory of Possessive Individualism*, 3, 263.

15. Locke, *Two Treatises of Government*, II § 79: 337–338, and § 87: 341–342.

16. Johann Gottlieb Fichte, *The Science of Rights*, trans. A. E. Kroeger (New York: Harper and Row, 1970), 403, 441.

17. Carole Pateman, "The Fraternal Contract," in *The Disorder of Women*, ed. Carole Pateman (Stanford, Calif.: Stanford University Press, 1989), 42f.; see also Pateman, *The Sexual Contract*.

18. Pateman, "The Fraternal Contract," 35.

19. From the extensive literature available, see, for example, Jean Bethke Elshtain, *Public Men, Private Women: Women in Social and Political Thought* (Princeton, N.J.: Princeton University Press, 1981); Carol C. Gould, "Private Rights and Public Virtues: Women, the Family, and Democracy" in *Beyond Domination*, ed. C. C. Gould (Totowa, N.J.: Rowman and Allanheld Publishers, 1983), 3–18; Kornelia Hauser, *Viele Orte überall? Feminismus in Bewegung* (Berlin: Argument, 1987); Karin Hausen, "Überlegungen zum geschlechtsspezifischen

Strukturwandel der Öffentlichkeit," in *Differenz und Gleichheit*, ed. Gerhard et al., 268–282.

20. Ute Gerhard, *Verhältnisse und Verhinderungen. Frauenarbeit, Familie und Rechte der Frauen im 19. Jahrhundert* (Frankfurt/Main: Suhrkamp, 1978), 154f.

21. For example, in the maintenance of a gender-specific division of labor in "housewife marriages" until the 1977 reform, in the resistance to legal equality on the issue of the laws pertaining to the wife's married name until 1993, and against the special protection of marriage as an institution by the constitutional commission; see *Gemeinsame Verfassungskommission*, Stenogr. Bericht der 6. Öffentliche Anhörung, zu Art. 6 GG, 10 December 1992, Bonn.

22. Rawls, *A Theory of Justice*, 490–491.

23. Carol Gilligan, *In a Different Voice: Psychological Theory and Women's Development* (Cambridge: Harvard University Press, 1982).

24. Seyla Benhabib, "The Generalized and the Concrete Other: The Kohlberg-Gilligan Controversy and Feminist Theory," in *Feminism as Critique*, ed. Seyla Benhabib and Drucilla Cornell (Minneapolis: University of Minnesota Press, 1987), 77–95 and 174–181, here, 84; reprinted from *Praxis International* 5/4 (January 1986): 402–424. Benhabib quoted from Thomas Hobbes, "Philosophical Rudiments Concerning Government and Society," in *The English Works of Thomas Hobbes*, ed. Sir W. Molesworth (Darmstadt: Wissenschaftliche Buchgesellschaft, 1966), 2:109.

25. Ibid., 85.

26. Ibid., 89. On page 137, Benhabib quoted from Rawls, *A Theory of Justice*, 137.

27. Susan Moller Okin, "Reason and Feeling in Thinking about Justice," in *Feminism and Political Theory*, ed. Cass R. Sunstein (Chicago: University of Chicago Press, 1990), 15–35, here, 32, 34; originally published in *Ethics* 99 (January 1989).

28. Okin, "Reason and Feeling," 35.

29. Foreword to the revised edition: Jürgen Habermas, *Strukturwandel der Öffentlichkeit. Untersuchungen zu einer Kategorie der bürgerlichen Gesellschaft*, new ed. (Frankfurt/Main: Suhrkamp, 1990), 19; not included in the 1989 English edition.

30. See also the chapter on feminist legal theory, which is relatively one-sided in its consideration of the discussion in the United States, in Jürgen Habermas, *Between Facts and Norms: Contributions to a Discourse Theory of Law and Democracy*, trans. William Rehg (Cambridge: MIT Press, 1996), 409–427.

31. Habermas, *Between Facts and Norms*, 31.

32. See Max Weber, *Economy and Society: An Outline of Interpretive Sociology*, ed. Guenther Roth and Claus Wittich, 2 vols. (Berkeley: University of California Press, 1978), 1:31–36.

33. See Rainer Döbert, "Männliche Moral—weibliche Moral?" in *Frauensituationen. Veränderungen in den letzten zwanzig Jahren*, ed. Uta Gerhardt and Yvonne Schütz (Frankfurt/Main: Suhrkamp, 1988), 88–113.

34. See Kathy Davis, "Die Rhetorik des Feminismus. Ein neuer Blick auf die Gilligan-Debatte," *Feministische Studien* 9 (1991): 79–97; previously published in *Amsterdams Sociologisch Tijdschrift*. See also Andrea Maihofer, "Ansätze zur Kritik des moralischen Universalismus. Zur moraltheoretischen Diskussion um Gilligans Thesen zu einer 'weiblichen' Moralauffassung," *Feministische Studien* 1 (1988): 32–52; Gertrud Nunner-Winkler, ed., *Weibliche Moral. Die Kontroverse um eine geschlechtsspezifische Ethik* (Frankfurt/Main: Campus, 1991).

35. See Herta Nagl-Docekal, "Jenseits der Geschlechtermoral. Eine Einführung,"

in _Jenseits der Geschlechtermoral. Beiträge zu einer feministischen Ethik_, ed. Herta Nagl-Docekal and Herlinde Pauer-Studer (Frankfurt/Main: Fischer, 1993), 7–32, here, 17f.

36. See Habermas, _Between Facts and Norms_, 105; and Gustav Radbruch, _Einführung in die Rechtswissenschaft_ (Stuttgart: Koehler, 1952), 16f.

37. See Ingeborg Maus, "Juristische Methodik und Justizfunktion im Nationalsozialismus," _Archiv für Rechts- und Sozialphilosophie_ 8 (1983), 176–196; Maus, "Gesetzesbindung" der Justiz im "Dritten Reich," in _Recht und Justiz im "Dritten Reich,"_ ed. Ralf Dreier et al. (Frankfurt/Main: Suhrkamp, 1989), 80–103; Neumann, "The Change in the Function of Law in Modern Society." Both authors refer to Hegel. See _Hegel's Philosophy of Right_, trans. with notes by T. M. Knox (London: Oxford University Press, 1967, 1978), § 211.

38. Ingeborg Maus, "Entwicklung und Funktionswandel der Theorie des bürgerlichen Rechtsstaats," in _Der bürgerliche Rechtsstaat_, ed. Mehdi Tohidipur (Frankfurt/Main: Suhrkamp, 1978), 1:13–81, here, 45.

39. Ingeborg Maus, _Zur Aufklärung der Demokratietheorie. Rechts- und demokratietheoretische Überlegungen im Anschluß an Kant_ (Frankfurt/Main: Suhrkamp, 1992), 309f.

40. See Habermas, _Between Facts and Norms_, 106–107.

41. Maus, _Zur Aufklärung der Demokratietheorie_, 336.

42. See Joan Wallach Scott, "Gender: A Useful Category of Historical Analysis," in _Gender and the Politics of History_ (New York: Columbia University Press; 1988), 28–50; reprinted from _American Historical Review_ 91/5 (December 1986): 1053–1075; see also Geneviève Fraisse, _Geschlecht und Moderne. Archäologie der Gleichberechtigung_ (Frankfurt/Main: Fischer, 1995), 22ff., including an insightful and critical summary of the various "ways of thinking gender difference."

43. Carole Pateman, "Equality, Difference, Subordination: The Politics of Motherhood and Women's Citizenship," in _Beyond Equality and Difference: Citizenship, Feminist Politics and Female Subjectivity_, ed. Gisela Bock and Susan James (London: Routledge, 1992), 17–31, here, 21.

44. Ute Gerhard, _Unerhört. Die Geschichte der deutschen Frauenbewegung_ (Reinbek: Rowohlt, 1990), 170ff.; see also chapter 6 in this book.

45. Judith Evans, _Feminist Theory Today. An Introduction to Second-Wave Feminism_ (London: Sage, 1995), 25.

46. Catherine A. MacKinnon, _Feminism Unmodified. Discourses on Life and Law_ (Cambridge: Harvard University Press, 1987), 34.

47. Adriana Cavarero, "Die Perspektive der Geschlechterdifferenz," in _Gleichheit und Differenz_, ed. Ute Gerhard et al., 95–111, here, 104; "Adapting to the Male Position" is still the main suggestion in Theodor Maunz, Günter Dürig, and Roman Herzog, _Grundgesetz Kommentar_ (Munich: Beck, 1996), note on Art.3 II, marginal no.11.

48. DIOTIMA, group of women philosophers from Verona, _Il pensiero della differenza sessuale_ (Milan: La Tartaruga edizioni, 1987).

49. Cavarero, "Die Perspektive der Geschlechterdifferenz," 97.

50. Luce Irigaray, "Über die Notwendigkeit geschlechtsdifferenzierter Rechte," in _Gleichheit und Differenz_, ed. Gerhard et al., 338–350, here, 338ff.; sections of this article were taken from an interview by Christina Lasagni, which appeared as "Il sesso della Lege" (The Gender of the Law) in the Bologna law journal: _Il diritto delle Dorne_, no. 1 (July 1989); see also Luce Irigaray, _Ethique de la différence sexuelle_ (Paris: Minuet, 1984).

51. Rossana Rossanda, "Differenz und Gleichheit," in *Gleichheit und Differenz*, ed. Gerhard et al., 13–29, here, 27.

52. Carol Hagemann-White, *Sozialisation: Weiblich – männlich?* (Opladen: Leske and Budrich, 1984), 78.

53. Judith Butler, *Gender Trouble: Feminism and the Subversion of Identity* (New York: Routledge, 1990), 6–7, 31–33, esp. 32.

54. Judith Butler, "Contingent Foundations: Feminism and the Question of 'Postmodernism'" in *Feminist Contentions: A Philosophical Exchange*, ed. Seyla Benhabib, Judith Butler, Drucilla Cornell, and Nancy Fraser (New York: Routledge, 1994), 35–57, here, 48; previously published in *Feminists Theorize the Political*, ed. Judith Butler and Joan W. Scott (New York : Routledge, 1992), 3–21; an earlier version appeared in *Praxis International* 11/2 (July 1991), 150–165; see also Judith Butler, "For a Careful Reading," in *Feminist Contentions*, 127–143; and Butler, *Gender Trouble*, 142–149.

55. Christine di Stefano, "Dilemmas of Difference: Feminism, Modernity, and Postmodernism," in *Feminism/Postmodernism*, ed. Linda J. Nicholson (New York: Routledge, 1990), 63–82, here, 75; di Stefano cites Nancy Hartsock, "Rethinking Modernism: Minority vs. Majority Theories," *Cultural Critique* 7 (1987): 187–206.

56. Nancy Fraser, "False Antitheses: A Response to Seyla Benhabib and Judith Butler," in *Feminist Contentions*, 59–74; also appeared in *Justice Interruptus: Critical Reflections on the "Postsocialist" Condition,* ed. Nancy Fraser (New York: Routledge, 1997), 207–223, and *Praxis International* 11/2 (July 1991); see also Nancy Fraser, "Pragmatism, Feminism and the Linguistic Turn" in *Feminist Contentions*, 157–171; and Alison M. Jaggar, "Sexual Difference and Sexual Equality," in *Theoretical Perspectives on Sexual Difference*, ed. Deborah Rhode (New Haven, Conn.: Yale University Press, 1990), 239–254.

57. Deborah L. Rhode, "The Politics of Paradigms: Gender Difference and Gender Disadvantage," in *Beyond Equality and Difference*, ed. Bock and James, 149–163, here, 149.

58. Various directed valid equal rights articles were also introduced in the 1949 constitution of the German Democratic Republic; in view of the dictatorial system there, however, the consequences were very different. This context cannot be dealt with any further here; for more information, see Ute Gerhard, "Die staatlich institutionalisierte 'Lösung' der Frauenfrage. Zur Geschichte der Geschlechterverhältnisse in der DDR," in *Sozialgeschichte der DDR*, ed. Hartmut Kaelble, Jürgen Kocka, and Hartmut Zwahr (Stuttgart: Klett-Cotta, 1994), 383–403.

59. See also Titia Loenen, "Different Perspectives in Different Legal Studies: A Contextual Approach to Feminist Jurisprudence in Europe and the USA," paper presented at the Conference on Feminist Approaches to Law and Cultural Diversity, European University Institute, Florence, Italy, 1993.

60. See Catherine A. MacKinnon, "Toward Feminist Jurisprudence," in *Toward a Feminist Theory of the State*, ed. Catherine A. MacKinnon (Cambridge: Harvard University Press, 1989), 237–249, here, 242; see also MacKinnon, *Feminism Unmodified*.

61. MacKinnon, *Feminism Unmodified*, 33ff.

62. As important as comparative legal distinctions are, it is notable that the different sides can nevertheless learn from each other in terms of legal doctrine. For details, see Ute Sacksofsky, *Das Grundrecht auf Gleichberechtigung. Eine rechtsdogmatische Untersuchung zu Artikel 3 Abs. 2 des Grundgesetzes* (Baden-

Baden: Nomos, 1991), 207f. Sacksofsky made an interesting comparison between equal rights of women in Germany and in the United States. In the expanded 1996 edition, she interpreted the amended Art. 3 Sec. 2 of the German Basic Law by referring to the U.S. and feminist discussion in explaining a "paradigm shift" connected with the prohibition of dominance (1996, 404).

63. Full equality of husband and wife regarding the married couple's last name was not achieved until 1994, when § 1355 BGB was revised.

64. Parlametarischer Rat, 42. Sitzung des Hauptausschusses, 18 January 1949, Stenogr. Protokolle, 538 f.; on this, see Barbara Böttger, *Das Recht auf Gleichheit und Differenz. Elisabeth Selbert und der Kampf der Frauen um Art. 3.2 Grundgesetz* (Münster: Westfälisches Dampfboot, 1990), 215ff.

65. Erna Scheffler, "Die Gleichberechtigung der Frau. In welcher Weise empfiehlt es sich, gemäß Art. 117 d. Grundgesetzes das geltende Recht an Art. 3 Abs. 2 d. Grundgesetzes anzupassen." Paper presented by Erna Scheffler at the 38th Meeting of German Jurists (Tübingen, 1951), quoted in Sacksofsky, *Das Grundrecht auf Gleichberechtigung*, 107.

66. BVerfGE 3, 225ff.

67. Ines Reich-Hilweg, *Männer und Frauen sind gleichberechtigt* (Frankfurt/Main: Europäische Verlags-Anstalt, 1979), 50.

68. On this, in detail, see Sacksofsky, *Das Grundrecht auf Gleichberechtigung*, 85f., 91f.

69. Bericht der Gemeinsamen Verfassungskommission gemäß Beschluß des Deutschen Bundestages, Drucksachen 12/1590 and 12/1670; Beschluß des Bundesrates, Drucksache 741/91 (Bonn, 1993), 31; see also Wolfgang Gitter, Manfred Löwisch, and Annemarie Mennel, *Welche rechtlichen Maßnahmen sind vordringlich, um die tatsächliche Gleichstellung der Frau mit den Männern im Arbeitsleben zu gewährleisten?" Gutachten zum 50. Deutschen Juristentag* (Munich, 1974); Karl-Heinrich Friauf, "Gleichberechtigung der Frau als Verfassungsauftrag. Rechtsgutachten," *Schriftenreihe des BMJ*, no. 11 (1981); Ernst Benda, *Notwendigkeit und Möglichkeit positiver Aktionen zugunsten von Frauen im öffentlichen Dienst. Rechtsgutachten im Auftrag der Leitstelle Gleichstellung der Frau in Hamburg* (Freiburg: Institut für öffentliches Recht, 1986); and Sacksofsky, *Das Grundrecht auf Gleichberechtigung*, with additional references.

70. Sacksofsky, *Das Grundrecht auf Gleichberechtigung*, 305f., 313; see also Susanne Baer, *Würde oder Gleichheit? Zur angemessenen grundrechtlichen Konzeption von Recht gegen Diskriminierung am Bsp. sexueller Belästigung am Arbeitsplatz in der Bundesrepublik Deutschland und den USA* (Baden-Baden: Nomos, 1995), 221ff.

71. See Hortense Hörburger, *Europas Frauen fordern mehr: die soziale Dimension des EG-Binnenmarktes am Beispiel der spezifischen Auswirkungen für Frauen* (Marburg: SP-Verlag, 1990); Baer, *Würde oder Gleichheit*, 181.

72. On this, see the introduction to part 1 of this book.

73. Though this is the view expressed in Andrea Maihofer, *Geschlecht als Existenzweise. Macht, Moral, Recht und Geschlechterdifferenz* (Frankfurt/Main: Helmer, 1995), 167f.

74. Joachim Perels, ed., *Grundrechte als Fundament der Demokratie* (Frankfurt/Main: Suhrkamp, 1979), 69.

75. See Jaggar, "Sexual Difference and Sexual Equality."

76. Johannes Schwardtländer and Heiner Bielefeldt, *Christen und Muslime vor der Herausforderung der Menschenrechte* (Bonn: Wissenschaftliche Arbeitsgruppe für Weltkirchliche Aufgaben der Deutschen Bischofskonferenz, 1992), 22;

Heiner Bielefeldt, "Die Menschenrechte 'das Erbe der gesamten Menschheit,'" in *Würde und Recht des Menschen*, Festschrift für Johannes Schwartländer zum 70. Geburtstag, ed. Heiner Bielefeldt, Winfried Brugger, and Klaus Dicke (Würzburg: Könighausen & Neumann, 1992), 143ff., 156.

77. Schwardtländer and Bielefeldt, *Christen und Muslime vor der Herausforderung der Menschenrechte*, 22.

78. Axel Honneth, *Der Kampf um Anerkennung. Zur moralischen Grammatik sozialer Konflikte* (Frankfurt/Main: Suhrkamp, 1992).

79. Barrington Moore Jr., *Injustice: The Social Bases of Obedience and Revolt* (White Plains, N.Y.: M. E. Sharpe), 1978), 15.

80. See Thomas Leithäuser et al., *Entwurf zu einer Empirie des Alltagsbewußtseins* (Frankfurt/Main: Suhrkamp, 1977).

81. See Oskar Negt and Alexander Kluge, *Öffentlichkeit und Erfahrung* (Frankfurt/Main: Suhrkamp, 1977), 59, 67.

82. See Helge Pross, *Die Wirklichkeit der Hausfrau* (Reinbek: Rowohlt, 1977).

83. Arbeitsgruppe Bielefelder Soziologen, ed., *Alltagswissen, Interaktion und gesellschaftliche Wirklichkeit* (Reinbek: Rowohlt, 1973), 22; see also Martin Kohli, *Soziologie des Lebenslaufs* (Darmstadt: Luchterhand, 1978), 15.

84. See Winfried Brugger, "Stufen der Begründung von Menschenrechten," *Der Staat* 31 (1992): 20–38.

85. Honneth, *Der Kampf um Anerkennung*, 148ff.

86. Hannah Arendt, "Es gibt nur ein einziges Menschenrecht" (1949), in *Praktische Philosophie/Ethik*, ed. Otfried Höffe, Gerd Kadelbach, and Gerhard Plumpe (Frankfurt/Main: Fischer, 1981), 2:152ff.; Hans-Richard Reuter, "Menschenrechte zwischen Universalismus und Relativismus," *Zeitschrift für Evangelische Ethik* 40 (1996): 135–147.

87. Rawls, *A Theory of Justice*, 62.

88. Brugger, "Stufen der Begründung von Menschenrechten," 19ff.

89. Thomas Humphrey Marshall, *Citizenship and Social Class* (Cambridge, U.K.: Cambridge University Press, 1950). This appears as part 1 in Thomas H. Marshall and Tom Bottomore, *Citizenship and Social Class* (London: Pluto Press, 1992).

90. On this in detail, see chapter 3 of this book.

91. See Olympe de Gouges's *Declaration of the Rights of Woman and Citizen*, Article 11, in the appendix of this book.

92. See appendix. For sources, see chapter 3, note 15, in this book.

93. "The Declaration of Sentiments," Seneca Falls Conference, 1848, taken from: Elizabeth Cady Stanton, *A History of Woman Suffrage* (Rochester, N.Y.: Fowler and Wells, 1889), 1:70–71. Accessed through the Internet Modern History Sourcebook.

94. On specific aspects, see chapter 3 of this book.

95. Louise Otto, "Die Freiheit ist unteilbar," in *Die Frauen-Zeitung* (Frankfurt/Main: Syndikat,1979), 41; reprint of no.1 (1849).

96. Dohm, *Women's Nature and Privilege*.

97. Habermas, *Between Facts and Norms*, 271.

98. Entry: "Frauen" in *Conversations-Lexicon, oder encyclopädisches Handwörterbuch for gebildete Stände*, 7 vols. (Stuttgart: Macklot, 1818–1819), 2:789.

99. Louise Aston, "Meine Emancipation, Verweisung und Rechtfertigung." Introduction in *Für die Selbstverwirklichung der Frau: Louise Aston*, ed. Germaine Goetzinger (Frankfurt/Main: Fischer, 1983), 61f.

100. Louise Dittmar, "Die männliche Bevormundung," in *Frauenemanzipation im*

deutschen Vormärz. Texte und Dokumente, ed. Renate Möhrmann (Stuttgart: Reclam, 1978), 64. This is an excerpt originally published in Louise Dittmar, ed., *Das Wesen der Ehe. Nebst einigen Aufsätzen über die soziale Reform der Frauen* (Leipzig: n.p., 1849).

101. See the petition of Allgemeiner deutscher Frauenverein, ed., *Einige deutsche Gesetzparagraphen über die Stellung der Frau*, with comments by Louise Otto (Leipzig: Schäfer, 1876); on the struggle against the German Civil Code, see Beatrix Geisel, "Patriarchale Rechtsnormen 'unterlaufen.' Die Rechts-schutzvereine der ersten deutschen Frauenbewegung," in *Frauen in der Geschichte des Rechts. Von der Frühen Neuzeit bis zur Gegenwart*, ed. Ute Gerhard (Munich: Beck, 1997), 683–697.

102. Marie Stritt, *Das bürgerliche Gesetzbuch und die Frauenfrage* (Frankenberg/i.S.: Reisel, 1898), 4, 13.

103. Katharina Scheven, "Was versteht man unter 'Reglementierung der Prosti-tution?'" *Der Abolitionist*, no. 1 (1902), 2.

104. See Anna Pappritz, "Die Teilnahme der Frauen an der Sittlichkeitsbewegung," in *Handbuch der Frauenbewegung*, ed. Helene Lange and Gertrud Bäumer (Ber-lin: Moeser, 1901), 154–192.

105. Agnes von Zahn-Harnack, *Die Frauenbewegung. Geschichte, Probleme, Ziele* (Berlin: Deutsche Buchgemeinschaft, 1928), 76f.

106. See Dora Peyser, *Alice Salomon. Die Begründerin der sozialen Frauenberufe in Deutschland* (Cologne: Heymann, 1958); Alice Salomon, *Charakter ist Schicksal. Lebenserinnerungen* (Weinheim: Beltz, 1983); Christoph Sachße, *Mütterlichkeit als Beruf* (Frankfurt/Main: Suhrkamp, 1986).

107. See Helene Lange, *Kampfzeiten. Aufsätze und Reden aus vier Jahrzehnten* (Ber-lin: Herbig, 1928), 2:8ff., 197ff.

108. Marshall, cited from Marshall and Bottomore, *Citizenship and Social Class*, 16; see also Anna Yeatman, "Beyond Natural Right: The Conditions for Univer-sal Citizenship," in *Postmodern Revisionings of the Political*, ed. Anna Yeatman (New York: Routledge, 1993).

109. See Charlotte Bunch, "Transforming Human Rights from a Feminist Perspec-tive," in *Women's Rights—Human Rights. International Feminist Perspectives*, ed. Julie Peters and Andrea Wolper (New York: Routledge, 1995), 11–17; Elisabeth Friedman, "Women's Human Rights: The Emergence of a Move-ment," in *Women's Rights*, ed. Peters and Wolper, 18–34.

110. See Eibe Riedel, "Menschenrechte der dritten Dimension," *Europäische Grundrechte-Zeitschrift* 16, no. 1/2 (1989): 9ff.

111. See Hillary Charlesworth, "What are 'Women's International Human Rights'?" in *Human Rights of Women. National and International Perspectives*, ed. Rebecca J. Cook (Philadelphia: University of Pennsylvania Press, 1994), 58–84, here, 75.

112. Sonja Wölte, "Der internationale Schutz der Menschenrechte von Frauen: Ansätze einer feministischen Kritik am UN-Menschenrechtsinstrumentarium" (Ph.D. dissertation for the department of social sciences, Universität Frank-furt/Main, 1996), 20ff.

113. Convention on the Elimination of All Forms of Discrimination against Women (CEDAW), adopted by the United Nations General Assembly on 18 December 1979 (Resolution 34/180).

114. See also Ruth Klingelbiel, "Kein Rückschritt und kein Meilenstein. Die 4. Weltfrauenkonferenz zwischen Neuinterpretation und Erweiterung des Menschenrechts-konzepts," *Wissenschaft & Frieden*, no. 4 (1995): 12–16; Ines

Holthaus, "Frauenmenschenrechtsbewegungen und die Universalisierung der Menschenrechte," *Peripherie*, no. 61 (1996): 6–23.

115. See Christa Wichterich, *Frauen der Welt. Vom Fortschritt der Ungleichheit* (Göttingen: Lamuv, 1995).

116. Of the wealth of literature on the subject, see especially *Human Rights of Women*, ed. Cook, and *Women's Rights*, ed. Peters and Wolper, including many national reports.

117. See Nahid Toubia, "Female Genital Mutilation," in *Women's Rights*, ed. Peters and Wolper, 224–237.

118. Beijing Declaration and Platform for Action, report of the Fourth World Conference on Women, United Nations (New York, 1996), no. 224; cited in *Human Rights Reader*, ed. Ishay, 497.

119. Bunch, "Transforming Human Rights from a Feminist Perspective," 17.

Appendix

IN COMPARISON WITH The Declaration of Rights of Man and Citizen (1789), the sentences or terms in italics in the version of *The Declaration of the Rights of Woman and Citizen* (1791) that is reprinted here were inserted or replaced by Olympe de Gouges. These deviations from the male text, sometimes merely subtle nuances, demonstrate the gender difference and constitute the starting point for my legal interpretation. Because the translations of the two French documents into different languages often do not correspond with each other, my comparison refers to the French originals. *

The Declaration of the Rights of Woman and Citizen
Olympe de Gouges

Preamble

The mothers, daughters, and sisters, representatives of the nation demand to be constituted into a national assembly. Considering that ignorance, disregard of or contempt for the rights of women are the only causes of public misfortune and of governmental corruption, they have resolved to set forth in a solemn declaration, the natural, inalienable and sacred rights of woman; to the end that this declaration, constantly held up to all members of society, may always remind them of their rights and duties; to the end that the acts based on women's power and those based on the power of men, being constantly measured against the goal of all political institutions, may be more respected; and so that the demands of female citizens, henceforth founded on simple and indisputable principles, may ever uphold the constitution and good morals, and may contribute to the happiness of all.

Consequently, the sex that is superior in beauty as well as in courage of maternal suffering, recognizes and declares, in the presence and under the auspices of the Supreme Being, the following rights of woman and citizen.

Article 1. Woman is born free and remains equal in rights *to man*. Social distinctions can be founded only on general utility.

Article 2. The goal of every political association is the preservation of the natural and irrevocable rights of *Woman and Man*. These rights are liberty, property, security, and *especially* resistance to oppression.

Article 3. The principle of all sovereignty resides essentially in the Nation, *which is none other than the union of Woman and Man*; no group, no individual can exercise any authority that is not derived expressly from it.

Article 4. Liberty *and Justice* consist of *rendering to persons those things that belong to them*; thus, the exercise of *woman's* natural rights is limited only *by perpetual tyranny with which man opposes her*; these limits must be changed according to the laws *of nature and reason.*

Article 5. The laws *of nature and of reason* prohibit all acts harmful to society; whatever is not prohibited by *these wise and divine laws* cannot be prevented, and no one can be forced to do anything unspecified by the law.

Article 6. The law *should be* the expression of the general will; all *female* and *male* citizens must participate in its elaboration personally or through their representatives. It should be the same for all; *all female and male citizens*, being equal in the eyes of the law, *should be* equally admitted to all honors, positions and public employments, according to their capacities and with no distinctions other than those of their virtues and talents.

Article 7. *No woman is immune;* she can be accused, arrested, and detained in cases as determined by law. *Women, like men,* must obey these rigorous laws. (Remark: De Gouges did not mention the sentence: To resist is to render oneself guilty.)

Article 8. Only punishments strictly and obviously necessary may be established by law. No one may be punished except under a law established and promulgated prior to the crime *and legally applicable to women*.

Article 9. *Once any woman is declared guilty, then the law must be enforced rigorously.*

Article 10. No one is to be disquited for his *very basic* opinions: (De Gouges did not mention "religious beliefs"). *Woman has the right to mount the scaffold; she must equally have the right to mount the rostrum*, provided that her demonstrations do not disturb the legally established order.

Article 11. Free communication of thoughts and opinions is one of the most *precious* rights of *woman, since this liberty assures the legitimate paternity of fathers with regard to their children. Every female citizen can therefore freely say: "I am the mother of a child that belongs to you," without a barbarous prejudice forcing her to conceal the truth*; she must also answer for the abuse of this liberty in cases determined by law.

Article 12. The guarantee of the rights of woman and female citizen [requires] *a major benefit*. This guarantee [should] be instituted for the advantage of all, not for the particular benefit of those to whom it is entrusted.

Article 13. For the maintenance of public forces and administrative expenses, the contributions *of women and men shall be equal; the woman shares in all forced labor and all painful tasks, therefore she must have the same share in the distribution of positions, tasks, assignments, honors, and industry.*

Article 14. *Female and male* citizens have the right to determine the need for the public taxes, either by themselves or through their representatives. *Female citizens can agree to this only if they are admitted to an equal share not only in wealth, but also in public administration, and by determining the proportion and extent of tax collection.*

Article 15. *The mass of women, allied for tax purposes to the mass of men*, has the right to hold every public official accountable for his administration.

Article 16. Any society in which the guarantee of rights is not assured, or the separation of powers determined, has no constitution. *The constitution is invalid if the majority of individuals who compose the Nation have not cooperated in writing it.*

Article 17. The right of property is inviolable and sacred *to both sexes,* jointly or separately. No one can be deprived of it, since it is a true patrimony *of nature* except when the public necessity, certified by law, clearly requires it, subject to just and prior compensation.

Postamble

Woman, awake! The tocsin of reason is sounding throughout the Universe; know your rights. The powerful empire of nature is no longer surrounded by prejudices, fanaticism, superstition and lies. The torch of truth has dispelled all the clouds of stupidity and usurpation. Man enslaved has multiplied his forces; he has had recourse to yours in order to break his own chains. Having become free, he has become unjust toward his mate. Oh Women! Women! when will you cease to be blind? What advantage have you gained in the Revolution?

* For various English translations of the Declaration, see chapter 3, note 15 of this book. The version printed here refers largely to the translation in *Women, the Family, and Freedom,* ed. Bell and Offen. Article 6 is a mixture of various translations and my own interpretation, and Articles 10 and 12 were taken from *Women in Revolutionary Paris, 1789–1795,* ed. Levy, Applewhite, and Johnson. Terms in brackets have been added to correspond more closely to the French original.

Index

About the Author

UTE GERHARD is the first professor of gender studies in social science in Germany. She is director of the Center for Women's Studies at the Johann Wolfgang Goethe Universität Frankfurt/Main. She has studied law, social sciences, and history and published on women's rights, social policy, the history of women and the women's movement, and feminist theory. She is a recipient of the Hessian Cultural Award for Science.

About the Translators

ALLISON BROWN has been a freelance translator of scholarly books and essays, largely in the fields of history and the social and political sciences, especially women's and cultural studies, since 1988. She has studied linguistics and German studies, and has an M.A. in translation science. She has been living in Berlin since 1982.

BELINDA COOPER is a law teacher, journalist, and translator, particularly of scholarly and legal books and articles. She holds a J.D. from Yale Law School and is a senior fellow at the World Policy Institute of the New School in New York and a visiting assistant professor of law at Ohio Northern University. She lived and worked in Berlin from 1987 to 1994.